COLUMNS TO CHARACTERS

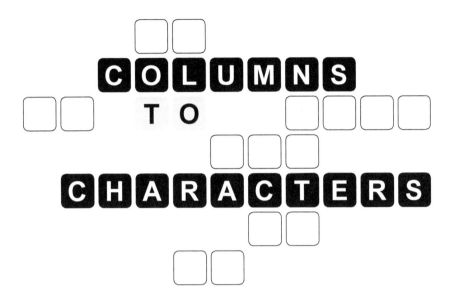

The Presidency and the Press
Enter the Digital Age

EDITED BY
Stephanie A. Martin

WITH A FOREWORD BY
Peter Baker

AND AN AFTERWORD BY
Jon Meacham

TEXAS A&M UNIVERSITY PRESS
COLLEGE STATION

This paper meets the requirements of ANSI/NISO Z39.48-1992
(Permanence of Paper).
Binding materials have been chosen for durability.
Manufactured in the United States of America

Library of Congress Cataloging-in-Publication Data

Names: Martin, Stephanie A., 1974– editor.
Title: Columns to characters: the presidency and the press enter the digital
   age / edited by Stephanie A. Martin; with an afterword by Jon Meacham.
Description: First edition. | College Station: Texas A&M University Press,
   [2017] | Series: Kenneth E. Montague presidential rhetoric series |
   Includes bibliographical references and index.
Identifiers: LCCN 2017013966 (print) | LCCN 2017022273 (ebook) | ISBN
   9781623495633 (ebook) | ISBN 9781623495626 (printed case: alk. paper)
Subjects: LCSH: Presidents—Press coverage—United States—History. |
   Communication in politics—Technological innovations—United
   States—History. | Press and politics—United States—History. | Social
   media—Political aspects—United States | Mass media—Political
   aspects—History. | United States—Politics and government. |
   Presidents—United States—History.
Classification: LCC JK554 (ebook) | LCC JK554 .C65 2017 (print) | DDC
   070.4/49320973—dc23
LC record available at https://lccn.loc.gov/2017013966

CONTENTS

FOREWORD

PETER BAKER

A few days after delivering his final State of the Union address in the majestic chamber of the House of Representatives in January 2016, President Barack Obama sat down to deliver his message in a different fashion. He sat down for an interview with a young man named Adande Thorne, a self-described "time traveler" and "professional cuddler" who hosted a popular YouTube channel under the screen name sWooZie. SWooZie asked about race relations and terrorism but then veered into a series of questions that presidents do not often get asked.

"If you had to pick from one of these 'Star Wars' characters, who would you be?" sWooZie asked.

Obama didn't hesitate. "I've got to go with Han Solo," he said. "He's a little bit of a rebel."

SWooZie then showed the president a drawing of two dogs, one with pants covering all four legs and another with the pants covering just the hind legs. "If you had to pick a pair of pants for your dog, A or B?" he asked.

With the same studious demeanor he used to discuss health care, Obama pointed to the dog with just two legs covered. "You've got to go with this," he said. Pointing to the other one, he added, "This, I think, it's a little too conservative. A little too much. Too much fabric."

The evolution of technology has transformed the way presidents interact with the public. For decades they have searched for ways to bypass the filter of the mainstream media and communicate directly with voters. Franklin D. Roosevelt famously used his fireside chats over radio. John F. Kennedy and Richard M. Nixon both appeared on the *Tonight* show with Jack Paar during the 1960 campaign, and eight years later Nixon appeared on *Rowan & Martin's Laugh-In*, asking, "Sock it to *me*?" Ronald Reagan launched a weekly radio address from the White House. Bill Clinton played the saxophone on the *Arsenio Hall Show* while a candidate and after taking office created the first White House website. George W. Bush had his State of the Union address broadcast live over the Internet.

But presidential use of technology made a quantum leap during Obama's tenure. Obama not only became the first sitting president to go on the *Tonight* show while in office—and made regular treks to the studios of Jon Stewart and David Letterman as well—but was the first president to set up a Facebook page, the first to post messages on Twitter, the first to answer questions on Reddit and Google+, the first to post an essay on Medium, and the first to have accounts with Instagram, Snapchat, Vine, Tumblr, and Flickr. "Obama will always be known as the president that opened the floodgates of social media," Erna Alfred Liousas, an analyst at Forrester Research, told the Associated Press.

The reasons are clear. With the fragmenting of the American audience, Obama found, as his successors will, that it is not enough to make a prime-time speech from the Oval Office or give an interview to the network news anchors. Obama's final State of the Union address reached just over 31 million Americans on various television networks, a far cry from the 52 million who watched his first address seven years earlier—and lower than any such speech since 2000. So while Obama invited the team from NBC's *Today* show to spend part of the day at the White House before his speech, he also followed up by sitting down with sWooZie and a couple of sWooZie's fellow YouTube stars for a series of one-on-one interviews. And why not? SWooZie boasted 3.7 million subscribers, more than the typical viewership of any of the historically influential Sunday morning talk shows such as *Meet the Press* or *Face the Nation*. Indeed, combined with the other two YouTube hosts who got time with Obama that day, the interviews in theory reached more than 10 million subscribers, about twice as many people as watch the *Today* show on any given morning.

Of course, Obama did not personally write most of the tweets and other messages sent out in his name. His White House Office of Digital Strategy had about twenty staff members who constantly churned out 140-character messages for Twitter and the like, more than worked in Bush's entire White House press office. But Obama was himself something of a gearhead, coming to office with a greater personal interest in technology than that of his predecessors. Clinton prided himself on being the first president of the Internet age, leading the country across the bridge to the twenty-first century, as he often put it, but in reality he was not much of an early adopter. Other than the two messages he sent for symbolic purposes, Clinton did not use email as president or all that much since leaving office. When his White House science adviser sat him down to show him how email worked, the adviser said, "It may have been the first time he sat down in front of a computer." Bush used email frequently before taking office and again after returning to Texas but made a point of staying offline for the eight years he lived in the White House, acutely aware that any messages he sent could be considered presidential records potentially subject to disclosure someday.

Obama, on the other hand, insisted on keeping his BlackBerry after being sworn in, despite the resistance of the Secret Service, which was not keen on the idea of a president carrying a device that could theoretically be tracked or hacked, giving away his location or allowing someone to listen in on his private conversations. In the end, he was given a supersophisticated version of the BlackBerry with extra encryption for security purposes, while the list of people who were given his email address was kept exceedingly short. The government's technology gurus reportedly even made it impossible for his friends or advisers to forward messages from the president or to send him attachments.

Over time, Obama expanded his digital opportunities, becoming the first commander in chief to receive his daily intelligence briefing on an iPad. He used the tablet late at night to scan the Internet for news stories or sports scores. During a trip to Alaska to highlight his policies to combat climate change, he was given a GoPro camera and a selfie stick to take his own photographs and video of disappearing glaciers, images that were then shared online.

Some of this experimentation led to questions about whether it was at times a little beneath the dignity of a president. Obama appeared on *Between Two Ferns,* an online talk show in which a celebrity sitting between two potted plants exchanged insults with the host, Zach Galifianakis, on a set that resembled a 1980s-era public-access show shot in someone's basement. The president later gave an interview to a YouTube host named GloZell Green, who was famous for wearing bright green lipstick and once on camera soaked in a bathtub filled with milk and Fruit Loops. And Obama took his motorcade to a Southern California garage so that he could appear on a podcast called *WTF with Marc Maron* (the cats were locked in the bedroom). As Bloomberg's Margaret Talev cheekily asked, "What would George Washington think?"

But the architects of the digital strategy concluded that they had little choice in an era where five hundred cable channels were no longer the only competitors for the attention of Americans awash in all sorts of specialized services and venues providing information and entertainment. "Ultimately what all of this is about is finding ways to communicate with people in a time when media has [*sic*] become so disaggregated that simply communicating through the traditional means is woefully insufficient," Dan Pfeiffer, who served as Obama's White House communications director and later senior adviser, told the *New York Times.*

It also provided what most of Obama's predecessors had long coveted: a convenient way around the White House press corps. While Obama gave many one-on-one interviews to carefully selected journalists who did not work in the briefing room, he all but ignored the reporters who covered him day in and day out and might be expected to ask questions he preferred not to answer. He took questions from the pool of journalists that covered him most closely barely a third as often as Bush and less than a fifth as often as Clinton. Even Reagan, famous for circumventing the media, took questions far more often than did Obama.

Along with the additional avenues for messaging, though, came an extraordinary acceleration in the presidency itself. The advent of instantaneous communication and such feedback loops as Twitter meant a relentless cycle of crisis, reaction, and counterreaction that transformed the way a president does the job. It moved faster than ever before, making it nearly impossible for a president to stop and catch a breath. Obama made it barely a few minutes into his State of the Union address before Americans were passing judgment on social media.

When Harry S. Truman ordered the first nuclear bomb dropped on Hiroshima, it took sixteen hours after the devastating explosion for word to reach him aboard a ship crossing the Atlantic. Today presidents are notified within minutes of far less consequential developments and expected to react shortly afterward. When a terrorist tried to set off bombs in his shoes aboard an American passenger jet in 2001, Bush did not offer a public reaction for six days. By the time a terrorist tried to set off explosives in his underwear aboard an American passenger jet in 2009, Obama waited three days before making any public comment and was savaged for taking so long. By the time terrorists bombed the Boston Marathon, Obama came out before cameras within hours, and then a second time the next day.

With speed, of course, came intensity. Despite all the focus on the bitter polarization these days, presidents have always endured harsh and even venomous public criticism. Long before a congressional representative shouted, "You lie!" at Obama, Thomas Jefferson was called a heretic, Andrew Jackson a bigamist, Abraham Lincoln a monkey, and so on. The difference is that today's social media have spread and intensified the vitriol that has always existed in American politics and given it a broader, more visible platform than ever before. Anger has been fueled by the easy means of protest. Where the disaffected once had to board buses, ride to the capital, and march in front of the White House in the tens of thousands to be heard, today they can register discontent with the flick of a button from the comfort of their living room. The most extreme voices, those once seen as cranks on the fringe left or right, have shouted their way into the mainstream of American politics through technology. And the political class has taken its cues from them, each party or campaign blasting out one attack email, tweet, and Facebook posting after another, reaching sometimes millions of recipients.

The swift changes during Obama's time in office reshaped the presidency in profound ways, and it seems safe to assume that his successors will continue to push the boundaries and experiment further as technology opens even more new possibilities. The candidates seeking his job in 2016 made extensive use of social media and built on some of the digital innovations of Obama's pioneering 2008 campaign. Donald Trump, in particular, used Twitter to especially provocative ends, including middle-of-the-night tweets in the aftermath of the first general election debate against Hillary Clinton to defend himself against charges he mistreated a Miss Universe contestant. Once elected, he continued to tweet, even going so far in late December 2016 to compliment Vladimir Putin as "very smart" when Putin withheld reciprocal sanctions against the United States in retaliation for President Obama's decision to punish Moscow for its alleged meddling in the US presidential election. Time will tell whether Trump will continue to be able to communicate with his more than eighteen million followers using Twitter once he is in office, or whether he will have to be hemmed in for security reasons.

But even as Trump showed his social media prowess on the campaign trail, Obama, the first social media president, was not content to call it a day while the campaign raged around him. Heading into his final year in office, he was determined to make use of all the tools available to him. Even sWooZie had some ideas for further advances. In a Twitter post after his interview with the president, he suggested, "Me and Obama might go head to head in *Mario Kart* next time!"

ON TRUMP

STEPHANIE A. MARTIN

Donald Trump will almost certainly never appear on the popular web series *Between Two Ferns with Zach Galifinakis*. I begin with this disclaimer because many of the contributors who follow in this volume—including me—note President Barack Obama's purportedly groundbreaking appearance on this short format internet program and argue that it epitomized the forty-fourth president's pioneering turn as chief executive during this digital age. Obama did more to take the presidency directly to the people—going around the so-called mainstream press, including the White House press corps—even when this meant engaging formats outside of historical norms. And so Obama, among other things, sat for chats with late night hosts, podcasters, YouTube vloggers, and, yes, maybe most famously, Galifianakis.

When the conference that led to this volume was held in Dallas, Texas, in early February 2015, no one in attendance could have imagined that there was yet to emerge a presidential candidate who would engage social media in even more provocative ways than Obama had done during his tenure. Nor can they be blamed for this oversight. Until his election on November 8, 2016, almost no one seriously considered that Donald J. Trump would become the forty-fifth president. With hindsight, however, I think the essays that follow in this book unwittingly foreshadow the emergence of the New York billionaire, at least in terms of his uncanny use of social media to both attack the establishment press and speak directly to his supporters. Trump, more than any candidate or president before him, has never shied away from speaking his mind or honed his message to focus group standards, but instead he has prized his image as an off-the-cuff everyman who just happens to have a much larger than average bank account. The result, some six months into his presidency, is a leadership and communication style that to supporters comes across as a mix between blunt businessman and tough outsider who's willing to tell it like it is and that to detractors seems more like angry incompetence that does little more than stoke division and fear.

If Obama was the nation's first social media president, then Trump is its first Tweeter in Chief. Sure, Obama also had a Twitter handle—@POTUS (President of the United States)—and he turned this handle and the keys to the Oval Office over to Trump in January 2017. But that's not the account Trump really uses. Instead, just as during the campaign, Trump continues to use his personal Android device to send out 140-character missives from his personal account, @realDonaldTrump. He uses his phone to make news, to react to news, and to object to news cycles as they are unfolding. The Washington press corps, in turn, responds by covering these tweets, even as critics contend they are actually little more than distractions from the things that really matter. It is a drama that began unfolding during the campaign and that has worsened in the months since Trump took office, as scandals about everything from alleged Russian interference in the election, to the firing of the FBI director, to the president's refusal to release his tax returns have taken over the public airwaves and the public sphere.

In fact, on the afternoon of February 17, 2017, Trump launched a tweet calling the *New York Times*, CNN, and all three major broadcast news networks—ABC, CBS and NBC—"fake news," undermining the legitimacy of some the nation's oldest and most venerable media sources. Even more stunning, the president declared that these establishment outlets were not his "enemy" but rather "the enemy of the American People!" (exclamation mark his). It was an astonishing media censure, especially in a nation that takes pride in its First Amendment—freedom of the press. Carl Bernstein, the journalist so often credited with an oversized role in helping bring down the Nixon Administration, quickly asserted that "Donald Trump is demonstrating an authoritarian attitude and inclination that shows no understanding of the role of the free press."[1]

It is precisely this tension between the president—and whether as an elected leader he is foremost responsible to the people or to his institutional role as head of the executive branch—and the free press that occupy center stage in this book. The American imaginary of the media typically situates reporters as watchdogs who keep elected officials on their toes. However, the same American imaginary also positions journalists as both biased and prone to sensationalism. For good or bad, Trump exposes this tension anew, and makes plain how the perception of the media very often depends on the perception of the inhabitant inside the Oval Office. When this happens, the question becomes how much "unfiltered" conversation between the president and the people is too much? Why do we critique the media for bias—or expect objectivity—but tend to look the other way when the person who holds elected power lacks for equanimity? Is not some level of evenhandedness also a good thing to expect from those to whom the public grants much responsibility and privilege? In the end, this is why Trump's claim that the media is the people's enemy is so problematic. First, media are plural. They have no unified message or claim. Their similar objective exists inside individual reporters to find stories and tell them as well as can be done on tight deadlines under the auspices of shrinking audience attention spans and increasing pressure from every imaginable source.

But second, Trump's tweet points to the reason why we came together to create this book. Our purpose is to look at how the digital age is changing both the press *and* the presidency, and to consider how the Internet and social media have created new challenges for the relationship, while also making the job of being president both harder *and* easier. Donald Trump and his 6 a.m. tweets clearly point to the fact that it is easier than ever before for the nation's chief executive to reach citizens without using a media filter. But reporters still get to write stories about those tweets—along with everything else—and sometimes those stories take on a negative tone.

That's the deal. The president speaks and acts as a human starting gun. The media hears and then responds. The relationship is mutually constitutive, beneficial, and, yes, adversarial. It's all three at once. On the Internet and off. On Facebook, on Twitter, and everywhere in between.

Only for Trump, probably not on *Between Two Ferns*.

Notes

1. Michael M. Grynbaum, "Trump Calls the News Media the 'Enemy of the American People,'" *New York Times*, February 17, 2017.

ACKNOWLEDGMENTS

This book is the outgrowth of a daylong conference about the presidency and the press held at Southern Methodist University in February 2015. Both that conference and this volume owe their existence to SMU's Center for Presidential History and its wonderful director, Jeffrey Engel. He is a scholar above all others, with a generous spirit that knows neither ego nor bounds. Others at the center who proved invaluable to the conference and this book included Brian Franklin, Ronna Spitz, and, especially, William Steding. SMU's Cary M. Maguire Center for Ethics and Public Responsibility was also an important conference sponsor, as was the Division of Corporate Communication and Public Affairs (CCPA). I express special thanks to Maguire Center Director Rita Kirk, Assistant Director Candy Crespo, and CCPA Chair Sandy Duhé for the long hours spent planning, talking, and getting every last detail in order. Your hard work was more than evident.

Thank you to the editors at Texas A&M Press for the patient and courteous ways in which they do their business. I owe a particular debt to Jay Dew.

The Meadows School at Southern Methodist University provided me with financial support to write and edit. I am especially grateful to Dean Sam Holland and Associate Dean Kevin Hofeditz. Special thanks, too, go to the division of Corporate Communication and Public Affairs, my home at SMU, and the senior faculty there who supported me every step of the way: Rita Kirk for her critical eye, Maria Dixon for her sense of humor, Owen Lynch for asking tough questions, Ben Voth for being a cheerleader and important critic, and Sandy Duhé for patiently answering every question I asked and never doubting that I had what it took to bring this book to print. Cara Jacocks and Chris Salinas are treasured colleagues, and their scholarly friendship makes me wiser. Two very smart SMU undergraduates, Emily Gullo and Sara Longone, worked long hours with me tracking down sources and citations. The book is better for what they did.

For each of the scholars and journalists who contributed to this volume, I am grateful and humbled. Jennifer Mercieca, in particular, did more than contribute. She answered emails and took calls from me about how to do the editing job well and cheered me on when I needed a boost near the end. I am grateful.

Robert Horwitz and Val Hartouni have mentored and guided me at every step of my academic journey, and this project is no exception. I could never thank them enough. Paul Lester and xtine burrough were the friends who have been there. Tracy Watson Campbell has been and remains an anchor and advisor whose wit and wisdom are irreplaceable in my life. My parents provided space, babysitting, lunches, dinners, and their unfailing support. I am lucky to be their daughter. During one critical time crunch, my mother, Joyce Martin, even helped proofread.

Finally, most importantly, my husband and partner, Francisco Aragon, never complained that the book was taking too long, but simply stayed near and felt proud of the work that I do. His unflagging belief in me is a grace beyond measure, as are the wonder of Niles and Tate. They remind me of what really matters: The sky and the stars and the moon.

INTRODUCTION

On March 11, 2014, the comedy website *Funny or Die* posted an interview between then-president Barack Obama and Zach Galifianakis for its Web series *Between Two Ferns*. The appearance was among many Obama made in an effort to encourage young Americans to sign up for health insurance as part of the Affordable Care Act—his signature healthcare legislation. But it was also something more, wrote Lauren Duca of the *Huffington Post*. The appearance was part of a larger project that Obama and his team had been working on since he first announced his candidacy in 2007, a goal best summarized as the ambition to make the president and his administration "go viral."[1]

Viral. What better word could there be to describe the atmosphere of the social media age or the president once known as BlackBerry One? And, of course, it would be easy to read this impulse on behalf of the Obamans as little more than an ego-driven itch so typical of this image-driven era as well as foolish distraction from the real business of government and an affront to the dignity of the Office of the President. Indeed, many Republicans and conservative media members took this position when it came to the Galifianakis conversation,[2] even as they also squawked about appearances and interviews Obama granted to other less traditional media outlets. For example, and to name but a few of these "nonserious" formats, over the course of his time in office Obama appeared on *The Daily Show with Jon Stewart* seven times—once as a senator, twice as a candidate, and four times as president. He rode along with Jerry Seinfeld on an episode of *Comedians in Cars Getting Coffee*. He was on Marc Maron's popular podcast *WTF*. And he read mean tweets about himself on *Jimmy Kimmel Live!* before moving on to talk with the host about more serious topics such as race relations in the United States and partisan gridlock in Washington, DC. But each of these appearances, along with the many others Obama gave to all kinds of media, mainstream and nonmainstream alike, articulate Duca's larger point about going viral. Obama's hope was that in a world where the people—the audience—are presumed to be ever more distracted, disinterested, and disheartened in the news in general and politics and government in particular, the president must do all he can to reach citizens where they actually are.[3] This means he must be present on the Internet along with the evening news, and on Comedy Central along with CNN.

"Our reduced engagement and penchant for viral consumption lends far more power to viral news items, images and videos than, say, The State of the Union," Duca wrote. "There are realities of this worth considering for the way we process information in general, but it has particular salience when it comes to the messages we receive from the president."[4]

Duca's insight points to a political question as much as it does a technical one. There is a tendency in considering technological revolutions—as well as in considering any kind of communications revolution—to say, This changes everything! Nothing will ever be the same. But on the other hand there is also the possibility that what really matters in any narrative or account (this is the possibility that historians and reporters like best) are the people: the actors who populate the pages, survive the storms, fight the revolutions, win the elections, and advance against the tides. According to this line of thinking, the story is what matters and is what makes history great; all that technology changes is how the tale gets told—whether through wires, pay phones, or Internet cables. But is this really true? Is there little more at stake for reporters, or for presidents, than knowing how to use the latest technology? Or, rather, does the technology itself alter the relationship between the media and the nation's chief executive, and so materially affect the arc of the American political narrative? Would Obama (or Clinton, or Reagan, or FDR, or even Lincoln) still have been Obama if he had served in a different, non-digital era? Would Eisenhower have been Eisenhower if he had served today?

Of course, these are impossible questions to answer, even as they are also fruitful to imagine. There is little doubt that Obama benefited from having a charming, almost electric personality that made him a natural fit for the pop culture demands of the early twenty-first century. It's hard to imagine that George H. W. Bush could ever have been so smooth, and perhaps that would have been to his detriment had he tried to run for office during Obama's time. However, when one looks exclusively at Obama's success with nontraditional formats, it is easy to overlook the ways in which his relationship with much of the political media was actually quite fraught. Indeed, according to a report by Susan Milligan published in the *Columbia Journalism Review*, by the time of the 2014 midterm elections the relationship between Obama and the press was as frosty as any relationship between the nation's chief executive and the media had been in fifty years.[5]

But then, even George Washington quarreled with the media. By the end of his first term, press critics had begun to contend that the nation's first president conducted his duties with a "monarchial" style, and was too aristocratic in nature. Near the end of his second term, newspaper attacks increased when Washington refused to heed public opposition to the Jay Treaty, an agreement intended to prevent war with England but at a cost to the American relationship with France.[6] Lincoln, too, faced his share of press antagonism, including from a "copperhead press" made up of northern newspapers who aligned with the Democratic party and "attacked the war and the administration in Washington on a more or less regular basis."[7] And so it went. Indeed, if there has been one persistent theme in the relationship between media and the nation's chief executive, it is that they are usually in a state of discontent.

Even so, the two are also mutually dependent, each unable to exist without the other. This can be complicated if it is also self-evident: the Washington press corps needs someone and something to cover; the president needs a mechanism for reaching the people. It is also not always straightforwardly obvious who the serious political media are, or whether they still matter in the same way they once did. This, in part, explains why Obama's so-called dalliances beyond the White House press corps caused so much angst and ire. Through the nineteenth century the term *press* meant just that: the printing press of newspapers and a few magazines. By the 1920s, radio had joined the scene, and by the 1950s television came along as well. Now, many newspapers and magazines are no longer printed at all, but exist only on the Internet; radio has gone satellite; television news has lost some of its gravitas as a source of public service, given the rise of 24/7 cable networks full of opinionated punditry, not to mention so-called political entertainment TV that includes programs such as *The Daily Show with Trevor Noah* (before Trevor, Jon Stewart) and *Real Time with Bill Maher,* among others; and then there is Web-based journalism that includes blogging, vlogging, Facebook, Twitter, Tumblr, Instagram, Vine, podcasting, snapchatting, and so on and so forth and more.

Each of these new technologies has disrupted the public sphere and made political journalism both more open and more difficult. Presidents, too, have had to respond to a world where news and information both get out faster and go more in-depth, even as the citizen's attention span may have shrunk. As the title of this book suggests, the press of ink on a page has yielded to the instant transmission of ones and zeros—from columns and reports drafted, edited, and considered for hours to tweets that leave the fingertips in just few seconds—soon forgotten and followed by another flurried bit. The result, as the following chapters reveal, is a media system full of reporters doing their best to take their jobs seriously, break important stories, and fulfill the public's right to know, but who often also feel frustrated by administration attempts to block access or supply them with prefabricated quotes and pictures that may very well miss the heart of the matter. On the other side of the coin are presidents and their administrations who have a story to tell and who believe—rightly or wrongly—that the reporters who cover them are more interested in drama and scandal than they are in whatever the nation's chief executive wants to communicate to the people. And so presidents work to manipulate the message and define the news, and they get irritated when reporters stray from the script too much. The question becomes, in an era of social media, how much is it fair to allow the president to transmit more or less directly to the people, and how much should still filter through the White House press corps? Does the new digital era fundamentally change the rules of the game? Are the hard questions still being asked? Perhaps more important, are they still being answered?

A Relationship Both Fraught and Dependent

In 1981 James Ceaser, Glenn Thurow, Jeffrey Tulis, and Joseph M. Bessette published an article titled "The Rhetorical Presidency." Six years later, Tulis published a book by the same name. Together, these works fundamentally reshaped how scholars of the president in both political science and political rhetoric understood and studied the relationship between the nation's chief executive, Congress, and the American people. The argument is best understood as an institutional one: It has to do with the rise of mass media technology, campaigns, and presidential leadership, especially as that leadership is negotiated with Congress and relates to the constitutional balance of powers. Where presidential rhetoric once aimed to be deliberative and logical, its main purpose the persuasion of House or Senate leaders to consider this treaty or pass that law, it now functions more on the level of emotion, as a tool of popular persuasion. "Presidents regularly 'go over the heads' of Congress to the people at large in support of legislation and other initiatives," Tulis wrote. "Today it is taken for granted that presidents have a *duty* constantly to defend themselves publicly, to promote policy initiatives nationwide, and to inspirit the population. And for many this presidential 'function' is . . . the heart of the presidency—its essential task." One indispensable way presidents bring this message to the people, of course, is through mass media.[8]

Tulis's argument soon earned detractors. Some said the presidency was always more rhetorical than he admitted.[9] Others, including George Edwards, who contributes the second-to-last chapter in this book, have gone so far as to argue that presidential rhetoric isn't of much consequence anyway, because even those commanders in chief who most frequently exercise their powers of speech from the so-called bully pulpit often fail to see much overall change in public support for the policies they espouse—or at least that's what the poll numbers show.[10]

Nonetheless, and in spite of Edwards's dubiousness that presidential rhetoric aimed at public address has any meaningful effect on public opinion, there does still exist a general consensus that, as Vanessa Beasley reminds us, "the realities of mass-mediated communication force chief executives to 'go public' to seek popular support for themselves and their policies." The media matter, and, when it comes to the president, they matter a lot. The rhetorical presidency, then, is not simply a matter for concern from the point of view of the chief executive, but from the point of view of the press as well. Journalists take their role as government watchdogs seriously and believe they are granted special access not because they are, in fact, special, but because someone must see and report the actions of government officials, especially the president. "Whether widely noticed or not, good journalism makes a difference somewhere every day," wrote Leonard Downie Jr. and Robert G. Kaiser, both editors for the *Washington Post*, in their book *The News About the News: American Journalism in Peril*. "Exposure of incompetence and corruption in government can change misbegotten policies, save taxpayers money and end the careers of misbehaving public officials. . . . Examination of the ways society cares for the poor, homeless, imprisoned, abused, [and] mentally ill . . . can give voice to the voiceless. News matters." And this is the frame through which the news media prefer to view themselves—a heroic portrait of objective reporting based in facts and hard-hitting questions. As Michael Schudson points out, "Political insiders are especially impressed with media power."[11]

Even so, we know that much like the theory of the rhetorical presidency, the notion of an unbiased, transparent press that exists to keep the White House on its toes is not as straightforward as Schudson's political insiders might like to believe. For example, there is good reason to think that what the media do especially well is affirm the status quo and legitimize government activities and positions. Reporters and broadcasters don't lead, they follow. Perhaps no recent episode more aptly captures this press tendency than the failures of media to fully cover and question members of the George W. Bush administration in the run-up to the 2003 invasion of Iraq. Moreover, that the White House press corps resides inside the West Wing—that is, inside the White House—calls into question its very independence, say some. Its presence within the halls of government, and its near

absolute reliance on official sources for news, make it a biased political institution, not an unbiased, trustworthy observer.[12]

And so these are the stakes. The presidency. The press. On the one
hand is a chief executive with a foremost interest in crafting persuasive messages for the people. On the other is a media system filled
with individuals who do their best to hold the powerful accountable
but who may not always be as neutral as the myth holds them out to
be. And then into the mix come the technologies of the Information
Age: the Internet, social media, smart phones, and more. Presidents
can now communicate with constituents in ways much cozier than
were possible in the past. For example, as Mary Stuckey posits in an
essay about the applicability of the theory of the rhetorical presidency in the modern era, while she never met President Obama personally, during his terms in office she almost daily received an email
from either him or a member of his inner circle. "It is not clear," she
writes, "whether this kind of communication creates an illusion of
intimacy with the person of the president, and if so, whether that
intimacy somehow differs in important ways from the relationship
someone like FDR, for instance, established with the nation."[13] But
this perceived coziness—or, more precisely, the efforts of the president to create this perception of coziness with members of the
public—comes at the expense of tending to his relationship with
the media. And this troubles members of the press. This leaves the
White House press corps to complain that just as the voting public
sends the president to Washington to represent their interests and
"get things done," so this same public expects journalists to hold the
chief executive accountable to his duties and the standards of the
Constitution.

One of those standards, of course, is that of the free press—the
American media are arguably the freest in the world. In addition, the
digital era makes it easier to deliver information faster than has ever
been possible in the past. These facts, however, only add to the media's
frustration with administration stonewalling. When administrations
like Obama's, or those in the future, prefer to use their own in-house
video, blogging, and social media outlets to put out news, rather than
go through the White House press corps, reporters fear they will lose
the ability to do the kinds of tough stories about White House policy
decisions the public expects. When this happens, in turn, the public

won't really know what's happening inside the Oval Office, but only what presidents and their teams want the people to know.

That's the argument, anyway, and it is an important one to have. This volume takes it as its point of departure, as each of the following chapters consider, at heart, how the relationship between the presidency and the press will continue to evolve given the realities of the digital age. Early chapters allow readers the chance to get their historical footing in terms of how the relationship has been and where it might be going; middle chapters move through history into specific and contemporary issues; and the final chapters return to the theory of the rhetorical presidency and contemplate whether it is time to update the tenets of the paradigm or even replace it entirely.

Outline of the Chapters

The book is broken into four parts, each with its own generalized theme. The first part of the book is called "Presidents, the Press, and the Times That Have Made Them." It begins with a chapter by Martha Joynt Kumar that is less focused than any of the others on digital media, but gives readers a chance to take a long view of the administrations of Presidents Ronald Reagan, George H. W. Bush, Bill Clinton, George W. Bush, and Barack Obama. This survey view of five separate presidencies makes plain how the relationship between the president and the White House press corps has changed as technology has changed. Kumar, who since 1975 has held a White House press pass as an academic, concentrates primarily in this chapter on those forums where presidents and reporters meet face-to-face: press conferences, short question-and-answer sessions, and one-on-one interviews. In so doing, Kumar demonstrates that while all presidents feel compelled to respond to press queries, each also prefers some formats over others, depending on his strengths and weaknesses as a communicator and also having something to do with changing media trends. For example, Reagan often held prime-time news conferences—in part because he enjoyed them and was quite good on his feet, but also because he presided as president during a time when the big three networks would still break from their nightly programming to cover the president. Now, they likely would not. As such, Obama preferred long-format interviews, which allowed him to target his audience and the message he wanted to deliver. These sit-downs included chats with bloggers who were favorites of the so-called millennials but that members of the older generation likely missed and the mainstream media found unseemly. Indeed, readers who are especially interested in this topic might like to turn ahead to chapter 5, where Stephen Smith examines this controversy in full, as well as chapter 7, where George Edwards discusses contemporary media trends.

Much as the theory of the rhetorical presidency has long preoccupied scholars of both political science and presidential rhetoric, so has the theory of narcotizing dysfunction puzzled scholars of media studies, especially those who specialize in citizen involvement and the makings of the public sphere. Narcotizing dysfunction is a phenomenon first described by Paul Lazarsfeld and Robert Merton in 1948 in the article "Mass Communication, Popular Taste and Organized Social Action." For Lazarsfeld and Merton, narcotizing dysfunction was an effect of too much media in people's lives; it left them feeling assailed and overwhelmed. In response, they became narcotized and began to tune out, or else confused knowledge with action and so behaved as though being aware of a problem was the same as doing something to solve it.

In chapter 2, Rita Kirk returns to this theory and differentiates the one-way media flow that went from elite media outlet to citizen from the contemporary two-way flow that grows in increasing importance by the day. The one-way flow, which existed from the advent of mass media through the mid-1990s, characterized the types of narcotizing dysfunctions Lazarsfeld and Merton described. Under the two-way flow, news, even political news, is no longer simply a matter of reporting noteworthy information about what's happening in the nation's capital, but rather constitutes what Kirk calls "the ever present now," a world that belongs to all connected citizens. This ever present now, in turn, is carried, forwarded, and commented on by anyone who chooses to participate—whether well-informed or not—through smart phones and tablets, a phenomenon of reposting that leads to further forwarding and commenting. Those seeking to influence opinion can access the modes of communication just as easily as can journalists, and sometimes with lower professional standards, while also microtargeting messages to voters based on a host of factors ranging from standard demographic features such as geography, age, race, and gender to more complex groupings of self-selected friends. This means that while the Internet and social media remove barriers to participation and give disaffected citizens a voice in the political process, they also create a fog of complexity that confuses as much as it elucidates. However, Kirk argues, this new level of citizen activity raises the question as to whether a new kind of narcotizing dysfunction has begun to take hold. As people engage in message posting, linking, forwarding, tweeting, commenting, and so on, she writes, they often do so without thinking deeply about what they are saying. This, for Kirk, is the equivalent of empty content. Citizens feel engaged, but they have actually said and done little that is of new or lasting value. That is, whereas earlier forms of narcotizing dysfunction sometimes occurred when citizens and voters who were bombarded with media confused knowledge with action, now citizens confuse media action with knowledge. The problem has inversed; the result is the same.

The two chapters of Part Two, "Presidents, People, and the Art of Expression," examine presidential and reportorial language and consider how chief executives and journalists craft messages to both inform and persuade and what kinds of storytelling techniques make them better or worse at each. Chapter 3, by Rod Hart, considers the words presidents choose to compose speeches as well as the words reporters choose to write stories about those speeches—and other political events—in both historical and contemporaneous perspective. As part of his analysis, Hart asks several fundamental questions that elucidate the presidential and journalistic genres for readers. These include queries about the essential difference between the role played in public discourse by presidents and reporters; how voters can tell, almost instinctively, the difference between who counts as a politician and who counts as a journalist; how the presidential and the reportorial voice have changed over time; and, finally, how new digital technologies, such as blogs, have altered the business of political reporting. To answer these questions, Hart takes a big-data approach to analyze distinctive and common linguistic patterns of reporters and presidents alike. In so doing, he finds that presidents are actually more vivid storytellers than are journalists and that the Internet is opening up opportunities for reporters to be more exploratory in their work. This suggests that the Web's permissiveness may be changing the fundamentals of journalism itself. In some ways this is an especially interesting chapter to read after Kirk's, because it troubles her claim that the Internet harms creativity through a narcotizing effect. Instead, Hart suggests there is plenty of innovation to be found if one looks in the right places.

In chapter 4, I consider the rhetoric presidents have used to tackle one of the biggest parts of their job: managing the economy. I further consider how presidents have used the new media of their day to engage the American public with their plans about financial issues. Many Americans deem the president a dependable source of information on the economy, and they especially look to his words for guidance during times of economic crisis. Given this, in this chapter I analyze the economic rhetoric of three presidents who served during moments of national financial catastrophe: Franklin Delano Roosevelt, Ronald Reagan, and Barack Obama. My intention is to give the reader a chance to see, up close, how presidents are technologically savvy, especially in times of economic upheaval. This may be when they trust the mainstream media the least to deliver their message without too much slant or editorializing. As such, and as the reader begins to move into the second half of the book, which raises questions about the ongoing viability of the theory of the rhetorical presidency, this chapter serves as a kind of pivot point. All three of the presidents I highlight in chapter 4 turned to technology for forwarding their economic policies at especially urgent moments in national economic history. However, only the first two, Roosevelt and Reagan, were able rhetorically to generate a unified American audience with their remarks, and so successfully narrate a new economic vision through words as articulated through media. As such, I argue that the contemporary fragmented media environment casts doubt on the possibility that any future president will be able to offer a unifying economic vision for the United States, even in times of financial crisis. This case study offers clues, then, about how—or whether—another president will be able to emerge as a transformational leader who launches a new kind of political regime, as did Reagan and Roosevelt (not to mention the likes of Lincoln or Jefferson), given the fractured nature of media platforms today.

The next, third, part of the book, "Information and Its Discontents," takes up several of the challenges of the Information Age and considers how presidents and members of the political press have dealt with some of the obstacles that digitized government and digital documents present. First, in chapter 5, Stephen Smith offers readers a history of how the White House initially got online, beginning with the inaugural WhiteHouse.gov Web page that went live during the Clinton administration, followed soon after with the first email sent by a president. (That was Clinton, too. He sent only two during his entire tenure as president.) Smith then takes an in-depth look at the tense relationship between the Obama administration and some members of the White House press corps when the president agreed to interviews with the nontraditional members of the media that I wrote about earlier in the introduction. In so doing, Smith argues that new communication technologies should not be read as dangerous or a closing down of access to the president. Rather, they are an evolution; new technologies have changed the ways citizens see the president and how they expect to be able to interact with the nation's commander in chief. Even so, this does not diminish the role of the elite political press. Democracy depends on their continued watchdog function, and presidents must remain visible and willing to respond to tough queries. As such, Smith concludes by contending that understanding republican government in the twenty-first century will require taking stock of conflicting accounts of power—whether dispersed or centralized—alongside attention to modern modes of persuasion and the responsibilities of civic engagement for elected officials and citizens alike. Readers who especially like the questions and quandaries Smith raises in this chapter might turn next to chapter 7, where George Edwards also takes up similar issues, but with an even more skeptical view.

If Smith in chapter 5 takes up the lighter side of who counts as a journalist, then Tony Pederson in chapter 6 gives the question a more serious look. Few things vex presidents or citizens more than how much access to give journalists and others to digital documents while also protecting the nation's national security from unauthorized information leaks and breaches of classified data. Indeed, in the aftermath of the 2016 presidential election and the possibility that Russia may have tried to influence its outcome through cyber-attacks on the Democratic National Committee, these questions are more imperative yet. Given this, Pederson analyzes how government and the media do, and should, negotiate the release of sensitive material. Pederson takes as his point of departure the disclosures of thousands of classified documents by Julian Assange of WikiLeaks and former NSA contractor Edward Snowden, noting that the disclosures have heightened already extant tensions between members of both the presidency and the press. This is because the rights of journalists and their ability to protect sources were already under assault by both the Bush and Obama administrations. Indeed, as much as anything, the Assange and Snowden episodes throw into stark relief how the digital age makes it easy for almost anyone to identify themselves as a journalist, making it all the more urgent that government and media work together to develop clear guidelines to follow in deciding when something should be publicly disclosed and when it should not. In a post–9-11 world, when people seem more willing than ever to permit presidents to raise national security concerns as plausible excuses not to be transparent, Pederson raises serious doubt as to how the news media can continue to fulfill their centuries-old task of serving as a check on government while also taking seriously true threats to public health and safety.

Finally, in the last part of the book, "Everything Old Is New Again," we return to the theory of the rhetorical presidency, particularly as it pertains to new media and the Information Age. In chapter 7, George Edwards, whose earlier research has called into question whether presidential rhetoric tends to move the needle of public opinion, casts a skeptical eye toward the modern relationship between the presidency and the press and questions whether much of a relationship still exists at all. He begins the chapter detailing how things have already come apart: Because citizens no longer watch (or respect) the news as they once did, the president has no choice but to try to go around the media filter to try to reach the people directly. This means using social media as much as possible while also engaging those "offbeat" channels that draw so much ire—whether on the Internet or on cable. Edwards explains that in the contemporary environment of multiplatform media fragmentation, presidents must use every tool in their toolbox if they are to have any chance of reaching constituents, including their most ardent supporters, with their messages. To illustrate this difficulty, and to make plain the changed relationship between presidents and the press, Edwards analyzes the difference between Barack Obama's success at using digital technology to campaign and reach voters as opposed to his relative failure at using this same technology to maintain citizen enthusiasm for his programs and policy proposals once in office. Edwards argues that there were several important factors at play that led to this discrepancy. First, the media environment has fractured and segmented to such a degree that it is difficult to maintain audience attention for extended periods of time. This means that even when the Obama team successfully sent messages, they were able only to reach their base, and only the very most interested members of the base at that. Second, Obama's opposition had access to the same tools: for every message the president's team sent to its base, the Republicans could send a countermessage to their own. And finally, perhaps most ironically, new media technology meant that Democratic activists could quickly and inexpensively create their own messages to pressure the president toward their own ends, which were often in a direction even more progressive than Obama and his team wanted to go. This meant that Obama had to fend off attacks from the left and the right, making it even harder to mobilize sufficient support, both inside Congress and out, to pass his legislative agenda. Thus, while the myth of new media is that it gives more people a voice in the governing process, the reality is that its power may be overstated outside of campaigning, and it may actually contribute to the ongoing gridlock between the two parties.[14]

Finally, in the last chapter of the book, Jennifer Mercieca invites readers to look beyond the rhetorical presidency. Mercieca's essay is the perfect closing chapter, as she builds on Edwards's chapter and makes plain for readers how the technologies they've been reading about through earlier chapters—from early World Wide Web pages to email to Facebook to Twitter, and so on—have come full circle in the digital age and allowed the president to go around the mainstream press, at will, to take their message directly to the people. Mercieca argues that the media have become for presidents merely an option for their message; as such, the press is but one conduit for popular persuasion; it is no longer *the* conduit for popular persuasion. Mercieca refers to this shift as the rise of the "post-rhetorical presidency." As an example, she examines Obama's unveiling of major immigration reform, an issue that polling shows a majority of Americans think is of pressing concern. And yet no major network preempted its programming to carry an important presidential announcement of major policy reform with regard to the issue. Moreover, the president's team did not initially announce its new policy—or the president's speech—from the White House press room, but instead did so via a Facebook video post. Mercieca argues that this evidences the fact that the chief executive no longer needs the media as much as was once true and helps explain why the relationship between the president and the press is more adversarial than it has ever been.

Each part of the book concludes with a "Reality Check," a short reflection by a working journalist on the presidential beat—or, in one case, a former White House advisor. Each of these writers contributes insights that are essential to the scholarly understanding of the American presidency, along with the media that keep the White House on its toes. Academics think they know what's true about life in Washington, DC, in general and about the Oval Office and the media that cover that office in particular. But theories can go only so far, and theories can tell us only so much. These reality checks are meant to fill in the cracks and point out the mistakes and misunderstandings, wherever they are. The contributions come from David Demarest, former White House communications director for President George W. Bush; Thomas DeFrank, a contributing editor at *National Journal*; Bob Mong, longtime managing editor for the *Dallas Morning News*; and Stacia Philips Deshishku, Washington bureau chief for ABC News.

From Kennedy's era of Camelot to Nixon's era of conspiracy to the contemporary moment of seeming digital chaos, the relationship between the presidency and the press will continue to evolve. Nonetheless, it will almost certainly remain true that the media will continue to criticize and presidents will continue to call this criticism unfair. The honeymoon period for new chief executives full of flattering profiles and goodwill pieces will continue to shorten; the final days full of mistrust will lengthen from months into years. And somehow, strangely, this is how we will know that the press is still free, still viable, still shining its light, however dim that light may sometimes seem.

Notes

1. *Between Two Ferns*, Funny or Die, 2014; Lauren Duca, "What a Viral Presidency Means for Obama," *Huffington Post*, December 11, 2014, http://www.huffington post.com/2014/12/10/middlebrow-obama_n_6303948.html.

2. See, for example, the following article posted by Mediaite, a website devoted to analyzing political media. Here, they follow Fox News the day Obama's interview was posted to Funny or Die and show that show after show, and guest after guest, found it improper, even as many also conceded the bit was humorous to watch. Matt Wilstein, "Fox Completely Loses Sense of Humor over Obama's *Between Two Ferns* Video," Mediaite, March 11, 2014, http://www.mediaite.com/tv/fox-completely-loses-sense-of-humor-over-obamas-between-two-ferns-video/.

In addition, on his own show Bill O'Reilly called the president's appearance "desperate," and said, "Abe Lincoln would not have done it." *National Post* Staff, "Bill O'Reilly Calls Obama's Between Two Ferns Segment 'Desperate,' Says 'Abe Lincoln Would Not Have Done It'," *National Post*, March 12, 2014, http://news.nationalpost.com/arts/television/bill-oreilly-calls-obamas-between-two-ferns-segment-desperate-says-abe-lincoln-would-not-have-done-it.

3. Jacob Koffler, "A Brief History of Obama's Daily Show Appearances," *Time*, July 21, 2015, http://time.com/3966335/a-brief-history-of-obamas-daily-show-appearances/; "President Barack Obama: Just Tell Him You're the President," in *Comedians in Cars Getting Coffee*, 2015; "The President Was Here: President Barack Obama," in *WTF with Marc Maron*, Los Angeles, June 22, 2015; David Jackson, "Obama Reads 'Mean Tweets' About Himself," *USA Today*, March 13, 2015; Jonathan M. Ladd, *Why Americans Hate the Media and How It Matters* (Trenton, NJ: Princeton University Press, 2013), chapter 1.

4. Duca, "What a Viral Presidency Means for Obama."

5. Susan Milligan, "The President and the Press," *Columbia Journalism Review*, March-April 2015, http://www.cjr.org/analysis/the_president_and_the_press.php.

6. The digital archives maintained by Mount Vernon, George Washington's historical home, include information about the first president's sometimes contentious relationship with the press. Included there are excerpts from the *Aurora General Advertiser*, a Philadelphia newspaper, including a clip that notes, among other things, an opinion that "the Jay Treaty was deeply subversive of republicanism, and destructive to every principle of free representative government." Sharon Duffy, "Press Attacks," Mount Vernon Ladies' Association, http://www.mount-vernon.org/digital-encyclopedia/article/press-attacks/.

7. George H. Douglas, *The Golden Age of the Newspaper* (Westport, CT: Greenwood Press, 1991), 61.

8. Jeffrey Tulis, *The Rhetorical Presidency* (Trenton, NJ: Princeton University Press, 1987), 4 (emphasis in the original). Also see Samuel Kernell, *Going Public: New Strategies of Presidential Leadership*, 4th ed. (Washington, DC: CQ Press, 2007).

9. See especially Melvin C. Laracey, *Presidents and the People: The Partisan Story of Going Public*, edited by Joseph V. Hughes Jr. and Holly O. Hughes, Presidency and Leadership Studies (College Station: Texas A&M University Press, 2002).

10. George C. Edwards III, *On Deaf Ears: The Limits of the Bully Pulpit* (New Haven, CT: Yale University Press, 2006). Edwards, of course, is not without his detractors. See, for example, David Zarefsky, "Presidential Rhetoric and the Power of Definition," *Presidential Studies Quarterly* 34, no. 3 (2004).

11. Vanessa B. Beasley, "The Rhetorical Presidency Meets the Unitary Executive: Implications for Presidential Rhetoric on Public Policy," *Rhetoric & Public Affairs* 13, no. 1 (Spring 2012); Leonard Downie Jr. and Robert G. Kaiser, *The News About the News: American Journalism in Peril* (New York: First Vintage Books, 2003); Michael Schudson, *The Sociology of News*, Contemporary Societies, edited by Jeffrey C. Alexander (New York: W. W. Norton & Company, 2003).

12. Daniel C. Hallin, *The Uncensored War: The Media and Vietnam* (New York: Oxford University Press, 1986); Lance W. Bennett, Regina G. Lawrence, and Steven Livingston, *When the Press Fails: Political Power and the News Media from Iraq to Katrina* (Chicago: University of Chicago Press, 2008), in which the authors argue that the media relied on the Bush administration for which stories to report and did not do enough double-checking of facts or seek out independent sources to verify their sources; and Timothy E. Cook, *Governing with the News: The News Media as a Political Institution* (Chicago: University of Chicago Press, 1998).

13. Mary Stuckey, "'The Joshua Generation': Rethinking the Rhetorical Presidency and Presidential Rhetoric," *Review of Communication* 10, no. 1 (2010).

14. Edwards, *On Deaf Ears*. For an interesting journalistic take on Edwards's scholarship and doubts about the persuasive power of presidential rhetoric, see Ezra Klein, "The Unpersuaded: Who Listens to a President?" *New Yorker*, March 19, 2012, http://www.newyorker.com/magazine/2012/03/19/the-unpersuaded-2.

COLUMNS TO CHARACTERS

PART

ONE

Presidents, the Press, and the Times
That Have Made Them

1

The Mediums That Matter

Presidential Press Relationships and How Chief Executives Respond to Shifting Technological Tides

MARTHA JOYNT KUMAR

In this, the so-called Information Age, it can be easy to overemphasize the technological changes that characterize the ways in which news is produced, at the expense of noticing the ways in which the relationship between the White House and the press has remained similar over the years. But this is a mistake. Because while some things have changed, important things have stayed the same. In particular, this chapter focuses on three elements in the relationship that have been consistently important to both presidents and news organizations over many administrations, even as both sides have had to adjust over time in order to maintain and facilitate a relationship of mutual need.

The three elements that are at the core of this relationship are continuity, adaptation, and personal choice. By continuity in the relationship, I mean recurring patterns in the ways presidents and their White House staffs use news organizations and the reporters working for them as well as how they respond to press interests and pressures. Adaptation encompasses the way presidents respond to changing political and media conditions and to their shifting fortunes in office. When, where, and with whom presidents conduct interviews, for example, reflect the strategies that White House staff use to target outlets that best match their policy goals. Adaptation also encompasses the way a president and his staff respond organizationally to new media elements and conditions by making changes in the basic White House communications structure. News organizations also adapt to financial and organizational conditions in the presidency and among their media. Personal choice represents the scope of responses from which presidents can choose in their dealings with reporters. Today there is a fairly broad range of forums presidents can draw from in determining when, how, and where to respond to press queries. There are permanent patterns, but there is also plenty of room for change and personal choice.

In the remainder of this chapter I will examine each of these three elements—continuity, adaptation, and personal choice—as they took shape in the administrations of Ronald Reagan, George H. W. Bush, Bill Clinton, George W. Bush, and Barack Obama. This will reveal much about how each of these presidents managed his relationship with the press in ways that were both the same and different from the others'. Tracking how each of these chief executives spent his time with reporters is useful because a president's time is the most valuable resource a White House has. How a president spends it tells us a great deal about the priorities, choices, and operations of a presidency. The forums in which presidents choose to meet reporters tell us about their comfort level with the media, as well as offering insight into a personal leadership style. Additionally, since the relationship with the press is a central one in the modern presidency, this significance is reflected in the communications structure a president builds as part of the overall communications strategy.

Post–World War II presidents have varied in party and political philosophy, but they have been single-minded in their efforts to find a direct channel to the public with as little interference as possible from the reporters and news organizations that provide them with those paths to the public. Indeed, writers throughout this volume, including Martin, Smith, Edwards, and Mercieca, will all describe presidential efforts to use the new media of the day to go around the press and take the message directly to the people. In his diary, President Eisenhower's press secretary James Hagerty articulated his reasons for distributing presidential information to the public through television. In a March 4, 1954, notation in his diary, Hagerty spoke about a news release that the administration put out without going through the typical White House press corps: "I'm glad we released the tape of the statement to radio, TV, and newsreels. To hell with slanted reporters, we'll go directly to the people who can hear exactly what President [Eisenhower] said without reading warped and slanted stories."[1]

Presidents and press secretaries who followed Hagerty shared an antipathy for what they considered the distortion of their messages and actions presented by news organizations and a longing for a direct connection to the public. President George W. Bush referred to press organizations as "The Filter."[2] In a 2005 interview with the *Times* of London, Bush expressed a sentiment similar to Hagerty's: "My job is to occasionally . . . go out above . . . the filter and speak directly to the people." That has been a mutually shared presidential goal. They have used different forums to reach their publics and they all involve news organizations and the reporters who work for those organizations.

Presidential Interchanges with
Reporters: The Forums

In order to consider the relationship between presidents and the press and, specifically, in order to zero in on the three elements of continuity, adaptation, and personal choice that I noted earlier are at the core of that relationship, I developed a data set over a period of several years. This data set primarily tracks presidential interchanges with reporters. There are three basic types of interchanges a president has with journalists: press conferences, short question-and-answer sessions, and interviews:

> **Press Conferences.**[3] We think of press conferences as the basic type of presidential interchange with reporters because President Woodrow Wilson and all sixteen of his successors have held them. There have been variations in the format of these sessions as well as their ground rules, but without exception all of the presidents I have studied have held them.
>
> Press conferences come in two basic shapes: Solo press conferences and joint press conferences. In a solo press conference the president typically answers questions for about forty-five minutes. Reporters prefer the solo sessions, which give them more of an opportunity to dig into the president's thinking on an issue or event than is the case in joint sessions. Joint press conferences are most often held with a foreign leader. President Obama's press conference with Chancellor Angela Merkel of Germany in February 2015

is an example of these sessions. While fewer reporters are called on than in a solo session—two per side as opposed to ten or twelve—one gets a sense of the atmosphere of the president's interactions with foreign leaders, as was the case in the conference with Merkel, where the subject of the US government's tapping of her cell phone came up.

Short Question-and-Answer Sessions with Reporters.[4] In this second type of interchange the president takes a question or two from reporters who are brought in as a pool to represent all of the reporters for that type of media, such as a print or television. These brief sessions usually deal with a single ongoing issue or event that is fresh in the news and are held in places that are restricted in the number of people who can be accommodated. One example is when President Obama met in the Roosevelt Room with people who benefited from the Affordable Care Act. However, the fact that the reporters are supposed to stay on topic doesn't mean they always do. To wit, at this event, just as the president began his discussion with the assembled group, a reporter called out a question to the president seeking his reaction to the news of a just-released ISIS video showing a captured Jordanian pilot being burned to death. The president responded with a strong denunciation of the pilot's captors.[5]

Presidential Interviews.[6] The third type of interchange is the interview. Presidents do interviews with one or more reporters and increasingly with a broad range of news organizations reflecting the current variety that exists across the media spectrum. These include print, television, radio, and online options. While most of these interviews are on the record, some are off-the-record sessions, such as the luncheon presidents traditionally have with the anchors of television networks prior to their State of the Union address. Audiences also vary, as some issues have only a local viewership, while others have national or international reach. President George W. Bush, for example, regularly gave interviews with foreign media prior to his trips abroad. Those interviews set the stage for his trip before he arrived in the country, with Bush saying in his own words what the goals of his visit were. President Obama, on the other hand, aimed his interviews more at domestic audiences and made a special effort to bring in interviewers from black and Latino news organizations.

And so, in sum, it is through press conferences, short question-and-answer sessions, and interviews that the basic aspects of the relationship between the president and the press become clear. As such, it makes sense to use these interactions as a means for analyzing how this relationship has changed and—more important—stayed the same despite the changes of the Information Age. Indeed, the requirement to be a present president is nothing new: George Washington took the presidency to the people, as did Theodore Roosevelt, Woodrow Wilson, and Franklin Roosevelt along with each of their successors and every commander in chief in between. In Washington's time, and well into the twentieth century, that meant taking what were called "swings around the circle," in which presidents took trips to meet the people.

Continuity: How the President Speaks and How the Media Listens

Since the nation's founding, every chief executive has had a message for the people. From stage coach to train to Air Force One, from newspapers to radio to television, and now through electronic media, presidents have wanted the latest tools in their communications kits. The recurring presidential goal during the thirty-four years spanning the time between President Reagan's taking the oath of office in 1981 and the end of President Obama's two terms in 2016 has been to have the audience listen and understand what the president is trying to say. To accomplish that end, presidents have had to adjust to the forums from which people are getting their news and the forms in which they get it. During that time period news organizations, in order to protect their proximity and access to the nation's chief executive, have been equally interested in how platforms have been changing.

For the most part, presidential messages are crafted by staff in the West Wing in the same offices their predecessors used. These messages are then launched from sites and sources that meet the twin needs of relevance to where people are getting their information and what venues are comfortable for the commander in chief.

Media as Information Vehicle

From a president's viewpoint, reporters are housed in the White House for the president's purposes, to carry the president's messages to the public who elected him. They are in the president's house. Presidents have seen their responsibilities—as distinguished from their power—grow as the federal government has assumed authority for a broad range of issues. The pressure for presidents to use the press has grown at a pace consistent with the public's increased policy demands. Some idea of the growth in the chief executives' scope of responsibilities can be found by examining the *Federal Register* and noting the growth in rules and regulations a president must abide by in order to communicate presidential actions and policies. Rules and regulations promulgated by presidents and those representing them in agencies and departments deal with the ways in which they are doing business. They do not take effect until they are published in the *Register*. In Eisenhower's time there were around ten thousand pages of these rules published each year. That number has grown in the intervening years, topping off at an annual rate of over eighty thousand pages in

Table 1.1. Presidential addresses and remarks at the sixth year

President Barack Obama January 20, 2009–January 20, 2015: 2,674 [21 addresses to the nation; 307 weekly addresses; 2,346 addresses and remarks]
President George W. Bush January 20, 2001–January 20, 2007: 2,962 [30 addresses to the nation; 312 radio addresses; 2,620 addresses and remarks]
President Bill Clinton January 20, 1993–January 20, 1999: 3,132 [24 addresses to the nation; 318 radio addresses; 2,790 addresses and remarks]
President George H. W. Bush January 20, 1989–January 20, 1993 (no second term): 1,678 [25 addresses to the nation; 21 radio addresses; 1,632 addresses and remarks]
President Ronald Reagan January 20, 1981–January 20, 1987: 1,931 [42 addresses to the nation; 232 radio addresses; 1,657 addresses and remarks]

Sources: Based on information found in *The Public Papers of the President at the American Presidency Project website,* http://www.presidency.ucsb.edu/ws/, *and the National Archives' Compilation of Presidential Documents,* http://www.gpo.gov/fdsys/browse/collection.action?collectionCode=CPD.

Obama's time in office.[7] That increase is symbolic of the demands on a president's time and the need of presidents to reach the public with explanations of their actions and goals.

Presidents and their White House staffs view the press as the vehicle and their best option as a resource in forming a bond with the public. Whether through television, print, or radio, the president needs to get to the targeted audiences with a message crafted to get them to listen and to garner their support.

In considering the number of addresses and remarks presidents give during their tenure, one notices similar pressures on presidents to speak publicly about what they are thinking and doing. Totaling up all of their speeches, large and small, from inaugural addresses to remarks with groups of business executives in the Cabinet Room, one can see the enormous volume of speeches presidents now give and how similar the numbers are among Presidents Clinton, Bush, and Obama. This pattern tells us that no matter who is president, or what party he represents, recent chief executives gave about five hundred speeches a year. This volume signals the enormous personal time presidents devote to communicating what they are doing and the similarities in the strategies they adopt. In part, the similarities in the totals of the three most recent presidents may also represent the limit of how many speeches the system and the public can support.

The Role of Precedent: From Press
Conferences to Weekly Radio Addresses

Acceptance of precedents is another aspect of continuity in the ways presidents interact with news organizations. In these figures, the role of precedent that is a significant aspect of the continuity in the relationship is discernible. A president establishes a precedent, and quite often his successors buy into it and continue the practice. Rarely do presidents drop media practices that their predecessors found successful. One example of a practice that became a followed precedent is the weekly radio address that President Reagan developed in his second year in office. He went to Camp David most weekends he was in Washington and enjoyed writing and giving a Saturday address to let the public know his priorities and one that he hoped would serve as a tool for guiding the conversation on the Sunday talk shows and so help set the agenda for the week in Washington.

George H. W. Bush adopted the radio address rather late in his presidency, but from their first weeks in office, Presidents Clinton, George W. Bush, and Obama all integrated a five-minute Saturday appearance as a part of their communications plans. It takes little time to prepare and deliver, and, additionally, recent presidents pre-

Table 1.2. Presidential press conferences at the sixth year

President Barack Obama Jan. 20, 2009–Jan. 20, 2015: 122 (50 solo, 72 joint) White House solo: 32 Nighttime East Room press conferences: 4 (Feb. 9, Mar. 24, Apr. 29, July 22, 2009)
President George W. Bush Jan. 20, 2001–Jan. 20, 2007: 154 (37 solo, 117 joint) Total, 2001–2009: 211 (52 solo, 159 joint) White House solo: 32 Nighttime East Room press conferences: 4 (Oct. 11, 2001; Mar. 6, 2003; Apr. 13, 2004; Apr. 28, 2005)
President Bill Clinton Jan. 20, 1993–Jan. 20, 1999: 167 (53 solo, 114 joint) Total, 1993–2001: 193 (62 solo, 131 joint) White House solo: 38 Nighttime East Room press conferences: 4 (June 17, 1993; Mar. 24, 1994; Aug. 3, 1994; Apr. 18, 1995)
President George H. W. Bush Jan. 20, 1989–Jan. 20, 1993 (no second term): 143 (85 solo, 58 joint) White House solo: 60 Nighttime East Room press conferences: 2 (June 8, 1989; June 4, 1992)
President Ronald Reagan Jan. 20, 1981–Jan. 20, 1987: 39 (all solo) Total, 1981–1989: 46 (all solo) White House solo: 36 Nighttime East Room press conferences: 31

Sources: Based on information found in *The Public Papers of the President at the American Presidency Project website,* http://www.presidency.ucsb.edu/ws/, *and the National Archives' Compilation of Presidential Documents,* http://www.gpo.gov/fdsys/browse/collection.action?collectionCode=CPD.

taped the appearances at a convenient time on Friday or earlier in the week.

The joint press conference demonstrates the strength of precedent in presidential communications. Many of our earlier presidents have had an occasional joint press conference with a foreign leader or with their department secretaries or their budget chiefs, but they did not do so as a regular pattern of presidential communications. It was President George H. W. Bush who developed the joint session as a diplomatic and communication tool. And then Presidents Clinton, George W. Bush, and Obama accepted the innovation with ease.

The press conference itself is an example of continuity in presidential communications. Each of the five most recent presidents accepted the notion that the press conference is a basic communications tool because, first, to not do so would prove costly with reporters who have long accepted it as something all presidents will do. In fact, since Woodrow Wilson first started them in his first two weeks in office, presidents have held them, even if only erratically. Presidents may not like them, but they recognize press conferences are an accepted part of the political landscape. Presidents must be able to answer questions from a tough and knowledgeable crowd independent of the chief executives and of government. The press fills that role as a surrogate for the public, which is not in a position to question a president on its own.

White House Reporters Cover the News

One of the reasons for the continuity in presidential speeches and in White House organization is the fact that the definition of what constitutes a White House story has remained similar for reporters covering the president. Reporters want basic information on whatever initiatives the White House is putting forward, including the specifics of the initiatives and their goals, what problems the initiatives are designed to solve, what role the president had in the development of these initiatives, and what the ultimate goals are; what, if any, alternatives were considered; who participated in creating the proposals, both within and outside of the White House; what the response is on the Hill; what groups are involved in the issue; and what the initiative's prospects for success are. The medium makes little difference;

reporters always want the same basic information. This, in turn, reinforces a press operation designed to meet these needs and shape
the outcomes of reporters' stories. They have different routines for
reporting that news, but the search for information is similar from
one administration to the next.

Presidential Adaptation to Changing Media Conditions and Resources

Because the presidency is situated in a fluid political and media environment, all chief executives must be ever ready to adapt. Through
time, presidents have adjusted to changes in the media structure
and used new players as a governing resource. Even if it takes some
time, change for presidents and their staff has tended to represent
opportunity more than it has been a burden. Today's new technology
that alters how messages go out is social media; earlier presidents
contended with media advances that included photography, radio,
and television.

Most often presidents take advantage of the latest technology
to reach their intended audiences and then make whatever technological adjustments their strategies require. Eisenhower's use of
television is a good example. He successfully used it in the 1952
campaign and then brought it into the White House as a governing
tool. Early on in the Eisenhower administration, his press secretary,
James Hagerty, saw the opportunity television offered to get close
to the public in a more direct way than presidents had been able to
do except by traveling to specific places and communities.[8] In his
first year as president Eisenhower changed his press conferences
from the traditional off-the-record status that had governed those
sessions from 1913 to 1953 and instead allowed them to be played
on television, albeit on a delayed basis.

Strategies for Reaching Fragmented Audiences in a Digital Age

As the media environment has changed, so too has the presidential
approach to managing the press. President Reagan, for example, had
far different press conference practices than his successors have had.
His press conferences were a kind of nighttime spectacle that repre-

sented a national moment when people gathered around their television at 8:00 p.m. to watch him speak. The three national networks
almost always preempted their primetime programming to carry his
exchanges with reporters. But no more. We are long past the time
when a president could talk to the public through nighttime East
Room press conferences. Whereas Reagan had twenty-seven prime-
time news conferences, Presidents George W. Bush, Bill Clinton,
and Barack Obama each held only four over their full eight years
in office. The major news networks are simply not inclined to grant
presidents prime speaking slots except in the most extraordinary of
circumstances, nor are voters (viewers) inclined to watch.

Indeed, only one president, George W. Bush, has been able to
command television coverage that even approached the frequency
of address that Reagan had. Moreover, this was only because of the
gravity of the attacks of September 11 and because these attacks happened relatively early in his term. When President Obama wanted
airtime for an address to the nation to inform people of significant
changes in the nation's Cuba policy, he had to do so during the day,
not at night.[9] Having cable available to carry presidential events has
allowed the networks to deny White House requests for airtime and
to stick to their entertainment programming, where their advertising revenue remains intact.

Developing Short Question-and-Answer Sessions

Press conferences are almost always on the record and so are regarded as quite risky by both presidents and their staffs. In response,
recent presidents have adapted and created a new forum, the short
question-and-answer session. These sessions are held with a pool of
reporters who come into the White House or West Wing usually at
the beginning or end of a meeting. These sessions are usually short
and held when the president wants to give out information, but in a
less formal setting where he is expected to take multiple questions.

These sessions are used as a balance with press conferences. When
a president prefers not to hold a press conference, short question-
and-answer sessions are an escape valve that relieves some of the
pressure from press demands for full media-president interchanges.
These sessions provide a quick response to something that is breaking. But as the figures demonstrate, some presidents have loved

Table 1.3. Presidential short question-and-answer sessions at the sixth year

President Barack Obama Jan. 20, 2009–Jan. 20, 2015: 152
President George W. Bush Jan. 20, 2001–Jan. 20, 2007: 427
President Bill Clinton Jan. 20, 1993–Jan. 20, 1999: 822
President George H. W. Bush Jan. 20, 1989–Jan. 20, 1993 (no second term): 335
President Ronald Reagan Jan. 20, 1981–Jan. 20, 1987: 213

Sources: Based on information found in *The Public Papers of the President at the American Presidency Project website*, http://www.presidency.ucsb.edu/ws/, *and the National Archives' Compilation of Presidential Documents*, http://www.gpo.gov/fdsys/browse/collection.action?collectionCode=CPD.

them, while others have avoided them. For example, Clinton held 822 of these sessions, while Obama has had only 152.

The benefit of these sessions is that they hold off pressure for a full press conference and get a presidential response to an ongoing situation. However, they have drawbacks as well. The temptation is for presidents to make a quick, off-the-cuff remark to a query, as President Bush did soon after September 11, 2001. Walking along a Pentagon corridor, in response to a question about whether he wanted bin Laden dead, Bush referred to a nineteenth-century Western poster advertising a sought-after criminal with the call: Wanted, Dead or Alive. The ensuing image of the president as a Texas sheriff was criticized, as was his response to a question in another short question-and-answer session that was held on July 2, 2003. There, he was asked about the readiness of Iraqi opponents to attack American troops. "Bring 'em on," Bush replied, seeming (to some) overly cavalier in tone. Bush later admitted that he regretted both comments. Nonetheless, even if he had trouble with some of his answers, Bush preferred the question-and-answer sessions over the long-form solo press conference. He held thirty-seven solo news conferences, compared to Clinton's fifty-three and Obama's sixty-four, but sat for 427 short question-and-answer sessions.[10]

Clinton liked to talk policy any chance he got. The short question-and-answer session provided that opportunity for him when he was in the White House. He had 822 such occasions at the six-year mark in his presidency. Until the subjects of such queries dealt with his impropriety with Monica Lewinsky, Clinton was an easy mark for reporters to draw out a response from him at an event open to the press. On the other hand, President Obama was noticeably wary of responding to impromptu questions and held the fewest number of these sessions of any president included in this study.

Their personal style shaped both Presidents Clinton and Obama in their willingness to answer reporters' queries. President Obama disliked being in situations in which he did not have all the information he believed he needed to provide a response. And even if he did, confusion sometimes ensued about his planned trajectory for a policy or response to an event. While Bush could get in trouble for his short answers, Obama sometimes created confusion with his long ones. In April 2009, after releasing Bush administration torture memoranda, President Obama responded with a 718-word answer to a question about whether he supported a commission looking at the torture issue. That answer dogged his press secretary over the next two weeks as reporters sought a clear yes or no response. Robert Gibbs responded that the administration would not entertain questions about hypothetical situations. When Major Garrett, then of Fox News, pointed out that the president had entertained such a question in that instance (because he had not clearly disavowed torture in the Bush administration case), Gibbs responded: "We'll have—trust me, we'll have no more of that for the remainder of this administration."[11]

Presidential Communication: Stability through Change

One of the aspects of continuity in the relationship between the president and the press is the established framework for White House communications. Since the Nixon administration there have been two basic parts of the communications operation. First is the Press Office, which deals with the daily information needs of the president, the White House staff, and reporters. Second is the Office of

Communications, which develops strategies and plans for the roll-outs of a president's policy initiatives and is responsible for laying the groundwork for the road ahead.

Rather than alter the structure in any basic way, presidents have chosen to graft on new units as different technologies emerge or to provide whatever additional resources chief executives and their staffs believe they can effectively use. Even President Nixon did not try to reorganize and eliminate the Press Office; rather, he developed a separate communications planning operation. Although both offices sometimes operate under one communications overlord, the two operations have had different and complementary strengths over periods that stretched through an array of changes in the media.

The official presidential photographer, with his or her team, is a separate operation, but their photos are well integrated into what the communications and press offices release. The Obama White House added in a videographer to the existing photographic team, allowing them to do many new things, including making the Saturday radio address and a YouTube video address (see chapters 4 and 7 for more about this). Another change the Obama team made had to do with how they distributed their photos. Rather than limit the release of official White House photos so that news organizations could feature pictures taken by their own photographers, the White House photographers released their photographs in bulk releases on Flickr so that the public could access the White House photos the president and his staff chose to release. The president's staff saw an opportunity to directly engage the public with presidential images, and they took advantage of the resource.

Social media were a rapidly developing presence during President Obama's tenure, as several authors in this volume point out. Obama's team worked diligently to leverage the public through the website WhiteHouse.gov (first launched during the Clinton tenure) as well as Facebook and then, when it appeared, Twitter. Nonetheless, even though the Obama team prioritized its digital presence, it did not make its online staff into an autonomous communications office. Instead, the unit was tucked into the already extant communications office. The basic White House press and communications units continued as they had in the administrations of President

Obama's predecessors. Additionally, the president and his team responded to the new digital media opportunities in much the same way as his predecessors had responded to new resources that became available during their years in office.

The Power of Personal Choice

For the most part, presidents accept—at least in principle—that they have to respond to reporters' queries. However, flexibility remains in where, when, and how presidents respond to those questions. All of them hold press conferences, but even there one can see change in what constitutes a press conference. Presidents Clinton, George W. Bush, and Obama all used press conferences, particularly joint ones with foreign leaders. But rather than spending his time with the press in short question-and-answer sessions, President Obama often chose a different forum for answering reporters' questions—the interview. Whereas his predecessors mostly eschewed this choice, President Obama employed it as a major avenue for his dealings with reporters. During his first six years in office, he had 872 interviews, more than any president in history. At their six-year mark, Presidents Reagan, Clinton, and George W. Bush had far fewer—only 415, 239, and 333, respectively.[12]

At the same time that some publicity opportunities have become more perilous than they once were, press conferences being a good example, others became more attractive. With an array of media now operating online as well as in print and on television and radio, there exist both new as well as long-established opportunities to reach specific audiences a president might want to target for his programs and for any other message he wants to deliver. For President Obama, one-on-one interviews turned out to be a good way of meeting his twin needs of reaching particular targeted audiences and fitting in with his personal style.

President Obama and his staff wanted to reach the largest audience he could and, at the same time, still reach an audience that was appropriate for whatever goal he had in mind at a particular time. It could have been as specific as doing thirteen interviews with urban radio outlets by phone from his office the day before and the day of the 2014 congressional elections to encourage Latino and black voters to vote, as President Obama did that year. Or, as another example, he did short interviews in person on January 22, 2015, close to the February deadline to sign up for health care. Here, and much to the chagrin of members of the more traditional media, as Smith explains in chapter 5, the White House arranged for Google to set up interviews for him in the East Room with three bloggers and several million youthful followers. In these interviews, Obama encouraged young people to sign up for health care, as members of that group were important for the viability of the Affordable Health Care Act program, yet proved to be a hard-to-reach constituency. As this example shows, interviews proved to be an especially effective way for Obama to reach different publics compared to the more typical routes through the White House press corps, because these one-on-one conversations allowed him to target specific groups as well as cast both broad and narrow topic nets.[13]

President Obama's decision reflected his personal style, but it also revealed a recognition of how the chief executive's media environment had changed. In Reagan's era, if the president wanted to get coverage of an event, he and his staff aimed for the three network evening news programs that devoted substantial time to covering individual presidential events. If President Reagan wanted television airtime for a personal appearance in the evening, he had little difficulty acquiring it. But a quick look at these numbers shows how things have changed: At the six-year mark in their presidencies, Ronald Reagan had delivered forty-two addresses, Clinton twenty-four, and Obama just twenty-one. These numbers include inaugural addresses, speeches to joint sessions of Congress, and those addresses that the National Archives categorizes as addresses to the nation in its *Public Papers of the Presidents of the United States* series. And so we see that Reagan delivered fully twice as many evening addresses as did Obama.

While we think of President Reagan as a television president, it was more because of his addresses and his prime-time press conferences than it was because of the interviews he gave. Like Obama, Reagan often used print for his interviews; 69.6 percent of his interviews were with print publications, and 61 percent of those were aimed at national audiences. Reagan regularly sat with Hugh Sidey of *Time* as well as with reporters for *Newsweek* and *U.S. News & World*

Report. Nonetheless, he regarded these interviews as supplementary; his press conferences and addresses to the nation were his main press events, by which he expected the public to truly get to know him.

President George W. Bush divided his time almost evenly between television (49.6 percent) and print (45.3 percent) and rarely did radio. President Clinton, however, favored radio. He did more interviews on radio (50.2 percent) than television (31.4 percent), but it is important to remember that he was taking questions almost daily in short question-and-answer sessions at a much higher rate than his predecessors and successors did. He did not need to do interviews to get his points across, and he did only 239 of them by the end of his sixth year. One of the reasons he enjoyed doing radio was that he regularly did interviews when he was governor of Arkansas and continued that practice when he became president. Like President Obama, he often wanted to reach a black urban audience to get out the vote and to explain any policies that would have an effect on them.

Presidents and their staffs acknowledge that viewers have moved away from network evening news programs and focus attention on primetime news programs as well as morning and evening network shows. One way of getting some primetime coverage is doing interviews with television networks that have news programs in the evening hours. The most popular of primetime news programs is CBS's *60 Minutes*, a broadcast President Obama appeared on multiple times. President Obama did eleven interviews with Steve Kroft of *60 Minutes* (appearing on eight programs) through his first six years in office, and some of that interview material was used on the *CBS Evening News* as well. When he spoke to Kroft, he spent time going into depth on issues. The average amount of time he spent with Kroft was one hour, almost all of which was used in the resulting *60 Minutes* episode. This long amount of uninterrupted time allowed the president to lay out his case for his issues and leadership in the way he wanted.[14]

Additionally, *60 Minutes* has a wide and vast audience. Television interviews reach a broad range of people. In a recap at the end of May in the 2014–15 season, CBS reported average audience ratings of 12.38 million viewers for *60 Minutes* and 7.24 million viewers for the *CBS Evening News*. The morning news shows also offer a president and his aides a good viewing audience when they want to get a message to the public quickly. The May 2015 figures for the *Today Show*, the network morning show with the largest audience, had an average of 4.878 million total viewers for the 2014–15 season. With fewer people reading newspapers and news magazines and the accelerating decline of print publications, President Obama aimed his attention at doing interviews with national television programs.[15]

For President Obama, national media interviews represented 38 percent of his total; regional and local interviews were 26 percent; and specialty presses were another 27 percent. Clinton liked to do local interviews—40 percent—many with regional and local news-

Table 1.4. Presidential interviews at the sixth year

President Barack Obama Jan. 20, 2009–Jan. 20, 2015: 872
President George W. Bush Jan. 20, 2001–Jan. 20, 2007: 333
President Bill Clinton Jan. 20, 1993–Jan. 20, 1999: 239
President George H. W. Bush Jan. 20, 1989–Jan. 20, 1993 (no second term): 383
President Ronald Reagan Jan. 20, 1981–Jan. 20, 1987: 415

Note: Unlike all of the other categories, statistics on interviews are only occasionally publicly released. They are regarded as the property of the news organization and, with some exceptions, the individual organizations control whether and when transcripts are released. For the Obama, George W. Bush, and Clinton administrations, my figures represent internal counts maintained by White House staff. For the interview numbers for Presidents Reagan and George H. W. Bush, I have used the President's Daily Diary, which is compiled from official internal records by the president's diarist, an employee of the National Archives and Records Administration. For Presidents Reagan and George H. W. Bush, the President's Daily Diary offers a more complete picture of the president's interactions with those associated with news organizations because the diaries captured the phone calls they placed and those they received. Even when they are brief, I include these phone contacts in my counts, because the information exchanged between the president and the journalists will be used in some way by them and/or their news organizations in their articles or planning of their news coverage. The information they exchange is also important for presidents for their planning and decision making. The President's Daily Diaries for Presidents George W. Bush and Bill Clinton have not yet been made public.

papers that no longer exist. President George W. Bush favored interviews with national audiences—46 percent—but he included a
larger percentage of interviews with foreign publications than did
his predecessors or his successor. Bush did 28.8 percent of his interviews with foreign news organizations, in contrast with 3.8 percent
for Obama, 11.3 percent for Clinton, and 15.0 percent for Reagan.
With two wars for which he needed to build alliances abroad, President Bush wanted to explain his policies to an international community. He also had a communications strategy by which to set the
table for his trips by holding interviews with correspondents from
the countries he was going to visit so that when he got there the
people in the country knew what he wanted from his trip. President
Obama's interview totals reflect a relative lack of interest in foreign
news coverage through personal interviews, even though foreign
policy was a major issue in his presidency with the winding down of
the wars in Iraq and Afghanistan and the rise of the threat posed to
the region by ISIS. He spoke about those issues to a domestic audience, but not to foreign ones.

Conclusion

Continuity characterizes the contemporary relationships presidents
have with the press. They come into office with expectations that
they will meet with reporters to answer their questions. Yet, there
has also been sufficient flexibility as to when and where the recent
presidents met with reporters. In fact, President George H. W. Bush
developed a new meeting place for presidents and reporters. As a
president interested in foreign relations who met often with government leaders from throughout the world, Bush made more frequent
use of joint press conferences with foreign leaders than did all of his
predecessors combined. In so doing he demonstrated that there are
alternate forums for presidents to meet with those who cover them.
Joint press conferences became so popular that his three successors
have held more joint sessions than solo ones.

The presidents I have written about in this chapter—Ronald
Reagan, George H. W. Bush, Bill Clinton, George W. Bush, and
Barack Obama—demonstrate the degree to which a commander in
chief can adapt to the current media constellation and choose how

and when he wants to meet with the press. All five responded to the pressures reporters exerted but managed to do so in a way that accommodated their own needs and strengths. At the same time, the presidents and their staffs had to adapt to where the public was getting its news. During Reagan's time, for example, the weekly news magazines were a favorite, but by Obama's tenure he and his team focused on those news organizations people attentively watched or where a message best fit, whether that was an interview on *60 Minutes* for an update about ongoing tensions in the Middle East, or appearing with blogger GloZell Green the day after the 2014 State of the Union address to encourage millennials to sign up for the Affordable Care Act. In so doing, each president I studied put into action the wise advice of Press Secretary Hagerty that the best way for a president to get a message through is to find a way to go directly to the people. This is the work of the rhetorical presidency in action.

Notes

1. James Hagerty, "James Hagerty Diary," March 4, 1954, Hagerty Papers, Dwight D. Eisenhower Library.

2. George W. Bush, "Interview with the London *Times*," June 29, 2005, American Presidency Project, http://www.presidency.ucsb.edu/ws/?pid=73885.

3. Press conferences are divided into solo and joint sessions. Solo sessions are ones the president has in which he alone answered questions from reporters rather than having anyone with him also to respond to queries. Joint press sessions are usually ones in which the president answers questions together with a foreign leader. With this format, each leader answers questions from an equal number of reporters divided between the foreign and White House press corps members present. Both leaders first make statements, usually about what was discussed in their meeting, and then they take questions. Solo sessions tend to be longer ones. I have noted how many solo sessions a president has held in the White House compound. I have also noted how many of the solo sessions were prime-time East Room press conferences. President George H. W. Bush is the first president to use joint press conferences on a regular basis, and his successors have continued the trend he began. Press conferences are a category used by the National Archives over several decades in its *Public Papers of the Presidents of the United States*. While I use their categorization of press conferences as a way of establishing comparability, I further break them down into solo and joint sessions, depending on how many people answered questions and whether the president asked reporters to direct queries to both leaders. News conferences are found at the American Presidency Project website, http://www.presidency.ucsb.edu/ws/, and the National Archives' *Compilation of Presidential Documents*, http://www.gpo.gov/fdsys/browse/collection.action?collectionCode=CPD.

4. Short question-and-answer sessions are events in which only a small number of reporters representing the White House press corps—a pool—is allowed in to question the president. This category is designated by the National Archives as "Exchanges with Reporters," events at which the President may or may not make remarks at the same time. If he has a speech that is designated by the National Archives as "Remarks and Exchanges with Reporters," it is counted twice in my tabulations. His remarks are counted separately in the "Addresses and Remarks" category, while the interchange with reporters is counted in the "Short Question-and-Answer Sessions." In the Reagan and George H. W. Bush years some of these sessions were titled, "Session with Reporters," although the greatest number were categorized as "Exchange with Reporters." The sessions are found at the American Presidency Project website, http://www.presidency.ucsb.edu/ws/, and the National Archives' Compilation of Presidential Documents, http://www.gpo.gov/fdsys/browse/collec tion.action?collectionCode=CPD.

5. Barack Obama, "Remarks at a Roundtable Discussion with Beneficiaries of the Patient Protection and Affordable Care Act and an Exchange with Reporters," February 3, 2015, American Presidency Project, http://www.presidency.ucsb.edu/ws/?pid=109342.

6. Unlike all of the other categories, interviews are only occasionally publicly released. They are regarded as the property of the news organization, and, with some exceptions, the individual organizations control whether and when transcripts are released. For all three recent administrations my figures represent internal counts maintained by White House staff. The President's Daily Diaries for Presidents George W. Bush and Bill Clinton have not yet been made public. For the interview numbers for Presidents Reagan and George H. W. Bush, I have used the Presidents' Daily Diaries, which were compiled from official internal records by the president's diarist, an employee of the National Archives and Records Administration. The Reagan personal diary and President's Daily Diary are online through the Reagan Foundation website at http://www.reaganfoundation.org/white-house-diary.aspx, and the President's Daily Diary for George H. W. Bush is available through the Miller Center at the University of Virginia, but it goes only through October 1990. Instead, I used the full President's Daily Diary for George H. W. Bush, which is available at the George H. W. Bush Presidential Library in College Station, Texas. For Presidents Reagan and George H. W. Bush, the President's Daily Diary offers a more complete picture of the president's interactions with those associated with news organizations, because the diaries capture the phone calls they place and those they receive. Even when the calls are brief, I include these phone contacts in my counts because the information exchanged between the president and the journalists will be used in some way by them and/or their news organizations in their articles or in planning of their news coverage.

7. Harold W. Stanley and Richard G. Niemi, *Vital Statistics on American Politics, 2013–2014* (Washington, DC: CQ Press, 2013).

8. Michael Baruch Grossman and Martha Joynt Kumar, *Portraying the President* (Baltimore, MD: Johns Hopkins University Press, 1981).

9. President Barack Obama, "Address to the Nation on United States Policy toward Cuba," December 17, 2014, American Presidency Project, http://www.presidency.ucsb.edu/ws/index.php?pid=108030&st=&st1.

10. George W. Bush, "Remarks to Employees in the Pentagon and an Exchange

with Reporters in Arlington, Virginia," September 17, 2001, American Presidency Project, http://www.presidency.ucsb.edu/ws/index.php?pid=65079&st=&st1; "Remarks Announcing the Nomination of Randall Tobias to Be Global AIDS Coordinator and an Exchange with Reporters," July 2, 2003, American Presidency Project, http://www.presidency.ucsb.edu/ws/index.php?pid=564&st=&st1; Dan Froomkin, "Second Thoughts About "Bring 'em On," *Washington Post*, January 14, 2005, http://www.washingtonpost.com/wp-dyn/articles/A9092–2005Jan14.html.

At the end of his term, Bush reflected in an interview with CNN that his comments were a mistake. In the same interview President Bush regretted his challenge to Iraqi opponents to "bring 'em on." Alexander Mooney, "Bush: 'I Regret Saying Some Things I Shouldn't Have Said,'" CNN, November 11, 2008, http://www.cnn.com/2008/POLITICS/11/11/bush.post.presidency/.

11. Obama made these remarks following a meeting that he was having with the king of Jordan. For more information, see "Remarks Following a Meeting with King Abdullah II of Jordan and an Exchange with Reporters," April 21, 2009, American Presidency Project, http://www.presidency.ucsb.edu/ws/index.php?pid=86029&st=&st1; "Press Briefing by Press Secretary Robert Gibbs," April 23, 2009, American Presidency Project, http://www.presidency.ucsb.edu/ws/index.php?pid=86046&st=&st1.

12. See note 6 above for an explanation of what constitutes an interview and the differences in the information available for when and with whom the five presidents did interviews.

13. The three bloggers are Hank Green, Glozell Green, and Bethany Moda, "Google Interview," https://www.youtube.com/watch?v=Q9NveDmfJBg.

14. The interviews were conducted on March 20 (2), September 8, and December 7, 2009; November 4, 2010; May 4, May 5, December 6, and December 9, 2011; January 25, 2013, with Secretary of State Hillary Clinton; and September 26, 2014.

15. Sarah Bibel, "CBS News' Sunday Morning & Primetime Broadcasts Close Out the Season & May Sweeps with Wins in Viewers & Adults 25–54," TV by the Numbers, May 22, 2015, http://tvbythenumbers.zap2it.com/2015/05/22/cbs-news-sunday-morning-primetime-broadcasts-close-out-the-season-may-sweeps-with-wins-in-viewers-adults-25-54/407435/; Sarah Bibel, "NBC's 'Today' Topped 'Good Morning America' in Adults 25–54 Last Tuesday," TV by the Numbers, May14, 2015, http://tvbythenumbers.zap2it.com/2015/05/14/nbcs-today-topped-good-morning-america-in-adults-25-54-last-tuesday/404191/.

Revisiting Narcotizing Dysfunction

*New Media, Interactivity, and Rapid Response
in Presidential Communication*

RITA KIRK

Numerous theorists have discussed the role of "disruptive" technologies and their impact on the world.[1] With each new disruption—whether the impact of papyrus on ancient oral cultures, the printing press and its introduction of communication to the masses, or the auditory and visual revolutions of the early twentieth century—profound changes produce opportunities and stimulate fear. I argue that in 2016 we are in the midst of another disruption that changes the way we communicate. It, too, has widespread implications for our society and, more specifically, the relationship between the public, the press, and the president.

In addressing the disruption of contemporary forms of new media, an important first step is to get a clearer picture of the tension created by change and make some observations about what we can see while we are in the midst of this shift. Of course, it is with some excitement and concern that we consider history as it unfolds. This shift is not yet fully understood, and these observations may not provide a determinative picture of the media landscape. Yet it does provide a moment of reflection in the midst of upheaval and permits future readers a glimpse into the environment as we see it unfold.

In this chapter I argue that it is useful to examine the analysis of leading critics during another seismic shift in technology use and consider the qualities of the current new media model from that vantage point. In particular, I argue that the concept of narcotizing dysfunction, first introduced by Paul Lazarsfeld and Robert K. Merton in the 1940s, has been upended. Rather than being narcotized by so much information that the public becomes inert, current users have become so engaged in responding to information that they experience frenetic dysfunction: a need to respond without time for contemplation, reflection, or assimilation of incongruent factors.

Narcotizing Dysfunction: Disruptive Shifts in Technology

The first documented shift of the media landscape happened in the late 1940s. Even though radio and film were introduced earlier, it wasn't until their innovative use in World War II and subsequent commercialization after the war that the media environment took a marked turn. In the mid-1950s radio became more easily accessible as transistors were developed, enabling smaller, more portable radios. Radio frequencies, once limited to local markets, now reached across the nation as transmitter power increased, and FM stations were introduced, providing clear, static-free sound. Television became more affordable and not only restructured the design of our living rooms but also the schedule of our lives.

This shift had two important distinctions: news *was*, in many ways, an essential component of family life. Earlier developments in radio brought families together for fireside chats and radio dramas; thus, it blended the functions of entertainment and news for the first time. Additionally, this shift ushered in a mass audience capable of experiencing mediated messages simultaneously and in real time. It changed the nation from a collection of communities to a nation with common information flow.

As with all disruptive shifts, this new environment created a sense of foreboding, which was a feeling expressed by some of the leading theorists of the time, including famed Columbia researchers Lazarsfeld and Merton: "There is . . . concern with the present effects of the mass media upon their enormous audiences," they wrote, "particularly the possibility that the continuing assault of these media may lead to the unconditional surrender of critical faculties and an unthinking conformism."[2] Conformism, in an era emerging from the propaganda-dominated media use during World War II, was a prime concern for media critics. Interestingly, the path to conformism they feared was not necessarily a government propaganda machine, although that was certainly a worry, but rather an abundance of information that they argued would create a narcotizing dysfunction. The exploration of this narcotizing dysfunction between what they observed back then to the frenetic dysfunction I observe in the current media culture guides this analysis.

The original claim of a narcotizing dysfunction was observed to be a direct result of the shifting media landscape. That 1940s shift cannot be underestimated, for it detailed a transformational change in how people became aware of—and supposedly consumed—political information. The most obvious distinction of that "new media" age was that the media seemed to be everywhere; they surrounded people. By 1948 some seventy million people went to the movies every week, forty-six million read newspapers, and thirty-four million homes had radios they listened to for an average of three hours a day. Lazarsfeld and Merton noted that the media became so pervasive that they went "largely unnoticed." Moreover, the insidious nature of the media created conditions that served as a public palliative. "This vast supply of communication may elicit only a superficial concern with the problems of society, and this superficiality often cloaks mass apathy," they wrote. "Exposure to this flood of information may serve to narcotize rather than to energize the average reader or listener." Public passivity, then, was identified as an inherent flaw of such media. Lazarsfeld and Merton considered public action, not passive information consumption, to be the key to promoting democratic values. They concluded: "In short, he [the public] takes his secondary contact with the world of political reality, his reading and listening and things, as a vicarious performance. He comes to mistake *knowing* about problems of the day for *doing* something about them." While acknowledging that this was certainly not the intent of newscasters, researchers were clear that media inadvertently produce effects that could, perhaps, be exploited.[3]

One of those claims was elitist, no doubt, as it proffered that the emergence of broadcast media, and especially television, lowered the intellectual barriers of public media consumption. The explosion of radio and television threatened the newspaper industry for various reasons. Newspapers require a literate public; radio and television do not. This fear was compounded by the concern that these new media might siphon off regular newspaper readers. Second, radio and television were able to get information to the listener with greater speed than newspapers, making them a more valuable source for those who wanted to know the latest breaking news. Third, the nature of news coverage changed. Instead of the more in-depth reporting of newspapers, the visual and auditory media began moving toward the sound bite. Issues became simplified for mass consumption: "Public issues must be defined in simple alternatives, in terms of black and white."[4] This dumbing down of the news was, therefore, seen as a threat to democracy. Fourth, the ability to reach mass consumers provided an economic opportunity for media owners through increased advertising revenue. Finally, in the aftermath of World War II, political leaders became aware of the enormous power of the media in shaping political information and opinion, although communication researchers were unclear as to precisely how that worked. In short, it changed the political climate forever.

Each of these shifts suggested that a new type of journalist was needed: one who looked and sounded trustworthy. Similarly, a new type of politician emerged: one whose image became as important as ideas.

These value shifts, and the presumed potential of the media to create a climate harmful to democratic thought, is at the heart of Lazarsfeld and Merton's concept of the narcotizing dysfunction. They considered it narcotizing because "In this particular respect, because mass communications may be included among the most respectable and efficient of social narcotics. They may be so fully effective as to keep the addict from recognizing his own malady. . . . It is termed *dys*functional rather than functional on the assumption that it is not in the interest of modern complex society to have large masses of the population politically apathetic and inert."[5] From the vantage of the twenty-first century, we can see that the one-way communication model of that era created challenging conditions for those message recipients who wanted more interaction and participation.

That very condition—the one-way model of information—provided an opportunity for journalists to fill a new role, one that had been envisioned earlier but lacked the power to be effective. Acting on behalf of the public, journalists became arbiters of facts and contextualized the news for viewers. They stood in the gap and made sure that elected officials were held accountable for their actions and did the work of speaking truth to power on behalf of the people. In fact, the media themselves began wielding a new kind of influence. Whenever citizens were narcotized, media would be awake: "The mass media *confer* status on public issues, persons, organizations, and social movements. . . . Recognition by the press or radio or magazines or newsreels testifies that one has arrived, that one is important enough to have been singled out from the large anonymous masses, that one's behavior and opinion are significant enough to require public notice."[6] That era of professional journalism radically changed the nature of the profession. Journalists became the impartial arbiters of news. They were viewed as the bulldog protectorate of the people against the abuses of government. They questioned authority, demanded accountability, and publicly skewered those who abused public privilege. And, perhaps with some degree of hubris, they defined what constituted "all the news that's fit to print."

Rather than mere challengers to authority, as were the muckrakers such as Ida Tarbell and Upton Sinclair, journalists became powerful. They were credited for righting the ship of state during the McCarthy hearings—the only institution powerful or brave enough to question the crusading senator and his anticommunist movement. Other notable examples of media prowess ranged from the Bay of Pigs to Watergate. Quite literally, the balance of power between the press and our political leaders changed. No one, not even the president, was beyond the reach of this institution.

Of course, as subsequent scholars have shown, Lazarsfeld and Merton underemphasized citizen and viewer agency in their theory, even as they may have overemphasized the power of the media. Even so, their initial insights with regard to narcotizing dysfunction proved revolutionary to the fields of communication and media studies. As such, this historical perspective provides insight into our present media disruption. As we consider the impact of the current media shift, we are equally aware of who gains and who loses and the impact these changes may have on the relationship of the public, the press, and the presidency.

New Media and the Shift toward Public Activism

If unthinking conformism characterized the 1940s, at least in part, the rapidity of change in our current age similarly outpaces our ability to comprehend and critically evaluate messages today. Once again, the disruption is having real consequences for the business of news. In many ways this new media era is addressing some of the excesses of the old and breathing life into democracy in a way that is both unexpected and yet puts us ill at ease. There is no doubt that the political landscape has embraced new media, in part as a way to bypass the entrenched power structures of government. Yet by contrast to the earlier era it circumvents media organizations.[7]

Today's new media are invasive. Few people would have imagined that Internet sites would be a standard feature of campaigns when they first began in 1996. Nor could we have envisioned the creation of a host of new media such as political blogs, widely adopted by the 2004 presidential campaign,[8] or the use of social media sites such as Facebook, Twitter, and Instagram that were routinely used in 2008 and 2012. The new normal means that things once inventive and new quickly become commonplace. Media are created, blossom, and become obsolete in a matter of weeks. Apps driven through smartphones can push news organizations to consider the form through which people want their news delivered as well as the speed of their access.

Importantly, the driver of these changes is often not the legacy media and the large companies that own them, but the public who uses them and the designers who feed those public desires.[9] Modern campaigns seek to find where people are gathered—the electronic watering hole, as it were—and then adapt their messages to the user's media. Few people would have envisioned that messages in 144 characters would play a significant role in the way people monitor their political environments. Fewer still would imagine that such tweets would serve as the first blush of unfolding news events, often stimulating coverage by the legacy media. The paradigm has shifted, then, from the introduction of new concepts by the legacy media to user-driven change. But there are other changes as well.

As I see it, there are several distinct changes in this current media disruption. First, there is a challenge of localism.

The Challenge of Localism

The early twentieth century led us to an era of national news prominence, but there was always a place for the local news. As the economic model changed in the age of new media, local papers began folding at an alarming rate. Today, there is a paucity of information access regarding local news. Alberto Ibarguen, president of the John S. and James L. Knight Foundation, said in a hearing before Congress led by then-Senator John Kerry:

> For the first time in the history of the Republic, it's easier for a high school student to learn about the crisis in Darfur online than about corruption in local government in many local papers. Until recently, the circulation area of a newspaper or the reach of a local television or radio signal roughly coincided with the physical boundaries of cities and counties from which we elected mayors and school boards and Members of Congress. Even if we didn't know what was happening halfway around the world, for us all politics was local, and so was daily news coverage, and it was the news coverage that was shared generally, connecting buyers and sellers . . . but also citizens to other citizens. Our information systems helped define American communities and helped give them individuality and character. Those systems have changed. The new systems are digital and mobile and not bound by geography. The citizen is a user of information more than a passive consumer.[10]

We have all heard of market-driven news, and now we are experiencing the fruits of that model. Journalists are rarely retweeted at a significant level for coverage of city hall or school board meetings or monitoring court dockets. In simple terms, those activities seldom lead to news that sells. Within a generation we may have no one who guards the public interest, at least at the local level, unless you live in a major media market or some unforeseen revisions are made.

Some sixty years ago journalist Walter Lippman said he was secure in his belief that American democracy would endure: "There is," he said, "a fundamental reason why the American press is strong enough to remain free. That reason is that American newspapers, large and small, and without exception, belong to a town, a city, at the most to a region." The secret of a truly free press, he continued, is "that it should consist of many newspapers decentralized in their ownership and their management, and dependent for their support upon the communities where they are written, where they are edited and where they are read."[11] But our mobile society has thwarted that claim. Our mobile society means that the geographic unity Lippmann heralded is no longer in play, or at least is significantly less likely to be in play.

Demographically, Americans in this era are prone to frequent moves. "New data showed that more than 1 in 10 Americans moved between 2012 and 2013. . . . More than 35 million Americans changed residences, meaning that 11.7 percent of the country over the age of 1 had a new address during that time period."[12] And with the shift of populations, news is nationalized (and sometimes internationalized) such that awareness of the Ebola health issue in Liberia has greater top-of-mind awareness than the plight of homelessness in our own backyards.

Yet people yearn for that personal connection. They desire to become players in their own communities. Social activism among the young is on the rise, and the need for effective reporting on local issues is of critical importance. The problem is that it costs real money to produce high-quality news and analysis. Jim Maroney noted that in 2005 the *Dallas Morning News* was spending $30 million a year on news-gathering, with "more reporters on the street than the ABC, NBC, CBS, and FOX affiliates in our market combined."[13] There *are* readers for that information—it's just that they prefer the information to be free and abhor advertising intrusions. The challenge, then, is to find a model that responds to the challenge of localism.

The Challenge of Economics

It follows then that the second challenge is the economic viability of news. By and large, new media are still largely free media. Sadly, in an effort to stay competitive, major television news services have reduced the number of reporters and have replaced them with rip-and-read analysts who merely retrieve news from other sources and spend their time offering point-of-view analysis. We do not know if such analysis encourages audiences to be better analysts of information themselves or if these news commentaries spark greater public

debate or awareness. But we can deduce that there are fewer reporters doing the real business of journalism.

The economics of news has changed the hard line between news
and advertising as well as news and entertainment. So-called native
advertising, which blends public relations and advertising, is a tactic
by which information is placed in news media so that the advertisement is indistinguishable from a news story. As Mitchell explains:
"In digital news, the overlap between public relations and news
noted in last year's "State of the News Media" report became even
more pronounced. One of the greatest areas of revenue experimentation now involves website content that is paid for by commercial
advertisers—but often written by journalists on staff—and placed
on a news publishers' page in a way that sometimes makes it indistinguishable from a news story. Following the lead of early adapters
like the *Atlantic* and Mashable, native advertising, as it is called by
the industry, caught on rapidly in 2013."[14]

Andrew Sullivan, former editor of the *New Republic* and a former
blogger as well, argues that the lines are sometimes so blurred that
readers cannot distinguish between them. As another critic notes, it
may "not bother consumers as long as they are a good read." In fact,
these advertorials are less intrusive than traditional advertising. In
a critique of this relationship, *Wall Street Journal* managing editor
Gerard Baker said in a speech at NYU's journalism school that such
advertising/news blur is a "Faustian pact." In essence, the public is
being seduced by ads posing as news.[15]

Critically, the way consumer and successful new media companies make money is radically changing. Marissa Mayer, who was at
the time vice president for search products and user experience at
Google, later chief executive officer at Yahoo, said in the 2009 Kerry
hearings that "digital music [has] caused consumers to think about
their purchases as individual songs rather than full albums. Similarly, the structure of the Web has caused the basic unit, the atom of
consumption for news, to migrate from the full newspaper to the
individual article. With online news, a reader is much more likely to
arrive at a specific article rather than, say, the home page."[16]

The measures of commerce have clearly changed. With legacy
media, the way viewers were categorized had to do with "reach"

and "frequency." That poses the questions, "How many people are exposed to a message?" and "How many times do they receive it?" By contrast, the new media model (NMM) measures a different set of variables. Terms such as *consumption* (unique visitors/devices/browsers), *stickiness* (or time spent), and *sharing* have entered our measurement vocabulary. Traditional measures gave little indication whether individual news stories were read, let alone whether they were discussed. In the NMM, how long people spend with a story and how many times they share or repost it is of great importance. Mitchell found "that half (50 percent) of social network users share or repost news stories, images, or videos, while nearly as many (46 percent) discuss news issues or events on social network sites."[17] In this era of new media, those are a more useful and insightful measure than mere message exposure.

Further, the most important current measurements of commerce are time and engagement. Time is calculated in milliseconds. The difference in how fast market conditions can be transferred to users is the very principle upon which media-conscious organizations move.[18] And while it is easier to measure how quickly a story gets posted than it is to quantify precisely how that story works, or does not, to change political opinion, there is little doubt that campaigns work hard as part of their overall communication strategies to try to be strong players in the media market and so first influencers of public perception. This was particularly noticeable in Donald Trump's 2016 campaign, as he used Twitter to communicate directly with the public on a regular basis, and he also called in to weekday morning and Sunday shows to talk with the hosts, and so directly to voters.

Engagement, the other key measure, is much more clearly applied in politics. Rather than simple measures of reach, campaigns measure social media in terms of user website interface, ongoing dialogue with users, harvesting information about voters, message targeting by interest issue, fostering word of mouth, formalizing advocacy campaigns, collaborating with voters, enabling peer-to-peer communication, and supporting peer advocacy. Big-picture responses such as engagement (retweets, comments, fans, likes, and followers), sentiment analysis (overall opinion of users), conversions of leads, and share of voice (or mentions) are now critical components of media success measures. These are measures that simply could not be affordably reached in the legacy media models. In essence, the model has changed from one that measures financial efficiency in reaching people to one that measures financial efficiency in meeting specific outcomes (awareness, seats filled, votes obtained, shared community). In many ways the financial challenges for legacy media have led to more interesting and strategic measurements to justify ad revenues.

The Challenge of Authority

In the era of professional journalism the media were the force strong enough to challenge government authority. In the new media era, the authority being challenged may well be the legacy media themselves. Four specific confrontations between the legacy media and the New Media moguls are notable.

Time

The first is the challenge to time. Japanese manufacturing developed the just-in-time (JIT) model in the 1950s, but it was not until the '80s that the model began permeating the United States. The model holds in part that organizations should strive to have the right material at the right time at the right place and in the right amount.[19] Although the model concerns itself with manufacturing and inventory control, when applied to communication the model is similarly insightful. The media challenge is to provide delivery systems that are fluid rather than static. Legacy media typically built their news content around set times—news at 6:00 or at the top of the hour, or papers delivered each morning. New media are delivered just in time— what the consumer wants when the consumer wants it.

The impact of time shifting is an important challenge, because it undermines the position of the legacy media as *the* source to turn to for breaking news. Bloggers and those in nontraditional media have been known to trump the legacy media, who often feel bound by self-imposed professional standards by which sources are verified before publication. In an age of instant information, those minutes— or even seconds—can spell the difference between success and failure. By contrast, no one much cares if the social media sites get it wrong before they get it right, unless it concerns financial news or is intentionally misleading. After all, their reputations are developed by giving users advance notice of news that might be true or may be significant, not by being accurate. Legacy media cannot afford to ditch their reputations for truth, because for them accuracy is still currency.

Legacy media have, indeed, adapted to the need for speed. The Pony Express revolutionized mail delivery in 1860 by delivering mail across the nation in a mere ten days; today consumers are unwilling to wait more than three seconds for information to load on their Web browsers. Consumer impatience means that they will abandon sites that are slow and return to sites that produce results quickly. Their loyalty is to the product, not the producer of news—and that changes the game.

Barriers to Participation

The second challenge to the authority of legacy media is participation. The reason is simple: Today there are too few traditional journalists producing news content. That results in fewer news stories and too little original content. Most cities and towns across America have only one newspaper, and nationwide there are fewer television stations doing less original reporting. In her overview of the Pew Research Center's 2014 report on the state of news media, Amy Mitchell wrote that "at this point, fully a quarter of the 952 US television stations that air newscasts do not produce their news programs."[20] As a result, much of the news is redundant content in a mediated echo chamber.

Legacy media can no longer claim the decentralized structure that Lippman celebrated, but have become both monolithic and concentrated. As such, they have become what many consider another center of power, attempting to broker influence and legitimacy. They do this by being:

Masters of complexity, creating a hierarchy of professionals and amateurs;

Controllers of raw materials for media, with footage of events and access to deep research databases;

Speed-driven, with advantages accruing to those who have the knowledge first but who can also get it to their market fastest;

Politically connected, with access to business done in back rooms or in the corridors of power; and

Financially strong, with the ability to afford high costs. "The cult of 'production value' in design, recording, television, and Hollywood movies makes it difficult for lower budget artifacts to compete for attention."[21]

Media monopolies most certainly have each of these characteristics: a strong prejudice among journalists that there is a distinction between professionals and amateurs, high costs that prove to be barriers for new legacy media to emerge, the power to close access to key sources, and slick production design. As just one example, the legacy media virtually control access to the halls of Congress and the corridors of power at national party nominating conventions, where the political parties use the congressional rules to determine who gets access to news events.[22] Among other things, the rules require that the majority of the reporter's income be derived from their role as a journalist. This tends to exclude start-up organizations or those who have yet to make money regardless of the breadth of their readership.

The NMM challenges that monopoly. It empowers people to speak, developing their own credibility in the marketplace of ideas. It has a very low cost of entry. Though the NMM still has limited access to traditional news conference events, its journalists find ways of being on the forefront of breaking news events.[23] There are hundreds of examples, such as Glenn Greenwald's breaking of the National Security Administration lead story in 2013, and blogger Brian Krebs's breaking of the story on Target's financial security breach. And access to relatively easy to use computer programs allows participants to create some fairly slick productions, though that is not the primary value in breaking news.

The bottom line is that people want to interact with their environment, and that is creating a titanic shift. Harold Innis, a political economist who wrote about communication and social change, believed that "change came from the margins of society, since people on the margins invariably developed their own media. The new media allow those on the periphery to develop and consolidate power and ultimately to challenge the authority of the center. Latin written on parchment, the medium of the Christian Church, was attacked through the secular medium of vernaculars written on paper." While the mainstream media model created enormous barriers for the participation of citizens, the NMM has opened the doors for participation. Howard notes "that the proportion of people producing and consuming political content online has increased, not decreased, with the infusion of digital technologies."[24]

Rejection of the Homogeneity of the Masses

The legacy media model evolved as a result of the creation of mass communication. No longer constrained by geographical boundaries, the mass media served to unite us as a nation. Yet as Lazarsfeld and Merton noted, "The manifest concern over the functions of the mass media is in part based upon the valid observation that these media have taken on the job of rendering mass publics decipherable to the social and economic *status quo*."[25]

The NMM challenges that as a model. It permits users to self-select media outlets, which organize people by interest or ideology, and permits them to share items of interest on personal networking sites such as Twitter or Facebook. Numerous news blogs and aggregators (like Zite, Yahoo, the *Drudge Report*, or the *Huffington Post*) let users opt in for the coverage they desire. Just because they are self-selecting does not imply that the user numbers are low or that they are undistinguished as news sites. According to eBizMBA's "Top 15 Most Popular Blogs" (2015), the *Huffington Post* is estimated to have 110 million unique visitors each month, and in 2012 it became the first digital media enterprise to win a Pulitzer Prize for David Wood's series on wounded veterans, *Beyond the Battlefield*. Words like *narrowcasting* have become widespread, and the targeting of messages is becoming an important skill for the journalist. In essence, the NMM is about the power of the individual.

Rejection of the Homogeneity of Legacy News

For a number of years there have been cries and complaints about the "liberal media" and their coverage—or lack of coverage—of news. In response, a number of (mostly) conservative sites have emerged that directly take aim at this perceived bias. For example, Andrew Breitbart, founder of Big Journalism and more recently Breitbart.com with over 12.5 million unique monthly visitors, said,

"Our goal at Big Journalism is to hold the mainstream media's feet to the fire. There are a lot of stories that they simply don't cover, either because it doesn't fit their world view, or because they're literally innocent of any knowledge that the story even exists, or because they are a dying organization, short-staffed, and thus can't cover stuff like they did before." Similarly, Tucker Carlson, cofounder of the *Daily Caller*, claims, "I believe that our coverage is the balance against the rest of the conventional press." These rising leaders of the NMM see themselves in opposition to the legacy (or mainstream) media, although not without controversy.[26]

This clarion cry for an alternative to the mainstream media has produced numerous political news websites. As of January 2015, not one of the top ten sites based on unique users is an outgrowth of a traditional media outlet.[27] But that does not mean that their journalists lack legacy credentials. In fact, a number of reporters are trained in traditional media outlets. Many reinvented themselves as a result of the layoffs in the conventional press, while others moved toward what they see as the future of journalism.

The media revolution is fundamentally about disruptive change. Neil Postman famously wrote that "the printing press opened a door upon which European culture had been anxiously knocking. And when it was opened, the entire culture went flying through." While that is true, it is important to note that it is not the technology itself that produced the change. Rather, the technology was a vehicle for expression. Stephen Talbott writes: "It is easier for us to think of the technological device as a 'thing' that somehow affects our thinking than to think of it as, in its essential nature, an expression of our thinking." Given our discussion so far, we can now begin to consider how our thinking has changed, particularly in the way public opinion, the press, and the president are entwined.[28]

Impact of Change on the Body Politic

The changing relationships among the president, the press, and the public begin during the campaign season and then change into more formal and routinized relationships once the election is done. The traditional news model that evolved during the media explosion of the 1940s and '50s firmly seated the control of the news cycle and news content in the hands of the mainstream media. To feed the press, campaigns developed strategies for serving press deadlines, staging media events with strong visuals, and utilizing media darlings ranging from popular actors and musicians to noted pundits in order to gain attention.[29] The driving force behind campaign strategy is to find ways of getting coverage from the legacy media, whether earned media (the development of campaign events worthy of news coverage) or placed media (the purchase of time in news cycles).

With the advent of new media, the scenario shifts from press control to a complex system that, while still preferring mainstream media coverage, is capable of circumventing it by feeding local media in down markets and using social webs to spread viral messages. While legacy media previously have dominated major political events such as the State of the Union address or political debates, that is no longer the case. Candidates and presidents, interest groups, and activists use social media to reach previously untouched publics and to bypass the filters imposed by MSM. A conservative political action committee manager recently explained, "I have the same goals as the activists. I'd like to get a million people. I want the Speaker of the House to be able to send an email to a million people about how the latest tax package benefits them. I want to be able to circumvent Peter Jennings."[30] Circumvention is an oft-touted goal.

Digital op-eds, six-second animated GIFs, tweets, and Facebook posts cover the social media landscape and can now attract more viewers than the MSM. Campaigns have embraced the new media model and have discovered innovative uses in each campaign cycle that become routinized afterward. At this juncture, it is unclear whether both models will find a way to coexist or whether they will both morph into some yet unseen operation.

So what does this mean for political relationships among the press, the public, and the president? First, in this shift we can detect the decline of the silent majority and the rise of the engaged citizen. Second, we are witnessing the increasing importance of collections of individuals. Third, measures of commerce are shifting.

The Decline of the Silent Majority and the
Rise of the Engaged Citizen

For years critics have suggested that candidates—and even presidents—govern by opinion polls.[31] The suggestion is made that politicians routinely take the pulse of the voter before taking positions on major issues. Innate to this supposition is that there is a great majority, often silent, whose opinions can be measured. Two things are making polling less useful in politics. One is that traditional public opinion polling is becoming methodologically difficult. With the rise of cell phones and caller ID, reaching a valid sample of voters is much more difficult and, therefore, more expensive. Even noted polling organizations Gallup and the Pew Center decided against the traditional horse-race polling in the 2016 primaries. The second is that traditional polling is norm centered. In essence, pollsters are looking for majority reactions and opinions. Inherently, polls ignore people on the margins, and they do not easily measure intensity of opinion. Until the new media model emerged, polling was pretty much the only game in town.

In traditional campaigns, polling-driven strategies are designed to target the highest number of people in an effort to sway voters to a particular candidate's direction. But what if there were an emergent, more cost-effective way to find and persuade voters? From 2012 to 2016, and surely continuing on, campaigns began using data mining and microtargeting to reach potential supporters. In 2012 Howard and his coauthors estimated that "four of every ten readers are profiled in exhaustive detail in terms of identity and political opinion. These detailed profiles are used to draw direct and indirect inferences in the commercial and political sphere. Political actors then use this information to design the messages we receive."[32]

For example, in the 2012 election both Obama and Romney hired data trackers for their websites. "These are companies, like ad networks and data brokers working on behalf of the campaigns, that collect information about users' online activities to show political ads to people tailored to their own interests and beliefs."[33] Using data mining tools, they sift "through mountains of information—in this case, voters' online habits—to find gems of actionable insight."[34]

Clearly, the Obama campaign was more skilled at social media. Based on the data, users could join one of eighteen different constituency groups on the Obama website that then sent messages directly addressing that group's interests (the Romney campaign did not use this strategy until August 2012). In one internal study the Obama campaign sent "a traditional fundraising mail request and a tailored data-based online request and found the online effort outperformed by 14 percent."[35] Evidence of the persuasion is measured by action, whether by giving money or by becoming part of the viral tribe that demonstrates their social membership through reposts, tweets, or clicks on the website. In 2012 the Pew Research Internet Project found that "66 percent of social media users (39 percent of American adults) have engaged in . . . political activities with social media"—activities that include things such as encouraging people to vote or take action, post links to stories, join an interest group, follow candidates, or post and repost comments. However, a 2016 update of this poll found that this online political activity was taking its toll. "More than one-third of social media users are worn out by the amount of political content they encounter," researchers wrote, "and more than half describe their online interactions with those they disagree with politically as stressful and frustrating."[36]

Even so, readership or viewership is not sufficient. Both media organizations and campaigns can determine specific stories that move the direction of conversations. This is often described as the distinction between pack journalism and the viral tribe. Pack journalism is an echo chamber. One person reports the story, and if it resonates, it may appear in newspapers or on news talk radio and television programs across the nation. In the traditional media, original reporting is often regarded as too expensive. In its place, viewers and voters get talking heads, horse race coverage, and scandal and rumor on repeat. This repetition and reuse of programming is a practice that weakens its uniqueness as a media source. By contrast, the viral tribe constitutes cocreators of news and commentary. The very nature of the "viral" descriptor is an indication that news mutates as various interest groups find the portions of a story relevant to them. Online users, then, are active users. As Howard once again noted, "The proportion of people producing and consuming political content online has increased, not decreased, with the infusion of digital technologies."[37] The tribe is also an important concept. Interestingly, the power of one person should not be underestimated, for the individual now has the capability to influence outcomes.

The The Individualization of Mass Media

So what starts the conversation with these engaged citizens? In our current mediated world, rarely do people simultaneously gather as a mass audience in front of some communication device to witness news. The new normal permits time shifting as opposed to set news cycles and staged events. Users can access the messages and the conversation when they are ready. In the hands of skilled strategists, the mediated conversation begins before the MSM can start their coverage. For example, President Obama had an Office of Digital Strategies whose job is to advance the president's message, skipping past the traditional media to deliver news to the public itself via online and social media outlets. This was a disruption of the expected normative protocol, and it was a distinction worthy of our consideration.

One of the main distinctions between the NMM and the MSM is where the conversation begins. In legacy media, political events created moments that drove interest among certain well-informed or interested segments of the population. In the NMM, the object is to find out where people are having conversations and join them. While it is true that most people still get their news from the mainstream media, new audiences are being activated. Dan Pfeiffer, Obama's senior adviser and outspoken advocate of social media, said, "To not have an aggressive social media strategy in 2015 is the equivalent of not having an aggressive TV strategy in the 1950s. . . . We have to go where the conversations are already happening."[38] That's a telling distinction. Finding those collections of conversations is far more interesting to students of the new media model because there is a sense that feeding into active conversations will be more persuasive than passive reporting to mass audiences.

Yet one aspect of the legacy model is becoming more powerful: the concept of the persuasiveness and influence of opinion leaders. Every president, campaign, and news organization wants to find them, since they drive others to join the conversation. To be clear, not everyone who comments or posts is an opinion leader. While "25% always agree or mostly agree with their friends' postings . . . 73% 'only sometimes' agree or never agree." While these disagreements are usually ignored, "some 18% of social networking site users have blocked, unfriended, or hidden someone" for political reasons. Yet there is a small, significant group who do indeed drive the conversations. In fact, some 16 percent of social network users say they have changed their views about a political issue after discussing or reading posts about it."[39]

The 1940s experiments to find support for the "hypodermic needle" theory sought to prove that the public responded to mediated messages in predictable ways. That hypothesis was mostly disproven and discarded. However, support was robust for the opinion leader hypothesis, which stated that high-information political users often become highly influential opinion leaders to their peers. These opinion leaders were deemed to be highly persuasive. In the new media model we can now document who is influential by learning how many people these individuals reach.[40]

These opinion leaders are the most sought after public of political campaigns. Kevin Madden, 2012 senior advisor to the Romney campaign and press secretary in the 2008 campaign, said, "Voter-to-voter contact became a more powerful way to persuade voters than a 30-second ad. . . . That was something in 2008 [that affected] how campaigns strategically made decisions and how the newsroom strategically made decisions on what to cover. Pack journalism essentially began to go viral." This is an important evolution. The rise of the political information industry makes it possible for political campaigns to understand how the public makes political choices. Howard notes, "Consultants combine the latest statistical methods with Web-based sampling techniques to generate reliable information about how political characters and policy options play in the public sphere." That is a model transforming the news industry. Learning how citizens process, learn, and recall information that leads to decisions is democratizing. No longer is the relationship with the public a one-way, static model. It is a highly interactive, targeted, and dynamic news process that has changed reporting as well as the financial picture for journalism.[41]

Conclusion

One of my favorite tweets, from @jeffjarvis in 2014, said, "It took 150 yrs after the printing press to invent the newspaper. We don't know what the Internet is yet." I believe that is true. Skilled journalists still need to be good writers, and the one thing that is relatively stable in the new media era is the use of the phone as a tool of reporting.[42]

For all our speculation, we are watching transformational history taking place. The new media model is the shiny new thing. It's what we find fascinating and alluring, but we are just now beginning to assess its impact.

In the 1940s, Merton and Lazarsfeld were concerned with the narcotizing dysfunction of the media—that people would become passive recipients of the news that pervasively surrounds them. The condition now is not that the public is passive but that it is over-active. To rephrase Merton and Lazarsfeld, "In short, he [the public] takes his secondary contact with the world of political reality, his retweets and Facebook posts, as a vicarious action. He comes to mistake *knowing* about problems of the day for *doing* something about them." The media have, in essence, developed a frenetic dysfunction: much action with little reflection.

Will the mediated environment become too much for the public to decipher over time? Will legacy media find a new role in adjudicating the noise that surrounds us? Will we indeed move back toward an era where the mainstream media become our willing guide as to what news is real and what is native advertising? Will we need to develop media-free spaces in our lives so we have the luxury of thought?

And what about those who have always been the newsmakers? The elected leaders and political activists? While it is still too early to prove, we can speculate that the less engaging, more passive recipients of information are the newsmakers themselves. Despite the flood of social media in the 2012 campaign, candidates declined to join the conversations they provoked. For example, of Obama's 404 tweets, only 3 percent were retweets "of a citizen generated post," while Romney retweeted just one post, and that was from his own son.[43] Here again, the media have the potential to assert a challenge for these newsmakers to do more than speak out; they must also actively engage the citizens they seek to lead. However, in 2016 this problem took on a new form, showing that mere engagement does not necessarily mean things get better, as Donald Trump, in particular, was routinely criticized for using social media as a means to dodge hard questions and spread lies and innuendos about his opponents while bragging about himself.

But the overarching message of this chapter is this: people are engaged—maybe too much. There is too much talking and not enough listening and dialogue. And this is the narcotizing dysfunction of this era. Just as Merton and Lazarsfeld contended that information saturation could render the public unthinking, the new media are having many of the same effects, but for different reasons. Rather than a lack of response, there is too much response. Little emphasis is placed on the quality of opinion, when merely having an opinion is self-satisfying to the user. According to one report, "Social networking already accounts for 28 percent of all media time spent online, . . . 18 percent of social media users can't go a few hours without checking Facebook, [and] 16 percent of people rely on Twitter or Facebook for their morning news."[44] In one of the more recent studies from more than a decade of research on Internet addiction (IA), researchers Cheng and Li found that some 6 percent of people worldwide have IA, a "threefold higher than [the rate] of pathological gambling."[45] Notably, a new term has entered the lexicon: *in real life* (IRL). The term distinguishes life lived outside social media in the land of human interaction from time spent online.

One thing is sure. Legacy media will have to find ways to adapt to the flood of data that is leading us to new understandings of human behavior.

Notes

1. See, for example, Manuel Castells, *The Rise of Network Society*, Vol. 1 in *The Information Age: Economy, Society and Culture* (Malden, MA: Blackwell Publishers, 1998); Yochai Benkler, *The Wealth of Networks: How Social Production Transforms Markets and Freedom* (New Haven, CT: Yale University Press, 2006).

2. Paul F. Lazarsfeld and Robert K. Merton, "Mass Communication, Popular Taste and Organized Social Action," in *Media Studies: A Reader*, edited by Paul Marris and Sue Thornham (New York: New York University Press, 2000).

3. Ibid. (emphasis in the original).

4. Ibid.

5. Ibid.

6. Ibid. (emphasis in the original).

7. Teun A. van Dijk, *News as Discourse* (Hoboken, NJ: Routledge, 2013); Ben H. Bagdikian, *The New Media Monopoly* (Boston: Beacon Press, 2004).

8. George Packer, "The Revolution Will Not Be Blogged," *Mother Jones*, May-June 2004, www.motherjones.com/politics/2004/05/revolution-will-not-be-blogged.

9. Homero Gil de Zúñiga and Amber Hinsley, "The Press Versus the Public: What Is 'Good Journalism?'" *Journalism Studies* 14, no. 6 (2013): 926–42.

10. *The Future of Journalism: Hearing Before the Senate Subcommittee on Communications, Technology, and the Internet of the Committee on Commerce, Science, and Transportation*, 111th Cong. (2009).

11. Ibid.

12. Jessie J. Holland, "Census: Americans Less Likely to Move Now Than in the 1990s," AOL, Finance, June 6, 2014, www.aol.com/article/2014/06/06/census-americans-less-likely-to-move-now-than-in-the-1990s/20907752/.

13. *Future of Journalism*.

14. Amy Mitchell, "State of the News Media 2014: Overview," Pew Research Center, Journalism & Media, March 26, 2014, www.journalism.org/2014/03/26/state-of-the-news-media-2014-overview/.

15. Andrew Sullivan, "Guess Which Buzzfeed Piece Is an Ad," The Dish, February 21, 2013, www.dish.andrewsullivan.com/2013/02/21/guess-which-buzzfeed-piece-is-an-ad/; Mitchell, "State of the News Media 2014"; Joe Pompeo, "'Wall Street Journal' Editor Gerard Baker Decries Native Advertising as a 'Faustian Pact,'" *Politico*, September 25, 2013, www.politico.com/media/story/2013/09/wall-street-journal-editor-gerard-baker-decries-native-advertising-as-a-faustian-pact-001773.

16. *Future of Journalism*.

17. Mitchell, "State of the News Media 2014."

18. In October 2014 top Bloomberg news producers and executives in Washington, DC, kindly lunched with a group of SMU undergraduates I was leading on a networking trip through the nation's capital. Included among those present were Craig Gordon, managing editor for the Washington bureau, and Jon Allen, Washington bureau chief. Gordon explained to students that his most important job is to beat his competition with a story and that beating the competition often meant posting something only seconds or milliseconds before they did.

19. T. C. Cheng and S. Podolski, *Just-in-Time Manufacturing: An Introduction* (New York: Springer Publishing, 1996).

20. Mitchell, "State of the News Media 2014."

21. Harold A. Innis, *Changing Concepts of Time*, Critical Media Studies: Institutions, Politics, and Culture (Lanham, MD: Rowman and Littlefield, 2004).

22. "Rules for Electronic Media Coverage," US House, Radio Television Correspondents' Gallery, https://radiotv.house.gov/for-gallery-members/rules-for-electronic-media-coverage-of-congress.

23. Robert J. Barro, "The Liberal Media: It's No Myth," *Business Week*, June 14, 2004.

24. M. Soules, "Harold Adams Innis: The Bias of Communications and Monopolies of Power," *Media Studies*, http://www.media-studies.ca/articles/innis.htm, accessed January 3, 2017; Philip N. Howard, "Deep Democracy, Thin Citizenship: The Impact of Digital Media in Political Campaign Strategy," *Annals of the American Academy of Political and Social Science* 597, no. 1 (2005): 153–70.

25. Lazarsfeld and Merton, "Mass Communication."

26. Stefano DellaVigna and Ethan Kaplan, "The Fox News Effect: Media Bias and Voting," *Quarterly Journal of Economics* 122, no. 3 (2007): 1187–234; Barro, "Liberal Media"; Matthew Gantzkow and Jesse M. Shapiro, "What Drives Media Slant? Evidence from U.S. Daily Newspapers," *Econometrica* 78, no. 1 (2010): 35–71; Brian Stelter, "Still a Conservative Provocateur, Carlson Angles for Clicks, Not Fights," *New York Times*, October 7, 2012, www.nytimes.com/2012/10/08/business/media/tucker-carlson-angles-for-daily-caller-clicks-not-fights.html.

The 2016 campaign brought the controversy over so-called conservative news to the fore, particularly with regard to the *Breitbart* site. *Breitbart*'s editor, Steve Bannon, eventually became a chief advisor to Donald Trump's campaign, and after Trump's election Bannon was appointed senior counselor to the president. Critics argued that Bannon had a history of racist, misogynistic, and anti-Semitic views. Michael D. Shear, Maggie Haberman, and Michael S. Schmidt, "Critics See Stephen Bannon, Trump's Pick for Strategist, as Voice of Racism," *New York Times*, November 14, 2016, http://www.nytimes.com/2016/11/15/us/politics/donald-trump-presidency.html?_r=0.

27. "Top 15 Most Popular Blogs: February 2015," eBiz MBA, https://web.archive.org/web/20150206043551/http://www.ebizmba.com/articles/blogs.

28. Neil Postman, *The Disappearance of Childhood*, vol. 1 (New York: Dalacorte, 1982); Stephen L. Talbott, "Media Ecology: Taking Account of the Knower," The Nature Institute, www.natureinstitute.org/txt/st/knower.htm.

29. Dan Schill, *Stagecraft and Statecraft: Advance and Media Events in Political Communication* (Lanham, MD: Lexington Books, 2009).

30. Howard, "Deep Democracy," 153–70.

31. Paul Brace and Barbara Hinckley, *Follow the Leader: Opinion Polls and the Modern Presidents* (New York: Basic Books, 1992); Richard S. Beal and Ronald H. Hinckley, "Presidential Decision Making and Opinion Polls," *Annals of the American Academy of Political and Social Science* 472 (1984): 72–84; Shea Bennett, "28% of Time Spent Online Is Social Networking," SocialTimes, Social Media/Trends, January 27, 2015, www.adweek.com/socialtimes/time-spent-online/613474.

32. Rita Kirk Whilock, *Political Empiricism: Communication Strategies in State and Regional Elections* (New York: Praeger Publishers 1991); Howard, "Deep Democracy," 153–70.

33. Natasha Singer and Charles Duhigg, "Tracking Voters' Clicks Online to Try to Sway Them," *New York Times*, Politics, October 27, 2012, www.nytimes.com/2012/10/28/us/politics/tracking-clicks-online-to-try-to-sway-voters.html.

34. Laurence Cruz, "2012: The Social Media Election?" Cisco, September 3, 2012, http://newsroom.cisco.com/feature-content?type=webcontent&articleId=1006785.

35. Ginger Gibson, "Jim Messina: President Obama Built Biggest Grassroots Campaign," *Politico*, November 20, 2012, http://www.politico.com/story/2012/11/messina-touts-grassroots-strength-084080.

36. Lee Rainie, Aaron Smith, Kay Lehman Schlozman, Henry Brady, and Sidney Verba, "Social Media and Political Engagement," Pew Research Center, Internet, Science & Tech, www.pewinternet.org/2012/10/19/social-media-and-political-engagement/; Maeve Duggan and Aaron Smith, "The Political Environment on Social Media," Pew Research Center, Internet, Science & Tech, http://www.pewinternet.org/2016/10/25/the-political-environment-on-social-media/.

37. Howard, "Deep Democracy," 153–70.

38. Michael D. Shear, "Obama's Social Media Team Tries to Widen Audience for State of the Union Address," *New York Times*, Politics, January 19, 2015, www.nytimes .com/2015/01/20/us/politics/doing-more-than-putting-an-annual-address-into-140-characters.html.

39. Lee Rainie and Aaron Smith, "Social Networking Sites and Politics," Pew Reseach Center, Internet, Science & Tech, www.pewinternet.org/2012/03/12/social-network-ing-sites-and-politics/.

40. Everette E. Dennis and Ellen Wartella, eds., *American Communication Research: The Remembered History* (Mahwah, NJ: Lawrence Erlbaum Associates, 1996), 169–80; Stephen Lacy Daniel Riff and Frederick Fico, *Analyzing Media Messages: Using Qual-itative Content Analysis in Research*, 3rd ed. (New York: Routledge, 2014); Gabriel Weimann and Hans-Bernd Brosius, "Is There a Two-Step Flow of Agenda-Setting?" *International Journal of Public Opinion Research* 6, no. 4 (1994): 323–41; Elihu Katz and Paul Felix Lazarsfeld, *Personal Influence: The Part Played by People in the Flow of Mass Communications*, 2nd ed. (Piscataway, NJ: Transaction Publishers, 2006); Bernard Berelson, Paul F. Lazersfeld, and Hazel Gaudet, *The People's Choice: How the Voter Makes Up His Mind in a Presidential Campaign* (New York: Columbia University Press, 1944).

41. Madden quoted in Kathleen Hall Jamieson, *Electing the President 2012: The In-sider's View* (Philadelphia: University of Pennsylvania Press, 2013); Howard, "Deep Democracy," 153–70.

42. Zvi Reich, "The Impact of Technology on News Reporting: A Longitudinal Per-spective," *Journalism & Mass Communication Quarterly* 90, no. 3 (2013): 417–34.

43. Maggie Dalton-Hoffman, "The Effect of Social Media in the 2012 Presidential Election," Trinity's Journals and Serial Publications, First-year Papers, 2013; Smith and Duggan, "State of the 2012 Election: Mobile Politics."

44. "Social Media Addiction; Statistics & Trends (INFOGRAPHIC)," SocialTimes, December 30, 2014, http://www.adweek.com/socialtimes/social-media-addiction-stats/504131.

45. Sujin Lee and Geunyoung Chang Leo Sang-Min Whang, "'Internet Over-Users' Psychological Profiles: A Behavior Sample Analysis on Internet Addiction," *CyberPsy-chology and Behavior* 6, no. 2 (2003): 143–50; Cecilia Cheng and Angel Yee-lam Li, "In-ternet Addiction Prevalence and Quality of (Real) Life: A Meta-Analysis of 31 Nations across Seven World Regions," *Cyberpsychology, Behavior, and Social Networking* 17, no. 12 (2014): 758.

REALITY CHECK

Ch-ch-ch-changes?

DAVID DEMAREST

This is a discussion about change, particularly change in the communications landscape to which every White House in history has had to adapt. As such, the White House (and its communications approach, apparatus, and strategies) is not immune to the technological changes that are constantly underway.

Looking back over the last thirty or so years, there has been a massive shift in how organizations communicate. This shift has been the result of at least three powerful and highly interrelated developments. First, the Internet has created platforms for communications that are radically different from those of the pre-Internet era. Second, globalization has eradicated traditional geographic and cultural boundaries for communications, while the absence of the ability to purely segment messaging has made almost all communications more or less fungible. Finally, the power of stakeholders (or, perhaps more precisely, interest groups) to advocate a point of view and leverage new media platforms to do so is far more central to the communications landscape than ever before.

I served as communication director of the White House in a far different communications environment than exists today. In short, ours was a landscape devoid of the Internet and cell phones (much less smart phones) as well as all those Internet-dependent platforms such as Facebook, Twitter, YouTube, and more. Cable TV was in its infancy. The big three networks, ABC, CBS, and NBC, still dominated TV news, while the *New York Times*, *Washington Post*, and *Wall Street Journal* commanded the field in print journalism. Blogs did not exist, and "citizen journalism" wasn't even a phrase in the communications lexicon. High-technology communications for us was doing a blast fax. In fact, in my time as communications director I cannot recall ever sending a single email. It would be several more years before that platform would become the indispensable business tool that it is today.

The magnitude of this technological transformation makes it easy to overfocus on its implications; that is, to suggest that the technology is everything and so nothing about communication in the post-Internet age is as it was in the pre-Internet age. But that is not so. Having served in organizations in government, politics, corporate and academic organizations, I can say that while some communications strategies have had to adjust because of the new communications landscape, many have not.

And, indeed, what has never changed, what can never change, is the requirement that administrations must value truth and transparency as part of the democratic process. This, in turn, means that while they should do what is necessary to protect their reputations and take the necessary steps to defend them from attack, all presidential administrations should also take care to engage the media with information; consistent and compelling policy narratives; and access to official events. The White House should be trying to work with—not against—the media, wherever possible, toward the development of a relationship of mutual trust.

Developing a trust premium is what allows a president to project moral authority domestically and internationally. Moreover, the ability to effectively convey and assert that authority depends at least in part upon presidents and their teams communicating with clarity, consistency, and conviction. Regardless of era, the White House is a unique institution, with its own traditions and approaches when it comes to media relations and communications management. However, the ways in which contemporary White House administrations behave, as compared to a White House of earlier times, might not be as unique as one might think. For example, every White House— at least every White House in the media age—has spurned spontaneity. Today's White House is no different. Predictability is king;

all presidents treasure flexibility in their own strategies yet insist on predictability in everyone else's. And oddly enough, often the media are a willing conspirator in such efforts.

I remember an article that was written by David Ignatius of the *Washington Post* in the early days of the George H. W. Bush administration. David interviewed me and wrote about our strategies for dealing with the media. He had observed the contrast that existed between our approach and that of the preceding (Reagan) administration. He noted that we were not as consumed with creating a script that we insisted the media follow. Rather, we set out to do the job at hand and let the media sort out what was and wasn't newsworthy. He then observed, ironically, that our approach was making reporters squirm—that for all their criticism of the Reagan communications operation as overly obsessed with news management, they (the media) actually liked it that way. His article was titled, "Press Corps to Bush: Manipulate Us!"

My quote in that article went as follows, "When you wade through all the rhetoric, the press corps is interested in access, and access helps them more than anything to do the job they are there to do. 'Familiarity breeds contempt' is the result [of] disingenuous access. By that I mean you go out when you have good news, but you stonewall when you have bad news. If the Administration can maintain access and create a sense of fair play, we're onto a new plane here."

Perhaps somewhat tongue-in-cheek, David Ignatius responded to my perspective by saying, "What a kind and gentle thought—that human beings (including reporters) will be fair to someone who treats them fairly. What a dubious proposition!"

One might suggest that the choice was not quite so binary—whether to hand-feed the news beast or to let it fend for itself. And there is truth to that thinking. There were certainly times that we did our best to manage the news line. But it is also true that we and, more importantly, the president we served were less institutionally consumed with news management than were those who came before and after us.

That there will always be tension between the White House and the media is a time-honored state of being. The challenge of today's radically changed media landscape may be creating some disincentives to a free and open dialogue between the White House and the media and, therefore, the public.

More so now than ever, the White House media operation is wary of the way seemingly minor moments can turn into significant distractions. That's not hard to understand. A misstatement, a mischaracterization, an offhand off-message comment by a presidential spokesperson (or even the president himself) can ruin the best-laid communications strategies. Such moments then live forever on the Internet. Unfortunately, White House wariness leads to the predictable: aggressive and sometimes punitive actions against individuals in the media as well as efforts to sanitize and routinize all media interaction to the point of stage-managed meaninglessness. As unsatisfactory as that may be from a policy standpoint, it has had the additional ripple effect at creating a far more stilted, and in some cases toxic, relationship between the White House and the media.

There is a notion that the twenty-first-century White House is using social media to bring the White House to the people in some more significant and more engaged manner. That misconception is based on an assumption that what is happening at the White House today is simply an extension of how candidates such as Obama and Trump used new media platforms in the 2008, 2012, and 2016 presidential campaigns. Those tactics generated very real enthusiasm and commitment (and money) from vast new audiences.

However, a hard look at the twenty-first-century White House and how it uses digital platforms reveals it is not very much about news-making. Nor is it about engaging with journalists. I believe that these new presidential social media strategies, like those used in the midst of political campaigns, were mostly about promotion and advocacy and connecting with supporters—constantly. Arguably, that construct is not particularly new. The platforms may be, but the effort is not. Beyond that, interpreting that effort as heightened engagement with the American people is neither new nor accurate. It is true that today's digital platforms have far-reaching implications. Unfortunately, since much of the intended use of those platforms touches people who already support White House policies and politics, few of those implications make the White House any less opaque to the people.

PART

 **TWO**

Presidents, People, and the
Art of Expression

The Press and the Presidency in Contrast

A Language Analysis

RODERICK P. HART

Politicians and journalists are not the same people. Everyone knows that. They have entirely different jobs, entirely different emotional predispositions, and entirely different intellectual and interpersonal skills. They also approach political ideas and commitments differently and, as a result, almost always have uneasy, if not hostile, relationships, a condition that no doubt finds the Founders smiling.

Sometimes politicians will turn into journalists (for example, MSNBC's Joe Scarborough of *Morning Joe* fame), or journalists will move in the opposite direction: Pat Buchanan, Al Gore, and Sarah Palin, for example. The United States has also seen "gimmick" candidates such as Ralph Nader, Gore Vidal, William F. Buckley, and Norman Mailer, journalists-of-a-sort who became politicians-of-a-sort, after which they write more books. Yet another permutation includes serious reporters—Karen Hughes, David Axelrod, and Strobe Talbott— who did not run for office but who took on significant roles in various presidential administrations. Generally speaking, though, politicians and journalists are not the same people. Everyone knows that.

But how do we know such things? That is the question being asked in this chapter. To answer that question, I make five basic assumptions: (1) people have a great deal of implicit knowledge about the world in which they live; (2) they use this knowledge to decide what is true and false, what actions to take, and how things work;

(3) because this knowledge is implicit, however, it is not always readily available even though it affects how we function; (4) our everyday language "leaks" these implicit understandings, but we are usually unaware of the leakage; and (5) by inspecting language behavior—especially large amounts of it—and by doing so systematically we can tap into people's presuppositions and, hence, learn how they know what they know.

In the pages to follow I inquire into the institutional differences between politics and journalism. I assume that while the surface differences between these two great institutions are intuitively obvious to most people, their deep structures have been undertheorized and, as a result, poorly understood.

Presidents and the Press: Who Affects Whom and When?

My aim in this chapter is to explore essential tensions between the press and the presidency—tensions built into the adversarial system a thriving democracy demands. Sometimes, though, collaboration rather than confrontation results. Jones and Sheets report, for example, that US news accounts characterized the infamous treatment of prisoners at Abu Ghraib as abuse or mistreatment, while European journalists called it what it was: torture. Along similar lines, Bates found a tendency in the US press to reinforce a president's preferred locutions (for example, as when Bill Clinton compared the slaughter in Kosovo to the Holocaust of World War II). Naturally, these linguistic echoes may have been unintentional. Even so, they show how tightly presidents and the press are joined at the hip.[1]

Accommodations like these are particularly visible when it comes to foreign policy. Baker found British tabloids reflecting establishment views of Islamic extremism, and Phelan and Shearer documented a preference for the term *radical* when activists were described in New Zealand newspapers. Although the press is popularly seen as adversarial to entrenched power structures, John and her colleagues found evidence that the press sometimes sanitizes governmental viewpoints before reporting them. Along these same lines, Squires and Jackson found the press unwilling to discuss systemic racism during Barack Obama's 2008 campaign, while Drury found British newspapers using the term *mob rule* to describe domestic protesters, ostensibly in an attempt to assuage traditional British sensibilities.[2]

But other studies find the opposite: that the press has become increasingly aggressive. Bucy and Grabe report, for example, that the average presidential sound bite has shrunk to 7.73 seconds and, as a result, that TV commentators now dominate TV commentaries. Esser finds, as a result, that the press effectively determines the news agenda no matter what the president may have in mind. In that same vein, Clayman and his colleagues show that reporters' questions during news conferences have become more aggressive over time. Finally, Parry-Giles details how journalists artfully deconstruct presidential actions, often framing the chief executive as inauthentic, manipulative, and inconsistent.[3]

Presidents take none of this lying down. As Cohen reports, they are increasingly "going local," traveling to the hinterlands to press the flesh. Eshbaugh-Soha and Peake conclude that such strategies help them dominate news coverage in the flyover states. Presidents have also made structural changes, adding to their Office of Communications staffers adept at "image and packaging," at prepping the president for news conferences, at making adjustments to the twenty-four-hour news cycle, and at helping the chief executive reach nontraditional journalists. The result? Scholars find that presidential coverage is more positive than congressional coverage, an effect that increases when international conflicts abound, as they did when the Bush administration pursued the war in Iraq.[4]

The press corps has also grown over the years, with specialized publications rising in importance because of the Web (for example, the *Huffington Post*) and with new television outlets (for example, Fox, MSNBC, HBO) also emerging. A larger media space both helps and hurts the presidency, resulting in a constant to-and-fro with the press. RealClearPolitics reporter Alexis Semindinger summarizes the results this way:

> No president can move an agenda forward or win reelection without majority support of the American people, and a free press continues to furnish voters with the best fact-based translations of the president and his chosen administration. History is littered with tales of newly inaugurated chief executives who vowed to soar over the heads of the media to control their messages and speak

directly with voters; all of them revised those goals when they dug into the job. Even with the explosion of the Web and other instantaneous, direct-connect forms of communication, presidents remain locked in a mutually dependent and politely adversarial relationship with the White House press corps.[5]

Researchers have taught us a good deal about the psychology of the presidency and the sociology of the press but we do not yet understand the deep structure of press/presidency relations. Understanding this requires us to know what distinguishes reporting from other symbolic activities, what gives presidential discourse its distinctive sound, what happens when presidents and the press confront one another directly (and whether they have done so differentially over time), and—given the growth of new media technology and the prodigious growth of the Internet—what might be expected to change about the presidency in the years ahead.

Presidents and the Press: What Texts to Examine and How?

Journalism is many things. Legally, it is an embodiment of the First Amendment, an acknowledgment of the people's right to interact with one another without fear of reprisal. Conceptually, it is a promise that the affairs of government will be monitored vigilantly and continually. Organizationally, journalism is a network of for-profit corporations that employ tens of thousands of people in the United States alone. Culturally, journalism keeps us in touch with our favorite ball teams as well as potholes, mortgage rates, immigrant children, and much else. Journalism is also a text, a complex of words and images produced in great globs each day. Government, too, is a text, but it is more than that as well. Government collects taxes, fights wars, builds rocket ships, ensures domestic tranquility. Government interpenetrates every aspect of human life—education, science, the workplace, medicine, and even religion and the arts. Government is a text, but a very complex one. That complexity is increased a thousandfold when journalism and government interact. Nonetheless, by examining three key rhetorical features, we can distill this relationship into something more understandable. Doing so, of course, is to be reductionistic in the extreme, since politics is a matrix within a matrix.

Journalism, too, is a matrix, ranging as it does from the *New York Times* to the *Fall River Herald-News* and from the *CBS Evening News* to *Entertainment Tonight*. In order to navigate these matrices, and remembering my earlier assertion that language is an important means for understanding institutional values, I deployed a computer program specifically designed to track people's lexical choices. Naturally, such choices are well beyond the ken of their makers. Who in their right mind, after all, can remember all the words they use? For jobs like this, a computer is helpful, especially if it can identify linguistic habits bearing on people's presuppositions—the intellectual grounds on which they stand.

The software used to do this work is DICTION 7.0, a program with the capacity to search a text with some ten thousand words fitted across thirty-three word lists or dictionaries. DICTION includes several calculated variables as well. None of the search terms are duplicated in these lists, giving the user an unusually rich understanding of a text. By combining counts of these variables in creative ways, DICTION's lexical layering sheds light on a passage's tone, something that becomes more prominent when word families are comingled.[6]

By stepping away from a text in these ways, DICTION notices things that people are sure to miss. Additional insight is provided by the program's built-in databank, which compares each passage to fifty thousand previously analyzed texts. Comparative work like this becomes critical when trying to understand a multifaceted conversation. For example, a race riot in Chicago will be discussed one way by the *Chicago Tribune*, another way by Fox News, and still other ways by the mayor's spokesperson, the riot's protagonists, the South Side religious community, the police department, and the busload of macroeconomists and urban sociologists subsequently interviewed in the media. When it comes to presidents and the press, DICTION is especially useful for generating the following measures:

Insistence: This variable measures a passage's discursive breadth: how aggressively it moves from topic to topic. Insistence helps identify the agenda control one expects in a clear piece of reporting. Passages high on Insistence are tightly focused, while those low on Insistence roam widely, producing a more conversational and less circumscribed discussion. Insistent passages are often repetitive, signaling an author's preference for an orderly world that keeps an audience on a short leash. To calculate this score, DICTION identifies all nouns and noun-derived adjectives and then performs this calculation: (number of eligible words × sum of their occurrences) ÷ 10.

Hortatory Style: As numerous authors have observed, politics has a distinctive sound, even though that sound is hard to describe.[7] American politics is especially complicated, since it is shot through with so many accommodations: the abstract and the concrete, the moral and the practical, the local and the federal, the expedient and the idealistic. Taken together, these tonalities produce the Hortatory Style, which taps the core beliefs of nationhood, religion, and community in assured and dramatic ways. To create this variable, two of DICTION's built-in scores and three customized dictionaries were combined: hortatory tone = patriotic language (*freedom, justice, republic,* etc.) + religious language (*worship, disciple, prophecy,* etc.) + voter references (*citizenry, constituents, nation,* etc.) + certainty (all-encompassing language) + embellishment (heavy use of adjectival constructions).

Narrative Force: Journalists are said to be the nation's storytellers, but they are hardly Mickey Spillane. Journalists explicitly reject the things that made Spillane popular: armchair psychology, brocaded descriptions, endless anecdotes, breathless denouements. Still, journalists must respond to "narrative necessity"—the need to render human actors understandable and their motivations and activities plausible. How do they do so? DICTION defines Narrative Force as the vivid description of people's activities at some particular time and place. Narratives are more than that, of course—plot, characterization, motivations, etc.—but they are rarely less than that. To assess narrative, DICTION combines human interest terms (*friend, baby, townspeople,* etc.), motion (*bustle, jog, fly,* etc.), temporal terms (*now, autumn, weekend,* etc.), spatial terms (*locale, border, Kuwait,* etc.), and embellishment (a selective ratio of adjectives to verbs).[8]

Hemingway would be put off by this crude reduction of narrative, and Martin Luther King Jr. would be left speechless by our mechanical understanding of Hortatory Style. But subtlety is not the goal of big data approaches. Their strength lies not in nuance but in functionality, as well as in scale and breadth. Such approaches look for underlying stabilities (and deviations) in the social world, but they must also meet the test of face validity: Does DICTION's output (its mathematical displays) do justice to its input (the texts it has processed)? I will show here that it does.

The corpus analyzed in this study was large and diverse, consisting of 5,325 political speeches delivered during US presidential campaigns or from the Oval Office between 1948 and 2012; 120 presidential press conferences conducted during that same timespan; 7,309 campaign stories published in the *New York Times*, the *Washington Post*, AP/UPI, and five regional newspapers; 1,219 transcripts of the evening news broadcast by NBC, CBS, ABC, PBS, and (in recent years) Fox News; 273 specialized news reports drawn from the political, financial, and technology sectors; 225 blogs from those same domains, a proxy for online journalism; and 1,102 stories in miscellaneous genres (TV drama, novels and short stories, theater scripts, and so on) to explore our measure of Narrative Force.[9]

Presidents and the Press: Who Says What, and Why?

The great advantage of computerized language analysis is that it lets researchers see the forest instead of the trees. Because the DICTION program has so many textual genres built into it, it can also differentiate one clump of trees from another. Standing so far back can, of course, result in one saying too little about too much or too much about too little. More positively, it can turn up some interesting results. I concentrate on four such results here.

Competitive Storytelling

Portions of Fig. 3.1 make intuitive sense, and other portions may be disorienting. It is not surprising, for example, that lawyers, philosophers, social scientists, and business writers avoid the narrative style. Lawyers and philosophers, after all, are argument-driven, producing texts that feature hierarchically nested assertions and counterassertions. While they may also exemplify things occasionally, their examples are often contrived or hypothetical and, hence, rather lifeless.

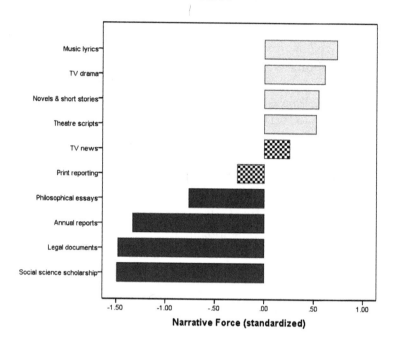

Fig. 3.1. Narrative force for print, broadcast, and other genres.

Social scientists and business writers eschew narratives for different reasons: (1) they are expected to produce quantitative rather than qualitative evidence, and (2) they are naturally suspicious of narratives. Stories, after all, are place- and time-bound, featuring colorful characters who represent populations no larger than themselves, thus failing the test of generalizability.[10]

In contrast, the aesthetic works in our sample scored highly on storytelling, a finding that validates our measure of Narrative Force. Whether it is artists telling small stories via music, producing narratives for theater or television, or crafting long-form stories for novels, readers receive sharply drawn descriptions of interesting people and places. They also find a combination of mundane and heroic events, counterposed characters, dramatic tension, and hints of the almost known and the still unfolding. Saul Bellow masterfully illustrates:

> On Broadway it was still bright afternoon and the gassy air was motionless under the leaden spokes of sunlight, and sawdust footprints lay about the doorways of butcher shops and fruit stores.

And the great, great crowd, the inexhaustible current of millions of every race and kind pouring out, pressing round, of every age, of every genius, possessors of every human secret, antique and future, in every face the refinement of one particular motive or essence—*I labor, I spend, I strive, I design, I love, I cling, I uphold, I give way, I envy, I long, I scorn, I die, I hide, I want.* Faster, much faster than any man could make the tally. The sidewalks were wider than any causeway; the street itself was immense, and it quaked and gleamed and it seemed . . . to throb at the limit of endurance.[11]

Most reporters do not sound like Saul Bellow. Their stories are less propulsive and also less presumptuous. Reporters operate more conservatively because they write for busy, demanding readers: "Get to the point, will ya? Enough with the 'gassy air' and the 'leaden spokes of sunlight.' How big was the 'great, great' crowd you're talking about? A hundred thousand? Two hundred thousand? What do you mean by 'antique secrets'? How could a sidewalk be bigger than a causeway? And what's with the fourteen verbs in a row—'I love,' 'I cling,' etc. What am I to make of that? Who's doing the clinging, the loving, the envying, the scorning? I'm on the train on my way to work. What's the bottom line here?"

Hence the dramatic differences between journalists and literateurs found in Fig. 3.1. Writers like Bellow, writers who careen across the landscape, make reporters nervous. So reporters slow down their narratives, interweaving them with facts and figures to ensure that point-making gets done. (Writers like Bellow, in contrast, keep their points submerged or camouflaged so as not to interrupt a reader's reverie.) Thus, when they talk about Christmas shopping, reporters operate quite differently from Bellow:

Over the weekend, shoppers across the country had noted unre-markable crowds.

"Back in the day, there used to be a lot of people," said Joyce Hudson, 54, one of several shoppers at a Kmart in Los Angeles who wandered the aisles at a pace seemingly no different from any other shopping day. Kmart's Black Friday sales began Thursday evening and the store stayed opened throughout the night.

Mrs. Hudson, shopping with her daughter, bought diamond earrings and several gold and silver necklaces, spending a total of $450, at deep discounts off the suggested retail prices.

"This year is really slow, there's a big difference from even last year," said a Kmart customer service manager, Indira Reyna, 44, who said she had worked the day after Thanksgiving for most of her 13 years on the job. "It's never been this slow. We still have all these deals."

Ken Perkins, the founder of Retail Metrics, an industry research company, said Black Friday was increasingly a thing of the past.

"The Black Friday hype has come and mostly gone," he said, thanks to "significant changes to the way consumers shopped, retailers promoted and the general importance of the day itself."

He warned against basing forecasts for the entire holiday season on Black Friday. But he added that the weak results could pressure retailers to cut their prices even more aggressively, which could hurt their bottom lines. He said discounts reaching 50 to 70 percent were becoming the norm.[12]

Here we find a piece of solid journalism, but we also find an arrested narrative. We learn very little about Joyce the shopper, her financial capacity, her inner desires, her attitudes toward parenting. We learn even less about Indira Reyna (did she, too, have a daughter? A son? A recent divorce?). To make matters worse, their saga is interrupted by Ken Perkins, who throws statistics at us. What started out as a pleasant story about American shoppers becomes an economic report in service to journalism's raison d'être: point-making.

Both journalism and literature are concerned with believability, but they earn their stripes differently. Literature unhinges readers, letting them wander into strange, intriguing places. Journalism features specific places in the world and documentable events. Even when writing feature stories, journalists rarely explore a character's full dimension—his problem with intimacy, her psychological hang-ups—features that become the raw stuff of novels. Journalism mixes tonalities from time to time, but literature mixes them wildly. Journalism is a modernist enterprise, emphasizing known knowns and known unknowns. Literature is often postmodern, constantly rearranging time and space. Journalism seeks closure, while literature prizes openings.

As we see in Fig. 3.2, print reporters and TV journalists also take a different approach to narrative.[13] These effects are persistent but also sensible: When TV news arrived on the scene in the 1930s, it fundamentally changed journalism: Suddenly, the reporter not only reported the news but also performed it. Dramatis personae came on the scene: governmental spokespersons, the person on the street, scientists in their laboratories. Just like that, news consumers were able to see people's faces, their gestures, their emotions. Old-line reporters worried that this would cheapen journalism, but who could turn their eyes away from the wreck on the highway or the wailing mother in Lebanon?

Over time, scholars began to describe how television changed the news: Patterson shows how the reporter became part of the story; Andres finds that TV's production values tend to privilege elite-level conflict; Lee notes that television gave members of Congress greater access to the populace, and that, too, amped up the wattage; and Esser reports the inevitable result of such trends: TV journalists work hard to produce counternarratives so the White House's media machine will not overwhelm them.[14]

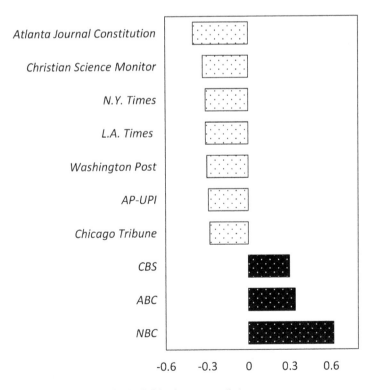

Fig. 3.2. Narrative force for individual press outlets.

In sum, print journalism *explains* what is happening, but TV journalism *shows* it. It does so with the help of dramaturgy: multiple voices, clever transitions, a fast pace, protagonists to whom one can easily relate. When television tells its story of Christmas shopping, then, things move quickly:

BILL WHITTAKER. 2014 is becoming known as the "year of the data breach." The theft of 40 million credit cards from Target late last year was followed by news of a breach at Michaels stores involving more than two million credit cards. Then came P. F. Chang's. And in September, Home Depot announced that 56 million of its customers' credit card numbers were stolen.

DAVE DEWALT. Nearly every company is vulnerable.

BILL WHITTAKER. Dave DeWalt is CEO of FireEye, a cybersecurity company that gets hired to keep hackers from getting into a company's network or getting them out after there's been a breach.

DAVE DEWALT. Even the strongest banks in the world—banks like JPMorgan, retailers like Home Depot, retailers like Target—can't spend enough money or hire enough people to solve this problem.

BILL WHITAKER. Cybersecurity is a misnomer? There is no cybersecurity it sounds like you're saying.

DAVE DEWALT. This isn't a lack of effort. Most of the large companies are growing their security spend. Yet 97 percent—literally 97 percent of all companies—are getting breached. So there's a gap here.

BILL WHITAKER. Ninety-seven percent?

DAVE DEWALT. Ninety-seven percent. In fact, we . . .

BILL WHITAKER. That's outrageous.

DAVE DEWALT. It is outrageous. It's pretty amazing.[15]

This, too, is storytelling, but it is storytelling of a different sort. Print journalism's point-making is also found in TV news, but its points are made more glacially there. Television uses dialogue to draw people in, creating a "fourth wall effect" whereby the viewer becomes part of the scene but is also removed from it. The back-and-forth between Whittaker and DeWalt keeps viewers involved and whets their appetites for further disclosures. Television news provides facts and figures, but it immediately personifies them, something that requires more work from print journalists. My findings show that TV news has increased in Narrative Force over time, and that adds even more energy to the political scene.[16] In short, while all journalists tell stories, their medium of choice changes how they tell them. But there are still other storytellers afoot—those we elect to office.

Evangelical Presidents

Viewed collectively, the data reported in Fig. 3.3 provide a handy summary of the essential differences between presidents and the press. Some of these data are predictable and some are not. One might have guessed, for example, that politicians would outstrip the press on the Hortatory Style scale. Barack Obama displayed the for-

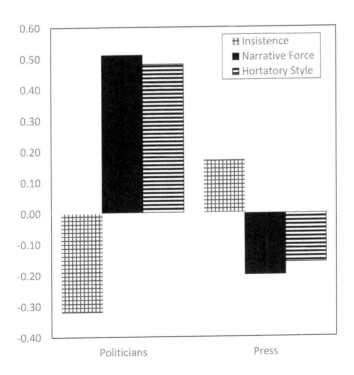

Fig. 3.3. Essential differences between politicians and press.

mulas associated with that style when announcing his presidential candidacy in 2007:

Call the roll: "It was here, in Springfield, where I saw all that is America converge—farmers and teachers, businessmen and laborers, all of them with a story to tell, all of them seeking a seat at the table, all of them clamoring to be heard."

Enlist the transcendental: "And that is why, in the shadow of the Old State Capitol, where Lincoln once called on a divided house to stand together, where common hopes and common dreams still live, I stand before you today to announce my candidacy for President of the United States."

Enlist the empirical: "That's why we were able to reform a death penalty system that was broken. That's why we were able to give health insurance to children in need. That's why we made the tax system more fair and just for working families. . . ."

Mix the empirical with the transcendental: "In the face of tyranny, a band of patriots brought an Empire to its knees. In the face of secession, we unified a nation and set the captives free. In the face of Depression, we put people back to work and lifted millions out of poverty. We welcomed immigrants to our shores, we opened railroads to the west, we landed a man on the moon, and we heard a King's call to let justice roll down like water, and righteousness like a mighty stream."

Repel the naysayers: "The cynics, and the lobbyists, and the special interests who've turned our government into a game only they can afford to play. They write the checks and you get stuck with the bills, they get the access while you get to write a letter, they think they own this government, but we're here today to take it back. The time for that politics is over."[17]

Journalists do not talk this way. They cannot abide the overstatements ("all of them with a story to tell"), the clever but vague charges ("a game only they can afford to play"), the hackneyed phrases ("face of tyranny"), the inexactitude. Voters are more tolerant, though. They may not speak like Barack Obama, but many still take shelter in his promises: (1) that someone is listening to them; (2) that he sees the big picture; (3) that history abides; (4) that having values and making money are not incommensurate; (5) that a savvy new sheriff is coming to town.[18]

The *New York Times* devoted twenty-eight paragraphs to the Obama announcement but quoted very little of it. It mentioned a few factual details ("wearing an overcoat but gloveless on a frigid morning," "trailed by his wife Michelle, and two young daughters," and so on) and it provided some historical context ("Mr. Obama invoked a speech Lincoln gave here in 1858 condemning slavery"), but it spent most of its time describing the dangers that lay ahead. It reported Walter Mondale, Gary Hart, and John Edwards telling Obama he had a lot to learn about campaigning. It spent a third of its time on Hillary Clinton and her brilliant strategist of a husband. It wondered how Obama would defend his thin political résumé and whether he could put together a viable campaign staff. It also asked questions: Would Republicans define him before he defined himself? Would his opposition to the war in Iraq make him seem unpatriotic? Would his race threaten his electability? In short, the *Times* cut through Obama's oratory with a cold, sharp scalpel. There was nothing surprising about that.[19]

What is surprising in Fig. 3.3 are the Narrative Style data that show politicians to be avid storytellers, even more so than the press.[20] These findings seem backwards until we consider the headlines that journalists write: "Is Storytelling the Secret Weapon of the 2012 Race?" (*Huffington Post*); "Barack Obama, Failed Storyteller" (*Human Events*); "Obama the Storyteller" (*American Thinker*); "Picasso, the President and Storytelling" (the *Economist*). What are these observers seeing? How can a president out-narrate the nation's designated storytellers? Mr. Obama shows how in the following passage:

So I'll just close with a story of a guy named Ramone—because we're rooting for guys like Ramone. Ramone spent eight years in the military, served in Afghanistan, served in Iraq. Ramone here? Raise your hand, Ramone.

So Ramone is somebody who fought for our freedom, fought for our security. But sometimes we give lip service to supporting our troops, and then when they come home they get lost. So when Ramone came home, he had a hard time finding a job because it was a tough economy. He didn't want to be a burden on his family, so he moved into a homeless shelter, took whatever work he could get. And then, one day in 2012, a VA counselor that he'd been working with handed him an application from Ford. Ford was hiring for new shifts.

Imagine what Ramone felt the day he knocked on his grandpa's door—his grandfather who had spent 25 years building Mustangs in Dearborn—and Ramone was able to tell his grandfather he got a job at Ford. And now Ramone has got his own place. And now Ramone has got a good job right on the line here in Wayne. And every day, he's doing just what his grandfather did. And he's proud. He's punching in and building some of the best cars in the world.[21]

Here Obama mixes the narrational and the hortatory. Combined, they constitute the rhetorical signature of American politics. "The stories our leaders tell us matter," says psychologist Drew Westen, "probably almost as much as the stories our parents tell us as children, because they orient us to what is, what could be, and what should be; to the worldviews they hold and to the values they hold sacred." Junot Díaz says, "We all know the importance of narratives, of stories; they are part of the reasons our brains are so damn big." And Barack Obama agrees, too. "The mistake of my first term," he said, "was thinking that this job was just about getting the policy right. And that's important. But the nature of this office is also to tell a story to the American people that gives them a sense of unity and purpose and optimism."[22]

Not everyone thinks that narrative is central to politics or that Obama was always good at it. While the president had "proved himself to be a fantastic storyteller on the campaign trail," says Díaz, "he has been unable to locate an equally engaging narrative for his presidency."[23] John Hayward of the conservative *Human Events* makes the opposite case: that Obama did little else but tell stories. Then he turned up the heat: "Obama is telling his squalling child-citizens that they wouldn't be crying about stagnant growth, trillions of dollars in new debt, "green energy" corruption, rampant abuse of executive power, and lost freedoms if Papa President had told them a better bedtime story before tucking them in. Politicians of every party have a tendency to blame poor messaging for their reversals of fortune, but Obama has raised this to the level of dementia."[24] Hayward is churlish here, but he also makes a point: that managing the narrative" has become all-consuming for politicians. The president's public relations folks now scout out appropriate settings for his storytelling events (for example, going to Michigan for the Ramone narrative), and they give his story of the day ample play on the White House website. The president's tales now compete directly with journalists', but the president has some distinct advantages: (1) his narratives command great attention (he is the leader of the free world, after all), and (2) reporters must avoid rhetorical excess (they are the guardians of objectivity, after all). But the press has another weapon, one that drives politicians crazy.

Steadfast Reporters

In *Politico*'s twenty-seven-paragraph story about the president's speech in Wayne, Michigan, Obama's friend Ramone was never mentioned.[25] Instead, the story contrasted the good jobs report and the myriad things getting in the economy's way: renewed fighting between Democrats and Republicans; internecine skirmishes within Obama's own party; the whimsies of Wall Street; the sorry legacy of NAFTA; the AFL-CIO's distrust of the Obama administration; and unfavorable public opinion polls. *Politico* relayed some good news as well—the rising job numbers seemed real, the auto bailout really had improved things, people really were buying houses again—but the bad news and the potentially bad news never abated. This rat-tat-tat of negativity suffused the story despite Obama's eloquence.

If strong narratives make politics politics, relentless focus makes journalism journalism. Fig. 3.3 shows how the press's Insistence scores easily top those of politicians, which is to say, the press repeats itself.[26] Journalists are said to be dogged when they refuse to forego a storyline. Journalists are said to hound the president on the campaign trail, to bark out questions they have asked countless times before. Journalists are said to run in packs, to have a taste for blood, to stay on the scent, and to sniff out the story behind the president's story. Journalists are said to be canine. That is their glory.

Journalists narrow discussions while politicians expand them. Journalists keep track of unfinished issues while politicians change the subject. In these ways and more, politicians and reporters talk past one another. Their contrasting styles are uniquely on display in press conferences. Presidents now begin these encounters with scene-setting remarks in an attempt to gain a tactical edge. They have also become adept at using the pivot; instead of directly answering a reporter's question, they say "let's talk about something else."

For example, in one free-wheeling press conference, George W. Bush was asked about his administration's performance in New Orleans after Hurricane Katrina.[27] He made a cursory response and then broadened the discussion with a paean to private enterprise. When queried about Supreme Court nominee Harriett Miers's knowledge of the law, he addressed her strength of character. When asked about his free-spending ways, he reminded reporters that the nation was at war in Iraq. When questioned about poverty, he moved to a discussion of education. When asked about political divisions in Congress, he spoke again of the war in Iraq. To be sure, all of these questions addressed complex matters, and all were part of a network of related issues. But increasingly in press conferences presidents respond to concave questions with convex answers.

Press conferences have also changed structurally, and that has altered the political scene as well. Consider, for example, a fairly typical exchange in one of Harry Truman's press conferences, an exchange that looks odd by modern standards:

REPORTER. Mr. President, in that connection, yesterday Mr. Olds, Chairman of the Board of United States Steel, indicated that a price increase of six and a quarter dollars a ton would not be sufficient to cover the 18 1/2 cents wage increase. Do you have any comment on that?

TRUMAN. I have none.

REPORTER. Have you any comment on the possible seizure of the steel industry by the Government?

TRUMAN. No further comment. I said something about it the other day. It isn't now under contemplation.

REPORTER. Not now?

REPORTER. Mr. President, do you have any comment on House action on your fact-finding bill?

TRUMAN. What was the House action on it?

REPORTER. The Case bill—the substitute.

TRUMAN. That was the action—not the action of the House but the action of the Rules Committee, wasn't it? The House hasn't yet acted on it, unless they voted within the last few minutes.

REPORTER. The House voted to take up the rule.

TRUMAN. The House voted to take up the rule? They still haven't acted.

REPORTER. To take up the bill—258 to 114.

TRUMAN. I have no comment on it. That's the business of the House.[28]

The insistence displayed by reporters here is rarely seen today. This direct, focused interchange has been replaced by a panoply of reporters' unrelated questions. Following the same, steady interrogative path has given way to journalistic grandstanding, president-baiting, and a general lack of deference.[29] Press conferences have become rowdier as a result, with reporters now covering far more territory than they had in the past and with presidents responding with their own practiced set-pieces.

Fig. 3.4 shows the inevitable result: the press has increasingly lost its collective focus during news conferences. What does the president do in response? He uses even more of the Hortatory Style (as we also see in Fig. 3.4).[30] Thus, the *Des Moines Register*'s Clark Mollenhoff doesn't have it quite right when complaining about his colleagues' "lobbed setups" and "blooper balls." Reporters do indeed ask such questions, but the more telling charge is that they have become too rivalrous with one another, hence making press conferences more diffuse. According to one tally, George W. Bush received an average of twenty-six different questions during his press conferences. In the encounter concerning Harriet Miers, for example, in addition to being asked about Miers, Hurricane Katrina, and the war in Iraq, Bush was queried about four different Supreme Court justices, Lyndon Johnson, Valerie Plame, the Bible, conservativism, female lawyers, lobbyists' gifts, political polling, and the chairman of the Federal Reserve.[31]

White House reporters defend their actions by noting how little contact they now get with the chief executive. As a result, they hit

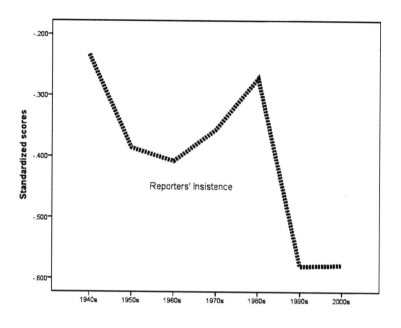

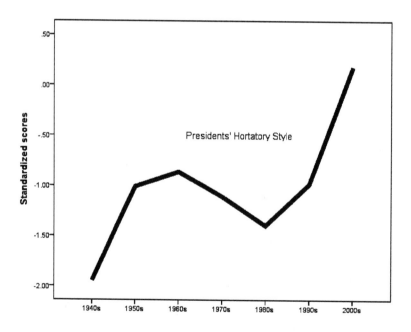

Fig. 3.4. Politicians' vs. reporters' styles in press conferences over time.

him with everything they have when the chance arises. But doing so has obvious costs—it lets the president retreat to higher ground (as we see in Fig. 3.4). While reporters are occasionally able to ask follow-up questions, their competitiveness for airtime attracts them to the gotcha question and the topper. Presidents respond to the press's disorganization by "transcending the miasma of petty politics" whenever possible. It is good to be the president.

It is also good to be a White House reporter, even though the job has its challenges. But that job has never been more important than it is today. Prioritizing a narrow set of issues is difficult in a 24/7 news cycle, but doing so keeps the nation focused on the most important questions (coverage of the Vietnam war is an example). Reporters' relentlessness also keeps the powerful and the privileged on their toes (Benghazi coverage is an obvious example). "Staying with it," "keeping on task," "digging in deeper," "trying once again," "not being deterred or intimidated"—these tools of Insistence keep power in check.

Changing Formats

Like so many other entities—music, book publishing, TV sitcoms, college teaching, and even taxicabs—journalism is being disrupted by the Internet. "We are all journalists now" crows attorney Scott Gant. "It is time to do away with the journalistic caste system we have created," he argues, "which elevates the employees of established news organizations above other citizens engaged in the practice of journalism." Gant concludes, "It is time to recognize that technology has caught up with the First Amendment."[32]

What are the new journalists bringing to the table? It is too early to tell, but scholars and industry leaders alike want to know. Here, we take a stab at that question by comparing a small set of bloggers (n = 225) to traditional journalists (n = 273) working in three areas: finance, politics, and technology. How do they differ from one another? Fig. 3.5 is suggestive, showing traditional journalists to be Insistent and bloggers to ramble or, to put it more generously, to embrace the Web's openness. Not having to worry about filling a predefined news hole, and having as much space as they want, bloggers constantly try out new things. Being unconstrained by traditional norms, they refer to themselves a good deal (a sin for longtime journalists), thereby increasing their brand and emphasizing their unique personalities.[33] There are reasons for this: Competing as they do with 180 million other bloggers, they must produce sprightly prose and update their sites constantly.[34] In such a hurly-burly world, worrying about conceptual focus is burdensome. So bloggers become exploratory (and larcenous), as *Outside the Beltway* did when reproducing Jake Tapper's denunciation of Barack Obama for missing the Parisian protests of the *Charlie Hebdo* massacre in 2015:

> I say this as an American—not as a journalist, not as a representative of CNN—but as an American: I was ashamed.
> I certainly understand the security concerns when it comes to sending President Barack Obama, though I can't imagine they're necessarily any greater than sending the lineup of other world leaders, especially in aggregate.
> But I find it hard to believe that collectively President Obama, Vice President Joe Biden, Secretary of State John Kerry, Secretary of Defense Chuck Hagel, Treasury Secretary Jack Lew and Attorney

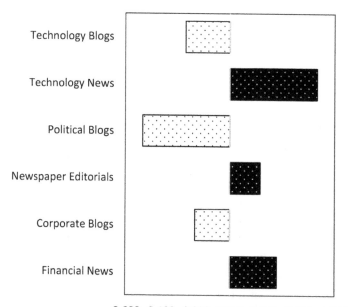

Fig. 3.5. Insistence scores for various blogs and press genre.

General Eric Holder—who was actually in France that day for a conference on counterterrorism—just had no time in their schedules on Sunday. Holder had time to do the Sunday shows via satellite but not to show the world that he stood with the people of France?

There was higher-level Obama administration representation on this season's episodes of "The Good Wife" on CBS. . . .

I imagine that Hillary Clinton and her husband are kicking themselves for not hopping on a corporate jet to get here. Can you picture Hillary and Bill walking in the front row, arm-in-arm with Netanyahu and Hollande?

Chris Christie, Scott Walker and Paul Ryan attended the Green Bay–Dallas football game Sunday and at least one of them sent his potential rivals mischievous tweets as if they were contemplating running for president of Beta Theta Pi. And Jeb? Mitt? Crickets.[35]

Tapper's remarks immediately went viral. There is a fury in them but also a certain jauntiness, qualities he had kept in check when reporting on air. But here, Tapper gets things off his chest, wanders across the political landscape, drops names, and makes pop culture allusions. We feel Tapper's personality as a result, something missing in CNN's "official" description of these same matters:

President Barack Obama didn't attend a unity march in Paris on Sunday, days after the deadly attack on the satirical newspaper *Charlie Hebdo*. Nor did his secretary of state, John Kerry, who has deep ties to France.

Kerry was in India, attending an entrepreneurship summit with new Prime Minister Narendra Modi—with whom the United States is hoping to develop much closer trade ties.

Instead, the United States was represented by US Ambassador to France Jane Hartley.

Attorney General Eric Holder was also in Paris, attending a security summit on combating terrorism. He recorded interviews that appeared on several US news outlets Sunday, but was not spotted at the unity march.

No one from the administration would speak on record about the US representation at the march.

"Attorney General Holder—a Cabinet level official—is representing the United States at the security meetings in Paris today. He is joined by the DHS Deputy Secretary [Alejandro] Mayorkas. The United States is represented at the march by Ambassador Hartley," a senior Obama administration official said.[36]

Like most traditional journalism, CNN's formal reportage does not point fingers, letting readers draw their own conclusions. Bradner the reporter writes briskly here, although some might call his prose dry. Yet there is merit in that too.

Does our cursory study of old-line vs. online journalism tell us where the profession is heading? Surely not. But DICTION does identify some of the freedoms the Web affords, while also identifying some of its dangers. Insistence—maintaining conceptual focus via word repetition—is a humble device, but my research over the years finds it to be journalism's most noble and most distinctive trait. Blogging and reporting are *not* the same thing. Journalism is at its best when it keeps its eye on the ball—telling us what happened and explaining what it means. All else is epilogue, or so I assert.

Conclusion

Although this chapter has covered considerable ground, its purpose was simple: to distinguish the press from the presidency. That seems like a shockingly elementary goal, but, strangely enough, nobody had tried to do so before, at least not in the manner I have attempted here. My studies identified two basic patterns: presidents tell stories and preach; reporters also tell stories (more sober ones) while focusing on issues. Presidents do not have the luxury of such focus, in part because their daily agendas are chock full and in part because the citizenry is so diverse. The inevitable result: presidents gallop off in a thousand directions and reporters try to corral them. One imagines that the Founders would be pleased with the tensions thereby created.

The arguments presented here are based on automated language analysis, a procedure that counts words. Such a tool misses *how* words are used and is thus something of a dumb clerk. But that is also its strength. Presidents and journalists are more than their words, but they are not less than them. That is, voters quickly learn that presidents are odd when listening to them. Sometimes they call their chief executive dilatory because of his endless narratives and sometimes they call him pretentious when he starts sermonizing. And yet during moments of crisis they will accept nothing less than a rich tableau from their president, a tableau showing that this, too, shall pass. Similarly, voters are often offended when reporters badger the president, but when reporters' questions expose corruption, they appreciate once again the Fourth Estate.

Will the Fourth Estate continue to be an estate? Will journalism stay vital in an age when the electronic and digital media offer compelling alternatives to the gray, gloomy story of everyday politics? One hopes so, but the challenges are formidable. The press's credibility is constantly being questioned in a cynical age. Its quotidian habits—get two sources, work up the background, double-check your statistics, ask a second question and then a third—seem quaint when an attractive website can be constructed on Monday, a digital following secured on Tuesday, virality assured by Wednesday. Everyone is not a journalist, but sometimes it seems that they are.

In times like these of turmoil and disruption, institutions are sorely put to the test. Journalism now confronts both technological and economic challenges. It would put its house in order if it knew where its house was located. Is Bill O'Reilly a journalist? Is MSNBC a news organization? Is *Salon* a newspaper? For its part, the presidency has virtually unlimited authority, and yet individual presidents often feel like Gulliver, tied to the ground by a thousand partisans. We live, as a result, in a place where power abounds but where it is also evanescent. We live in a provisional place where authority must be renegotiated each day. Thus, vigilance is required. Language lets us see into ourselves, into our history, into our culture. When it comes to politicians and journalists, then, we must keep an eye on the words they generate.

Notes

1. Timothy M. Jones and Penelope Sheets, "Torture in the Eye of the Beholder: Social Identity, News Coverage, and Abu Ghraib," *Political Communication* 26 (2009): 278–95; Benjamin R. Bates, "Circulation of the World War II/Holocaust Analogy in the 1999 Kosovo Intervention: Articulating a Vocabulary for International Conflict," *Journal of Language and Politics* 8, no. 1 (2009): 28–51.

2. Paul Baker, "Representations of Islam in British Broadsheet and Tabloid Newspapers, 1999–2005," *Journal of Language and Politics* 9, no. 2 (2010): 310–38; Shean

Phelan and Fiona Shearer, "The 'Radical,' the 'Activist,' and the Hegemonic Newspaper Articulation of the Aotearoa New Zealand Foreshore and Seabed Conflict,"
Journalism Studies 10, no. 2 (2009): 220–37; Sue Lockett John, David Scott Domke,
Kevin M. Coe, and Erica S. Graham, "Going Public, Crisis after Crisis: The Bush Administration and the Press from September 11 to Saddam," *Rhetoric & Public Affairs*
10, no. 2 (2007): 195–220; Catherine R. Squires and Sarah J. Jackson, "Reducing Race:
News Themes in the 2008 Primaries," *Harvard International Journal of Press/Politics* 15,
no. 4 (2010): 375–400; John Drury, "'When Mobs Are Looking for Witches to Burn,
Nobody's Safe': Talking about the Reactionary Crowd," *Discourse & Society* 13, no. 1
(2002): 41–73.

3. Erik P. Bucy and Maria Elizabeth Grabe, "Taking Television Seriously: A Sound
and Image Bite Analysis of Presidential Campaign Coverage, 1992–2004," *Journal of
Communication* 57 (2007): 652–75; Frank Esser, "Dimensions of Political New Cultures:
Sound Bite and Image Bite News in France, Germany, Great Britain, and the United
States," *International Journal of Press/Politics* 13 (2008): 401–28; Steven E. Clayman,
Marc N. Elliot, John Heritage, and Megan K. Beckett, "A Watershed in White House
Journalism: Explaining the Post-1968 Rise of Aggressive Presidential News," *Polit-
ical Communication* 27, no. 3: 229–47; Shawn J. Parry-Giles, "Political Authenticity,
Television News, and Hillary Rodham Clinton," in *Politics, Discourse, and American
Society: New Agendas*, edited by Roderick P. Hart and Bartholomew Sparrow, 211–27
(Lanham, MD: Rowman & Littlefield, 2001).

4. Jeffrey E. Cohen, *Going Local: Presidential Leadership in the Post-Broadcast Age*
(Cambridge: Cambridge University Press, 2010); Matthew Eshbaugh-Soha and Jeffrey
S. Peake, "The Presidency and Local Media: Local Newspaper Coverage of President
George W. Bush," *Presidential Studies Quarterly* 38, no. 4 (2008): 609–30; Elvin T. Lim,
*The Anti-Intellectual Presidency: The Decline of Presidential Rhetoric from George Wash-
ington to George W. Bush* (New York: Oxford University Press, 2008); Martha Joynt
Kumar, *Managing the President's Message: The White House Communications Operation*
(Baltimore: Johns Hopkins University Press, 2007); Corey Cook, "The Contemporary
Presidency: The Permanence of the 'Permanent Campaign': George W. Bush's Public
Presidency," *Presidential Studies Quarterly* 32, no. 4 (2002): 753–64; Richard Davis and
Diana Owen, *New Media and American Politics* (New York: Oxford University Press,
1998); Stephen J. Farnsworth and S. Robert Lichter, *The Mediated Presidency: Televi-
sion News and Presidential Governance* (Lanham, MD: Rowman & Littlefield, 2006);
W. Lance Bennet, Regina G. Lawrence, and Steven Livingston, *When the Press Fails:
Political Power and the News Media from Iraq to Katrina* (Chicago: University of Chicago
Press, 2007).

5. Alexis Simendinger, "Lessons Learned the Hard Way: Questioning Presidents,"
Presidential Studies Quarterly 38, no. 4 (2008): 693–99.

6. Roderick P. Hart and Craig Carroll, DICTION 7.0: *The Text-Analysis Program*, 2014,
http://www.dictionsoftware.com/. DICTION also lets scholars build their own dictionaries for specialized purposes. A user may construct up to thirty such dictionaries (up to two hundred words each in length), which DICTION will then use in its
search routines. For more about the intellectual architecture of the program, see the
various descriptions provided at www.dictionsoftware.edu, and Roderick P. Hart,
"Redeveloping DICTION: Theoretical Considerations," in *Theory, Method, and Practice
of Computer Content Analysis*, edited by Mark D. Wes (New York: Ablex, 2001), 43–60.

7. Murray Edelman, *Constructing the Political Spectacle* (Chicago: University of

Chicago Press, 1988); Robert Hariman, *Political Style: The Artistry of Power* (Chicago: University of Chicago Press, 1995); Kathleen Hall Jamieson, *Eloquence in an Electronic Age: The Transformation of Political Speechmaking* (New York: Oxford University Press, 1988).

8. Jerome S. Bruner, "The Narrative Construction of Reality," *Critical Inquiry* 18, no. 1 (1991): 1–21. For additional studies using the measures of Insistence and Hortatory Style, see Roderick P. Hart, Jay P. Childers, and Colene J. Lind, *Political Tone: How Leaders Talk and Why* (Chicago: University of Chicago Press, 2013). For a study employing the Narrative Force index, see Hart and Carroll, *DICTION 7.0*, and Hart, "Redeveloping DICTION."

9. For more complete descriptions of the texts analyzed here, see Hart, Childers, and Lind, *Political Tone*; Roderick P. Hart and Joshua M. Scacco, "Rhetorical Negotiation and the Presidential Press Conference," in *The Language of Public Affairs: Computational Research with DICTION*, edited by Roderick P. Hart, 59–80 (Hershey, PA: IGI-Global Publishers, 2014); and Roderick P. Hart, "Genre and Automated Text Analysis: A Demonstration," in *Rhetoric and the Digital Humanities*, edited by Jim Ridolfo and William Hart-Davidson (Chicago: University of Chicago Press, 2015), 152–68.

10. Narrative Force for print reporting = –0.2996; for TV news = 0.1726; for novels and short stories = 0.4482; for theatre scripts = 0.4684; for music lyrics = 0.6880; for TV drama = 0.5563; for corporate reports = –1.4035; for legal documents = –1.4999; for social science scholarship = –1.4532; for philosophical essays = –0.7883; $F [9, 9620] = 182.709$, $p < .000$.

11. Saul Bellow, *Seize the Day*, excerpted in Patrick Kurp, "The Inexhaustible Current," Anecdotal Evidence: A Blog about the Intersection of Books and Life, August 15, 2008, http://evidenceanecdotal.blogspot.com/2008/08/inexhaustable-current.html.

12. Hiroko Tabuchi, "Black Friday Fatigue? Thanksgiving Weekend Sales Slide 11 Percent," *New York Times*, November 30, 2014, http://www.nytimes.com/2014/12/01/business/thanksgiving-weekend-sales-at-stores-and-online-slide-11-percent.html?_r=0.

13. Narrative Force for NBC = 0.6104; for ABC = 0.4013; for CBS = 0.2945; for *Chicago Tribune* = –0.2462; for AP-UPI = –0.2615; for *Washington Post* = –0.2647; for *Los Angeles Times* = –0.3083; for *New York Times* = –0.3083; for *Christian Science Monitor* = –0.3387; for *Atlanta Constitution* = –0.3875; $F [9, 6906] = 65.212$, $p < .000$.

14. Thomas E. Patterson, "Political Roles of the Journalist," in *The Politics of News: The News of Politics*, 2nd ed., edited by Doris A. Graber, Denis McQuail, and Pippa Norris, 23–39 (Washington, DC: CQ Press, 2007); Gary Andres, "The Contemporary Presidency: Polarization and White House/Legislative Relations: Causes and Consequences of Elite-Level Conflict," *Presidential Studies Quarterly* 35, no. 4 (2005): 761–70; Frances L. Lee, "Dividers, Not Uniters: Presidential Leadership and Senate Partisanship, 1981–2004," *Journal of Politics* 70, no. 4 (2008): 914–28; Cohen, *Going Local*.

15. Bill Whitaker, "What Happens When You Swipe Your Card? As Hacking of Top Retailers Make Headlines, Bill Whitaker Discovers How Insecure Your Credit Card Information Is This Holiday Season," CBS News, November 30, 2014, http://www.cbsnews.com/news/swiping-your-credit-card-and-hacking-and-cybercrime/.

16. Narrative Force for TV news in 1980s = 5.0696; in 1990s = 5.5911; in 2000s = 5.9954; $F [2, 1437] = 24.303$, $p < .000$.

17. Barack Obama, "Illinois Sen. Barack Obama's Announcement Speech," *Washington Post*, February 10, 2007, http://www.washingtonpost.com/wp-dyn/content/article/2007/02/10/AR2007021000879.html. For additional insights on this marriage of the political and the theological, see Roderick P. Hart and John Pauley, *The Political Pulpit Revisited* (West Lafayette, NJ: Purdue University Press, 2004), and David O'Connell, *God Wills It: Presidents and the Political Use of Religion* (Piscataway, NJ: Transaction Publishers, 2015).

18. Hortatory Style for presidential remarks = 0.6485; for press reports = 0.0273; F [1, 11498] = 1419.102, p < .000.

19. Adam Nagourney and Jeff Zeleny, "Obama Formally Enters Presidential Race," *New York Times*, February 11, 2007, http://www.nytimes.com/2007/02/11/us/politics/11°bama.html?pagewanted=print&_r=1&.

20. Narrative Force for presidential remarks = 0.5163; for press reports = –0.2321; F [1, 11498] = 1996.620, p < .000.

21. Barack Obama, "Remarks by the President on the Resurgence of the American Auto Industry, Michigan Assembly Plant, Wayne, Michigan," White House, January 7, 2015, https://www.whitehouse.gov/the-press-office/2015/01/07/remarks-president-resurgence-american-auto-industry.

22. Drew Westen, "What Happened to Obama?" *New York Times*, August 6, 2011, http://www.nytimes.com/2011/08/07/opinion/sunday/what-happened-to-obamas-passion.html?pagewanted=all&_r=0; Junot Díaz, "One Year: Storyteller-in-Chief," *New Yorker*, January 20, 2010, http://www.newyorker.com/news/news-desk/one-year-storyteller-in-chief; Lindsey Boerma, "Obama Reflects on His Biggest Mistake as President," CBS News, July 12, 2012, http://www.cbsnews.com/news/obama-reflects-on-his-biggest-mistake-as-president/.

23. Díaz, "One Year."

24. John Hayward, "Barack Obama, Failed Storyteller," *Human Events*, July 13, 2012, http://beta.humanevents.com/2012/07/13/barack-obama-failed-storyteller/.

25. Edward-Isaac Dovere, "Obama Pushes His Economic Record in Detroit: But Labor Groups Accuse Him of Hurtling Auto Industry by Backing Trade Deals," *Politico*, January 7, 2015, http://www.politico.com/story/2015/01/obama-pushes-his-economic-record-in-detroit-114058.html.

26. Insistence for presidential remarks = –0.3912; for press reports = 0.2289; F [1, 11498] = 932.736, p < .000.

27. George W. Bush, "Transcript of President Bush's Press Conference," *Washington Post*, October 4, 2005, http://www.washingtonpost.com/wp-dyn/content/article/2005/10/04/AR2005100400584.html.

28. Harry S. Truman, "The President's News Conference," Truman Library, January 31, 1946, http://trumanlibrary.org/publicpapers/viewpapers.php?pid=1469.

29. Blair Atherton French, *The Presidential Press Conference: Its History and Role in the American Political System* (Washington, DC: University Press of America, 1982); Martha Joynt Kumar, "Source Material: Presidential Press Conferences: The Importance and Evolution of an Enduring Forum," *Presidential Studies Quarterly* 35, no. 1 (2005): 166–92; Samuel Kernell, *Going Public: New Strategies of Presidential Leadership*, 4th ed. (Washington DC: CQ Press, 2007).

30. The statistical effects are not overwhelmingly large here, mostly because the corpus of reporters' questions is quite small even when analyzed by DICTION in the aggregate. The corpus of presidential remarks, in contrast, is quite sizeable (since

the chief executive can talk as long as he wants). Still, the overall trends for both reporters and the president are persistent. Although the trend lines in Fig. 3.4 appear to be causally related, no such argument is being made here. Additional studies will be needed to determine if any direct effects on presidential speech have been occasioned by the wide variety of questions reporters are now packing into White House press conferences.

31. Mollenhoff quote in Kernell, *Going Public*, 186; Martha Joynt Kumar, "Source Material: 'Does This Constitute a Press Conference?' Defining and Tabulating Modern Presidential Press Conferences," *Presidential Studies Quarterly* 33, no. 1 (2003): 221–37.

32. Scott Gant, *We're All Journalists Now: The Transformation of the Press and Reshaping of the Law in the Internet Age* (New York: Free Press, 2007).

33. Insistence for traditional journalists = 0.31859; for bloggers = –0.3071; F [1, 496] = 50.107, p < .000; Self-references for traditional journalists = 1.4180; for bloggers = 8.3179; F [1, 496] = 158.523, p < .000.

34. For an interesting discussion of the size of the blogosphere, see "Buzz in the Blogosphere: Millions More Bloggers and Blog Readers," Nielsen Newswire, March 8, 2012, http://www.nielsen.com/us/en/insights/news/2012/buzz-in-the-blogosphere-millions-more-bloggers-and-blog-readers.html.

35. Doug Mataconis, "Obama's Absence from Paris Rally: Egregious Diplomatic Error, or Much Ado about Nothing?" Outside the Beltway, January 12, 2015, http://www.outsidethebeltway.com/obamas-absence-from-paris-rally-egregious-diplomatic-error-or-much-ado-about-nothing/.

36. Eric Bradner, "Obama, Kerry Absent from Unity Rally in Paris," CNN, January 12, 2015, http://www.cnn.com/2015/01/11/politics/obama-kerry-paris/.

4

Speaking of the Economy

Transformational Presidents, New Media Strategies, and the Necessity of a Universal Audience

STEPHANIE A. MARTIN

All presidents want to make history. Some, however, make more than others. Conventional wisdom holds that the best presidents are charismatic leaders who surround themselves with great teams and use the power of personality and good ideas to make the nation great. But what if the story is more complicated? What if a president's ability to create lasting change depends on external factors as much as it does individual political skill? And how much does media matter when it comes to upending the status quo, especially new media? When presidents innovate technologically, is public persuasion easier because messages can be sent directly to the people without being filtered through the White House press corps, as other authors in this book have claimed?

Take, for example, Barack Obama. When Obama was first elected in 2008, many posited that he would be a leader for the ages. For one thing, Obama was the first African American president. And, indeed, no matter how else he is remembered, this fact will undoubtedly always be of primary biographical import. In addition, Obama came to office articulating a rhetoric of high expectation; many Americans believed he would be an exceptional president, based largely on his oratorical ability to state lofty goals with a lyricism that allowed hearers to feel both inspired and invited to take part in his movement.[1] Plus, he advanced that rhetoric not only through traditional formats such as speeches and mainstream media interviews, but also online. He wasn't just the first black president; he was also the first social media president. This made him especially accessible and appealing. Finally, Obama came to the presidency soon after the onset of one of the worst financial crises the United States has ever faced. The 2008 economic recession was so large and significant, in fact, that figures as ideologically distinct as Paul Krugman and Peter Wallison described it as a world-historical event, "equivalent in its initial scope—if not its duration—to the Great Depression of the 1930s."[2]

In fact, national economic disruption often precedes public perceptions of presidential greatness. To wit, the two most influential commanders in chief of the twentieth century—Franklin Delano Roosevelt and Ronald Reagan—entered the Oval Office in moments of widespread financial tumult. Roosevelt defeated incumbent president Herbert Hoover in 1932, in the first election that took place after the great stock market crash of 1929 that set off the Great Depression. Reagan defeated incumbent president Jimmy Carter in 1980, largely due to stagnant economic conditions at home combined with perceptions that America had grown weak in the eyes of the world. And so Obama, too, came to the presidency facing an economy in peril, including a broken housing market, high unemployment, and low consumer confidence. As such, and particularly given Obama's aforementioned skills as an orator, social media savant, and perceived public unifier, some wondered whether Obama would emerge as a leader as significant as Roosevelt and Reagan before him. That is, would Obama be able to leverage his skill and the moment of economic crisis to create a new kind of American politics?

The answer, it seems, is both yes and no. By the end of his time in office Obama had overseen a dramatic rise in the Dow Jones average, a better than 3 percent drop in the unemployment rate, and had cut the budget deficit and passed his signature health care reform bill. In short, as his most ardent supporters were keen to point out, he had saved the economy from the brink of collapse. Nonetheless, he had also struggled to raise taxes on individuals even at the highest levels of income—a signature issue for him in both of his campaigns—and he had also not been able to secure funds for widespread infrastructure spending or expanding access to community college. This mixed result suggests that Obama operated more in the mode of a preemptive leader, to use Stephen Skrownek's term, than as a transformative one, as were both Roosevelt and Reagan. Preemptive leaders do not bring political revolution but rather find ways to both embrace and resist an already prevailing political ideology. In Obama's case, that ideology was Reaganism (neoliberalism), or the privileging of small government, low taxes, private investment, and personal responsibility for financial success. As a preemptive leader, Obama could not fully repudiate a legacy that he had actually campaigned against. Instead, he could only modify that legacy and then work to claim it as his own. This meant pushing for financial reform without engaging in "populist denunciations of Wall Street and the banking industry." It also meant foregoing tax increases and—to the horror of the liberals in his party—at one point even offering to cut Social Security and Medicare in an effort to secure a "grand bargain" with congressional Republicans during negotiations over the nation's debt limit. These kinds of moves on Obama's part meant that his economic reputation was mixed, at best, even among progressives. Many suggested his failure to promote a truly liberal economic agenda that addressed wage stagnation and income inequality led many Democrats to rally behind the democratic socialist candidate, Bernie Sanders, in the 2016 presidential primary rather than support Obama's preferred successor, Hillary Clinton. This, in spite of the fact that Obama remained at that time a hugely popular figure within his own party.[3]

But is it really fair to judge whether Obama—or any president—is transformational, and so especially historically significant, based on his policies and performance when it comes to the economy? After all, the president cannot walk into the Oval Office and press a button that works to lower the price of groceries for working families, or raise wages, or give insurance to everyone in need, or cut fuel prices, or do any such tangible thing to boost a struggling economy. Even so, citizens and voters make judgments about presidents largely based on the nation's financial state; it is more important to the public's impression of a president's job performance than is any other singular issue. Nevertheless, while it is true that commanders in chief have treasury secretaries and teams of economic advisers and are ultimately responsible for appointing individuals (including heads) to the Federal Reserve System, the only real tool they have for affecting economic change is their public rhetoric, especially as that rhetoric passes through the mass media channels of the day. Presidents are financial cheerleaders in chief. But this is all they are.

And so this is the conundrum: On the one hand, members of the public and historians, alike, hold presidents responsible—and measure their greatness, at least in part—based on how well they manage the nation's economy. On the other hand, presidents can only do so much. There are other factors at play. These factors include historical context and the media environment in which a president serves. In his book *The Politics Presidents Make*, Stephen Skowronek introduces the concept of "political time" as he argues that the transformative power of individual presidents has as much (or more) to do with the electoral moment in which each serves as it does with any particular actor or agenda. As such, the "blunt disruptive force" of the presidency is best understood in the context of *when* a chief executive holds office, alongside focused attention on *who* he happens to be. Skowronek further posits that political time is not a matter of strict historical chronology. Rather, political time articulates to (1) whether a president demonstrates allegiance or enmity to the policies of an established regime and (2) whether these presidential commitments are vulnerable or resilient. (By regime, Skowronek refers to dominant political orthodoxies such as neoliberalism or New Dealism that have bipartisan appeal.) Skowronek identifies four kinds of plausible regimes that presidents serve under: disjunction, reconstruction, preemption, and articulation. Regimes of disjunction are those that are falling apart; think Jimmy Carter. Regimes of reconstruction launch new eras; think Thomas Jefferson or Abraham Lincoln. Regimes of preemption stand in the gap, neither fully repudiating the prevailing political wisdom nor fully embracing it; think Dwight Eisenhower. And regimes of articulation continue what came before; think George H. W. Bush.[4]

A more robust explanation of Skowronek's theory is not necessary here. All the reader need realize is this: While the historical consequences of presidential leadership vary from one term to the next, the nature of these variations cannot—and should not—be reduced simply to the particular skills and styles of the men who happen to have held office. Rather, context matters, and it matters a lot. In addition, as "institutional thickening" has occurred, which is to say, as "organized interests and independent authorities" with the ability to exert different forms of pressure on presidents have increased, the possibility for launching a transformative, reconstructive presidency has lessened.[5] There are now too many cooks in the kitchen, and the media environment has become too fragmented for a single, unifying message to get through. Or so it seems. This sheds some light on Obama's limited success at implementing the ambitious agenda and platform on which he campaigned, even in spite of the fact that the Illinois senator came into the Oval Office facing a macroeconomic climate so abysmal many thought it had thrown the controlling ideology of neoliberalism into doubt and so would set off a new political era, as had happened for Ronald Reagan and Franklin Delano Roosevelt before him.

And so, let us ask, how did Roosevelt and Reagan manage the financial crises they faced, particularly from a rhetorical point of view? Were FDR and the Gipper more successful than Obama in crafting their economic messages and more successful at transmitting those messages through media, as well? That is, did they write better speeches and get more people to pay attention to their words? These are the questions that animate this chapter. Here, I consider how each of these three presidents framed their fiscal agendas—how they developed their vocabularies and cast their audiences—in an effort to understand how they developed a national economic worldview as part of the creation of a new political ideology. I then rhetorically examine one economic speech, in particular, as a means for showing how this new worldview and ideology took shape, and either worked to persuade the public to the president's side or else did not. In so doing, I pay particular attention to how each president—Roosevelt, Reagan, and Obama—used the new media of his time to speak directly to the people and so tried to reach as wide an audience as possible, while also avoiding too much filter and interpretation from the traditional media of their day. In each of these analyses, Skowronek's theory serves as a backdrop. Skowronek identifies both Roosevelt and Reagan as reconstructive, transformative presidents who changed the arc of American politics, in part by ushering in new economic policy agendas. There is little doubt that Obama aspired to be a great liberal president in the tradition of FDR, even as he also admired Reagan's approach to governing.[6] And yet, while the economic circumstances of his election suggested Obama might also emerge as a reconstructive leader, by the end of his term he was regarded as having performed more as a preemptive leader in the vein of Bill Clinton than as a president who altered national politics in a lasting (generational) way.

In exploring these questions I do not mean to argue that Skowronek's work suggests that rhetorical mastery is at the heart of political regime change. In fact, quite the opposite: Skowronek emphasizes that regime change has as much to do with time—that is, whether a dominant political narrative has run its course and so been exhausted, thus creating an ideological opening—as it does with personality. Nor do I posit that media are determinative. Instead, my aim is to reveal, first, how presidents *craft* messages in times of economic crisis, and second, how they *deploy* the new media of their time to reach the public with their messages and so both supplement the mass media effort that is also ongoing and important while also trying to set and control the news cycle to underscore presidential aims. The White House press corps is present in the analysis I present here, but its role is not in the foreground. Instead, I consider foremost how presidents used communication innovations to advance their economic arguments and agendas and, in so doing, tried to transform their political reality—both successfully and not. Roosevelt, of course, created the fireside chat that he hoped would have the effect of reaching a mass audience with a personal and cozy tone (it did); Reagan inaugurated the weekly radio address with much the same goal in mind; and Obama engaged in both social media and online video messaging to bring Roosevelt's and Reagan's rhetorical vision into the twenty-first century.

FDR's First Fireside Chat

In the fall of 1929, the United States descended into the Great Depression. In response, then president Herbert Hoover initially insisted that the economic trough would be temporary and that the nation's return to prosperity would come at the hands of the nation's businesses. Hoover had confidence that the natural forces of the market would lead to a quick correction. This meant that the president opposed extending federal aid to needy citizens, believing that such action "established politicized bureaucracies, . . . undermined free enterprise, [and] was illegal—a violation of local responsibility and states' rights." It was against this political rhetoric that Franklin D. Roosevelt positioned himself as he took to vociferously arguing for an active federal response to the growing Depression. In 1932 Roosevelt was elected president, largely based on a platform that called for a large government response to the ongoing economic catastrophe, including the creation of a social safety net that would, over time, come to include unemployment insurance, social security, work relief programs, and more.[7]

As president, Roosevelt made good on his platform that promised programs of collective responsibility for providing individual financial security, programs that were quite popular until—as we shall see—the late 1970s, when Ronald Reagan rose to power largely by leveraging rhetoric against their efficacy. And this is an important point, one that underscores and makes plain Skowronek's concept of a political regime: FDR's administration instantiated an economic legacy that would last through six more presidencies—both Democratic and Republican—and that denied that private enterprise on its own could motor the market machine. Instead, the idea was that regulation was always necessary to keep business in line, and a strong social safety net had to be in place to protect citizens from the always extant deficiencies of the marketplace. As such, the language (and the policy program) of economic conservatism was considered politically unviable for decades, made rubbish by the catastrophic nature of the Depression.

Even so, Roosevelt had to do the work of leading the people and persuading them during times of economic cataclysm to give his programs a shot. How was he able to convince the public his proposed actions were the right ones to take? How did he garner the support it would take?

By most accounts, Roosevelt was a masterful presidential persuader —among the best in the nation's history. Moreover, "as a rhetorical president," writes Halford R. Ryan, "Roosevelt exploited the technology of his time to its fullest potential. By radio, he spoke to the entire nation in his major addresses in the prototypic Fireside Chats." These remarks, along with portions of his major speeches, then often made their way into the motion picture newsreels of the day, giving citizens the chance to hear and see the president, and "the sound of his superb voice was reinforced by the visual dynamism of his delivery." And, more than was true of any of his predecessors in office, FDR scheduled frequent press conferences—he gave 999 of them to reporters during his thirteen years in office—in order to develop a consistent and ongoing relationship with the media that he used to influence the reportorial agenda, including his economic policy plans. And so while Roosevelt did find ways to go around the mainstream political press when he needed to, he also engaged them on a regular basis for putting his message out.[8]

In the fall of 2011, the Archive of American Television posted to its site and to YouTube an interview with the legendary David Brinkley, who was a White House correspondent for NBC News for the last year or so of Roosevelt's presidency. Brinkley explained his impression of the format of FDR's press conferences—as well as what made them so effective. Unlike the press conferences presidents give today, which Martha Kumar explains so well in chapter 1, and which are typically held either in the press briefing room of the West Wing or in the East Wing of the White House, Roosevelt invited reporters right into the heart of the Oval Office, twice a week—once in the morning to meet the needs of morning papers, and once in the afternoon to meet the needs of evening papers. The journalists gathered in a kind of semicircle around the president's desk, "standing up, smoking cigarettes, dropping ashes on the rug." Included in the gaggle of correspondents were reporters both for and against FDR's policies and programs. "He hated many of the newspapers because they hated him," Brinkley said. "He reciprocated as best he could by making nasty remarks about them—particularly the Republican papers that were always attacking him and tearing him apart." The informal environment of the conference allowed for a kind of biting jocularity that still provided a workable collegiality, Brinkley explained—a stark contrast to the careful and nuanced (but too often terribly toxic) relationship that so often exists between the president and the press that other writers in this book have so keenly explained, particularly Jennifer Mercieca in chapter 8 and Stacia Philips Deshishku in the final "Reality Check" of the book. In fact, this toxicity may at least partly explain Obama's ultimate failure to bring reconstructive change.[9]

Even so, that the relationship could be fraught meant that Roosevelt felt compelled to go around the Washington press corps and to leverage then emerging forms of mass media to take his message directly to the people, including developing the aforementioned fireside chat. Perhaps unsurprisingly, his first fireside chat was about the country's economic dire straits. Roosevelt delivered that address only eight days after taking office. On March 4, the president's third day, he had declared a national bank holiday, a saccharine term for describing what had been, in fact, a dramatic response to a deeply menacing financial situation. It was a wonder the entire economy did not collapse, and in many ways, it had. Most immediately concerning to Roosevelt and his team was the banking system. Thousands of financial institutions had gone under in the time between his election and when he actually took office, leaving many American citizens penniless. This led to bank runs as individuals rushed to remove their money before it was too late, actions that worked, like cascading dominoes, to cause more banks to fail. Additionally, gold reserves, which had been weakening in the months between Roosevelt's election and his inauguration, tumbled so dramatically that by late February it was not clear whether they could still back the nation's currency. And so the president's first act was to do that which had caused Hoover much hesitation: He ordered the banks closed.

The bank holiday, then, was Roosevelt's first major act as president. Once the banks were closed, he worked quickly to push the Emergency Banking Act through Congress, and it passed the Senate on March 9 by a vote of 73–7. The law was not without its detractors. These critics urged that it would prove dangerous because it granted the president the authority to intervene in the economy at will. Nonetheless, the law's most important provision was one that "compelled [banks] to close their doors until they could show stability in their reserves."[10] Most banks, in fact, could do this, and so once the bill had passed, most banks were able to reopen within a day, although some did need longer. This was an important step for the ailing economy, because it showed that most financial institutions retained the necessary solvency to continue operating. For those that didn't, the act also provided the Treasury Department with the authority to supply funds to help shore them up.

However, the passage of a bill doesn't automatically inspire confidence in the public. For that to happen, the citizens have to know the law exists, and—even more important—they have to believe its measures will work. For Roosevelt and his administration, this task looked doubly difficult because the public was deeply shaken by years of Depression, the shock of the bank holiday, and the new president's nascent moves and rhetoric toward a new kind of economic approach that aimed for collective action and responsibility, what we now know would become the New Deal. In fact, Roosevelt worried about the possibility that rather than support the measures he had taken to shore up the economy and the wobbly financial system, "as soon as the banks reopened, depositors would rush in and pull every penny out."[11] And so the president knew that a media strategy would be every bit as necessary for responding to the crisis as a legislative strategy had already been; if the plan was to work, the people were going to have to believe the president's words.

During his tenure as governor of New York, Roosevelt often spoke directly to the citizens of the Empire State over the radio, and so he decided to do the same thing as president. The hope was that a direct appeal would inspire confidence and so dissuade people from running to the banks to withdraw their money the minute they opened their doors. At 10:00 p.m. eastern time on Sunday, March 12, Roosevelt sat down in the Oval Office next to the fireplace there and began to speak. Using "an inflection of intimacy that came to define the New Deal for an entire generation," he explained the banking crisis in comforting, easy-to-understand terms and also urged the public to place confidence in any—and so every—bank the government would allow to reopen. Of course, this required listeners to have faith in something that hadn't happened yet. Roosevelt was speaking after a long and deep banking crisis, he had only just taken the oath days before, and the banks were only set to reopen on Monday morning. To this end, Roosevelt used his radio address to acknowledge this fact in straightforward terms: "The success of our whole great national program depends, of course, upon the cooperation of the public—on its intelligent support and its use of a reliable system." As Amos Kiewe so ably explains in his short book *FDR's First Fireside Chat*, this rhetorical move on Roosevelt's part was essential for two reasons. First, Roosevelt's language invited the people to see themselves as intelligent participators in Roosevelt's plan. And second, it empowered them to follow his requests. As such, the president and citizens were engaged in direct conversation, negotiation, and deal-making through the president's remarks. There was no real need for additional mass media (that is, news) interpretation; just the president and the people, speaking heart-to-heart. In that way Roosevelt used his fireside chats as an essential avenue for advancing his progressive economic agenda in the face of the Great Depression, as a kind of parallel messaging stream to the one moving through the regular mainstream press.[12]

It is impossible in this one short chapter to exhaustively detail Roosevelt's every rhetorical ploy and media interaction about his economic agenda and plans for saving the country from the Great Depression. Indeed, I have only barely begun the job here. But what I mean to show in this quick glance is this: Roosevelt invited the media—supportive and suspicious, alike—into the Oval Office by having his press conferences there, and he invited the public there, too, by means of the fireside chats, and these two gestures can be understood as rhetorical markers toward collective action in response to the Depression. This change in approach helped propel his change in rhetoric, a move that I suggest was ultimately central to the advancing of his reconstructive regime. Roosevelt was the first commander in chief to go from framing business as necessarily good and, instead, rendering it as something that required close watch and regulation and from which citizens required federally funded insurance protection. This rhetoric and these policies typify his terms of reconstructive transformation. In hindsight, this seems obvious. But if the banking holiday had failed—if Roosevelt's first fireside chat had proven unpersuasive and so there had been another banking run on Monday morning—there is no telling how deep the financial trough might have gone. If he had not been able to persuade the public, then his program, quite simply, would have failed.

In sum, that Roosevelt was able to use his presidency to launch not only the New Deal but also a kind of liberal consensus in American government was no small feat. Presidents of all stripes, from Truman to Eisenhower to Kennedy to Nixon, embraced that consensus, which held that government spending (Keynesianism) would grow the economy and enrich the nation's citizenry. Stability would come and unemployment would be minimized as long as everyone remembered that prosperity could be, at least in part, propelled through government programs. Private industry *alone* would never again be enough. This was the message of the Rooseveltian regime, and the regime held because the program worked until it didn't. That was when another economic ideology, long thought made moot by the ignominy of the Great Depression, was presented again to the American people by another orator every bit as skilled as FDR. He, too, would use media in new and innovative ways and so change the language the people would use to talk about both the economy and business. Like FDR, he would also engage the rhetorical presidency to leverage the mass media and take his message that championed freedom and enterprise straight to the people.

His name, of course, was Ronald Reagan.

Reagan and the Development of the President's Weekly Message

Recasting the nation's macroeconomic narrative is no easy feat and is usually only possible during political times of regime change. As I noted above, for several decades after the calamity of the Great Depression, the most compelling strands of the national conversation about the nation's economy had to do with the power of business to do harm and the need for a strong safety net to protect citizens against the inevitable tumults of the marketplace. But where the Rooseveltian conversation had emphasized economic equality, and making sure the forgotten man had food, clothing, and shelter, even if doing so meant high taxes, large government, and always growing federal bureaucracies, the discourse Reagan would initiate highlighted individual liberty as well as the notion that government programs do more harm than good. Reagan's emergence into national politics was not merely the advancement of an obvious leader, the quintessential American hero whose rise could have been neither thwarted nor denied, as many on the right now like nostalgically to insist. Rather, talented and charismatic a politician though he was, Reagan, like FDR before him, was the right man for the moment of reconstructive change.

The decade of the 1970s delivered enormous upheaval to both the political and economic environments in the United States. Where government spending had, for nearly forty years, mostly worked to deliver prosperity (at least to white Americans), and corporate America had more than willingly participated in delivering citizens both the products they wanted to buy and the wages they needed to buy them, suddenly there was rising unemployment, fiscal stagnation, and steep inflation. The popular term for this, of course, was stagflation, a macroeconomic condition thought impossible under the policies and programs FDR had popularized and that his presidential followers-on had (mostly) gladly continued to pursue. But when a disastrous and unpopular war in Vietnam dragged on to a seemingly endless conclusion and put enormous upward pressure on prices, at the same time as the Organization of Petroleum Exporting Countries (OPEC) provoked oil shocks, public skepticism emerged about the government's ability to manage the nation's economy. The policies and the language of the economic and political regime FDR initiated began to ring hollow: It was no longer straightforwardly obvious that a rising tide would lift all boats, if for no other reason than it was no longer straightforwardly obvious that the tide was still rising at all. According to the Bureau of Labor Statistics, in 1975 the average, annualized, unemployment rate stood at 8.5 percent, the highest it had been, by far, since the Great Depression. By 1980 it had only recovered to 7.1 percent. These numbers made again possible what had for decades been unthinkable: economic conservatism had hope.[13]

Hope, however, also requires a media strategy. While the cause of conservatism had never been entirely moribund, it had long been operating underground, getting its ducks in a row. Certainly it appeared sometimes in bursts (of defeat), only to recede again and await another opportunity. To this end there were the conferences of the Mont Pelerin Society, a kind of fraternity for elite, conservative-minded economists that included Friedrich von Hayek and Milton Friedman, among others. And there was the failed candidacy in 1964 of the *über*-conservative Barry Goldwater, who many at the time said sealed the fate forever of the far right wing in the United States but scholars now say actually started the movement that led to the rise of Reagan in 1980.[14] Movement activists took his defeat seriously and reorganized themselves to building a grassroots effort that included developing a think tank presence in Washington and—just as important—increasing the visibility of their media reach through better publicizing of their own periodicals, such as William F. Buckley's *National Review*. These same conservatives also worked hard to gain access to the mainstream media wherever they could.

In the last, Milton Friedman was an invaluable resource. He was a faculty leader at the world renown Chicago School of Economics, with the added credibility of having served FDR during the New Deal—a stint he said he both regretted and disavowed. Friedman could speak math—the preferred language of economists by the twentieth century—but, more important, he also had a knack for speaking and writing well in plain English and was able to simplify dry and complex monetary theory into language that voters would come to embrace. For Friedman, and for Reagan, it was all about freedom, most especially the notion that "economic freedom is an indispensable means toward the achievement of political freedom"—a force they thought most especially applied to individuals and that would be unleashed through leveraging hard work, personal grit, and expanding opportunity.[15]

Friedman provided for Reagan two important things. First, he endowed Reaganism with real academic gravitas. Whereas the administrations between Roosevelt and Carter were said to draw their economic inspiration not from themselves but from John Maynard Keynes, Friedman pointed his acolytes—including Reagan—back to Adam Smith himself. Members of the Reagan administration became so enamored with Smith, in fact, that the *New York Times* ran a story detailing how neckties embroidered with the classical economist's likeness had become a popular attire choice for "all [the] guys" on the president's team.[16]

Second, Friedman articulated his economic philosophy widely in the mainstream media, making it familiar to voters, and with language that Reagan could closely emulate in his own speeches, not to mention formal government documents. Friedman's writings often appeared in some of the nation's most influential newspapers and magazines throughout the 1970s and 1980s, including a biweekly column in *Newsweek* and occasional op-ed pieces in the *New York*

Times, the *Boston Globe,* and others. Friedman's book *Free to Choose,* coauthored with his wife, Rose, was reformatted into a television series for PBS.

Indeed, as economist Elton Rayack deftly demonstrated in his book *Not So Free to Choose,* if one compares the writings of Friedman with the formal policy documents issued by Reagan and his team, one finds striking similarity. Rayack details how the president's 1982 economic report includes nearly verbatim passages from Friedman's 1962 text *Capitalism and Freedom.* Both manuscripts begin by detailing the close relationship between political and economic freedom; both insist that where government is necessary its power is best exercised at the local and not federal level; both describe the freedom of "voluntary exchange" as an inherent magic of the market that ensures optimal outcomes; and both concede that although the trouble of negative externalities—such as pollution—must be handled by government, much attention must still be taken to ensure government does not go too far, as it will surely be inclined to do.

The similarity between Friedman's and Reagan's economic rhetoric, as well as Friedman's ability to make his ideas accessible to non-academic readers through the media, is important to notice, because creating and then disseminating an understandable, if technical, discourse is essential for transformative change to happen under the Skowronek framework. In addition, as I noted earlier, while the contemporary imagination often rhetorically frames Reagan in a kind of singular heroic light, his words were crafted in tandem with others and drew in both obvious and hidden ways from the philosophies of others. His revolution was not personally achieved. It happened in a particular moment of political time, under a particular set of economic circumstances, and with an ongoing press presence.

Nonetheless, Reagan himself was a master rhetorical performer, and, like FDR before him, he used mass media in unexpected and innovative ways. Here, as was true in my analysis of Roosevelt's engagement with media and, in particular, his innovative development of the fireside chat, I only have space in this essay to briefly consider Reagan's enormous gifts as a communicator. Many volumes have already been written about the Gipper's skills on camera and his administration's unyielding insistence that "pictures always mattered more to public opinion than words." Because of this, Reagan made it a point always to look presidential and to follow the script.[17]

Less attention has been paid, however, to another part of Reagan's strategy, which was his use of a nonvisual medium, radio, for resetting the national discourse, including the economic discourse. After FDR left office, and in spite of his success with the fireside chats, no other president until Reagan routinely used radio as a way to reach out to American citizens. But Reagan deeply admired the Depression-era Democrat, in spite of their ideological differences, and was keen to emulate his ability to connect with the American people.[18]

In April 1982 Reagan launched a weekly radio address to the nation. His motivation for doing so was twofold. First, he believed that regular radio addresses would give him the opportunity to speak directly to citizens without any filter or interpretation from news media. Second, he planned to use the radio address as a way to influence the conversation on the Sunday political news shows. On that front the weekly radio address became, over time, a remarkably effective means for driving the elite national news agenda.[19] Of late, this influence has dwindled some, due largely to fragmenting audiences.

Like Roosevelt, and as will also be true of Obama's first address that I will analyze in the section to come, Reagan's inaugural radio message had a fiscal theme, as it took up his administration's economic recovery plan. This points again to how important financial issues and rhetorics are to the president's relationship with the people. On April 2, 1982, the day before Reagan spoke, the Department of Labor had issued a jobless report showing that unemployment was up and was as high as it had been in 1975, when the country had been exiting a recession. Reagan, of course, had campaigned largely based on Friedman's economic theory, which proposed that fiscal growth and full employment would be best achieved through a program of low taxes, controlled government spending, and small, consistent infusions of money into the financial system by the bank of the Federal Reserve. These are the central tenets of monetarism, the economic theory for which Friedman won the Nobel Prize in 1976. So, for Reagan and his administration, that the new policies were slow to work (or were not working at all) represented a reality that required presidential explanation and personal cajoling. Again, as was true of Roosevelt in the first fireside chat, Reagan needed to engage his listeners as participants and partners in his economic program, and, more particularly, he needed to garner from them a willingness to stay the course in spite of its difficulty. However, where FDR had appealed to the public's intelligence as a means to empower them to take action and share in his plan, Reagan used metaphorical language that asked his listeners to have more patience, because the game was still unfolding.

In spite of Reagan's success during his first two years at cutting taxes and some spending, inflation remained troublesome, as the prime rate hit 18.63 percent on October 9, 1981, the highest rate ever recorded. This, along with continuing unemployment, meant that even though the administration had had success in pushing through Congress a smaller federal budget and, as he told his listeners, had been able to pass "a tax cut program which increased depreciation allowances for business and began a 25-percent cut in income tax rates for individuals, to be phased in over 3 years," some had begun to doubt the wisdom of the president's plans.

For Reagan, this dubiousness was premature. Yes, some individuals were struggling. In retort, he noted that "ninety-nine and a half million of our people are employed." Moreover, Congress had only agreed to the budget cuts the previous October, barely six months earlier. Progress was happening, he said, albeit too slowly. It wasn't fair, and it wasn't according to plan. "By all the rules of the game, interest rates should be down around 9 or 10 percent," he said. It hadn't worked that way because too many jobless people had meant high costs in jobless benefits, coupled with low tax revenues. "Fewer people working meant fewer people paying taxes," he continued. The deficit went up, and so inflation stayed too high. Wall Street was nervous. Where many were feeling fear, Reagan counseled patience: "Now, I know you've been told by some that we should do away with the tax cuts in order to reduce the deficit. That's like trying to pull a game out in the fourth quarter by punting on the third down. You've also been told our program hasn't worked. Well, of course it hasn't; it hasn't really started yet."[20]

Like a coach with his team down midway through the first quarter in the first game of the season, but who remains confident a

championship is all but inevitable, Reagan invited his listener to assume abundance even in the absence of evidence. Where Roosevelt
needed his listeners to feel empowered to act and to trust, Reagan
urged his listeners to maintain confidence and belief in spite of the
statistics or, even, the truth of their circumstances. In many ways this
represents Reagan's great power as an orator, his sunny optimism
that is at the heart of so many analyses of his talent as a great communicator. What is remarkable is that he was able to use that talent
in the nonvisual medium of radio as much as he could on television
and in person. He painted a picture with words that invited the
listener—the citizen—to share Reagan's economic worldview. This
approach would ultimately prove successful (enough), as Reagan
was able to maintain enough popular support to continue forward
with his program and plans and so successfully transform the nation's politics.

In all, Reagan made 331 weekly radio addresses, and, as was the
case in the first one, he often made economic matters a central topic
of conversation. As a transformational leader, in his appearances
Reagan "consistently played the role of a cheerleader" who would
exhort citizens to do their part to bring about financial recovery,
even as he blamed the media for their "doom and gloom" stories
that did little more than make things worse. As president, Reagan
insisted that the economic problems the country faced were not the
result of the new policies his administration sought to implement,
but rather stemmed from a "forty-year non-stop [spending] binge"
by the previous regime. Reaganism meant prudence, restraint, and
the possibility that individuals, not government, would finally be
allowed to prosper.[21]

Over time the rhetoric, if not all of the policies, worked. In 1983
GDP increased by a healthy 3.6 percent, and in 1984 it went up by 6.8
percent, helping the president cruise to an easy reelection. Indeed,
"the most remarkable attribute of this period of economic growth
was its durability. It lasted 92 months, which was more than twice
the average length of expansion since 1945."[22] This meant that, true
to Skowronek's theory, even Bill Clinton, rather than being seen as
a Democrat in the mold of FDR, is regarded by most as having been
made electable by following economic policies in the mold of Reagan
and implementing welfare reform and programs of free trade over

an expanded welfare state. But by 2008 the world had changed, and changed dramatically. It was then that the United States—and the world—faced the worst financial crash since the Great Depression, an event that might have upended the country's economic rhetoric and economic policy making. This time, another seeming transformational leader stood at the podium, promising to use technology to do what Reagan and Roosevelt before him had done. The question was: Would Barack Obama be able to deliver?

Obama's YouTube Chats

When Barack Obama was elected president in November 2008, expectations were high. Obama came into office having won 52.93 percent of the national popular vote—the highest cumulative total since the senior George H. W. Bush's drubbing of Michael Dukakis in 1988—and carrying 365 electoral votes. Elected on a platform of "hope" and "change," the new president also found himself overseeing an economy deep in peril. In the months and weeks leading up to the election, the American housing market had basically collapsed, as the world's largest banks teetered on the verge of outright failure too. Unemployment in January 2009, when Obama officially began his term, was over 7 percent; by year's end it would hover near 10 percent.[23] Indeed, many economists believe that only the Great Depression of the 1930s was worse.

Because of this crisis, and because of Obama's status as a seemingly transcendent leader, some at the time believed the new president's rise to power would signal a turning back from the Reaganesque policies of the previous four administrations that favored low taxes, little regulation, and individual responsibility for financial success. Soon after the inauguration, however, it became clear that implementing change would be much harder than the new president's campaign rhetoric had promised or relatively easy election had made it seem. Although Obama's own Democratic Party controlled both the House of Representatives and the Senate, the new chief executive struggled to pass the major stimulus package that he had proposed upon taking office.

Perhaps more surprising, Obama's message promising hope and change was swamped by a resurgence of free-market, up-by-the-bootstraps rhetoric almost as soon as he came to office. Almost from the moment of his inauguration in 2009, Obama was on the defensive, a situation that made it all the more urgent for the president to speak out forcefully on behalf of his agenda. But that effort was usually an uphill and unsuccessful slog. In fact, Obama could not even marshal support to raise taxes on individuals at the very highest levels of income, which had been a signature campaign issue for him. By the time of the midterm elections in 2010, the new president's approval ratings had steeply declined, as the Democrats suffered historic losses in both the House and the Senate. And so the question emerged as to whether Obama could still emerge as a transformational leader, or if he would be remembered as an inspirational orator and campaigner whose time in office would never amount to much. Under Skowronek's framework, Obama began to seem much more in the mold of a preemptive leader than a reconstructive one, in spite of the dire financial circumstances that met his time in office. His inability to garner bipartisan support for a new way of managing the nation's economy was an important reason for this.

But that Obama would ultimately be unsuccessful in transforming the nation's economic discourse, and so its politics, didn't mean the president and his team didn't try, and try from the start. In fact, even as they were struggling to overcome the many obstacles and opponents they faced, the members of the president's team continued to look for innovative ways to use new media to connect with constituents. Sometimes characterized as the "social media president," Obama from the earliest days of his candidacy for president had set as a goal the use of "technology to bring people together" as well as allow citizens to leverage "technology to organize on their own."[24] As a candidate in 2007 and 2008, Obama had enlisted the services of videographer Arun Chaudhary to produce frequent short pieces for reaching supporters. These videos proved especially effective as campaign tools, because while they were kept brief, they still highlighted "one of their greatest assets: the eloquence and charisma of Barack Obama." The videos were also effective and useful because voters could access them no matter their actual geographic location—anyone with an Internet connection could watch—and they allowed Obama's message to be distilled into manageable chunks. Rather than watch entire speeches, viewers could watch smaller (five minutes or so) versions on the campaign's YouTube channel that could also easily be shared with family and friends. Finally, critically, the videos gave viewers a way to speak back. "An important part of the YouTube community's philosophy is the ability to post a video response," explained new media strategist Rahaf Horfoush. "Video responses on Obama's videos led to increased traffic, because when someone posted a comment on their own channel it would encourage those who came across that video response to link to the original speech to see what it was about."[25] In essence, Obama was trying to create a conversation with constituents through video and social media to create conversations, all without having to go through the conduit of the traditional mainstream media.

Once in office, the president and his team were eager to continue the campaign's habit of reaching people through screens. To this end the new administration added a cinematographic component to the weekly radio address and began to upload the remarks to both the WhiteHouse.gov website and YouTube as well. However, motivating citizens to engage the work of citizenship proved to be much harder than inspiring supporters to vote. As George Edwards explains so well in chapter 7, whereas candidate Obama had "deftly used technology to shatter fundraising records, organize supporters locally, repel attacks, and get out the vote en route to a strong victory," it was not always clear how these same communications technologies could be leveraged after the electioneering was over and the governing had begun. But the Obama team was determined to try, and they thought maintaining their video operations from the campaign would be an innovative and smart place to start. "I knew this was something President Obama was good at, but also was going to be a huge pain. . . . We [were] actually agreeing to make a movie every Friday night," Chaudhary told the *Boston Globe* in 2014.[26]

The first of these movies had an economic theme and an economic message.[27] Exactly like Roosevelt and Reagan before him, Obama used new media technology to reach out to the people with words about financial crisis. However, unlike his predecessors, Obama found his oratorical task much more difficult. He made his remarks on Saturday, January 24, 2009, only four days after he had taken office and during the period of time when he was riding a relatively high tide of popular support, on which he hoped to capitalize. Nonetheless, as I mentioned above, deep partisan divide and rancor also greeted him, particularly in the halls of Congress. He did not have the kind of broad support in crisis that both Roosevelt and Reagan had enjoyed, or at least he did not have it to the same degree.[28] Instead, Republicans remained stalwart in their rhetoric against government spending, even in the face of macroeconomic calamity, and they meant to do whatever they could to block any attempt by Obama to engage a Keynesian-inspired approach as a means for digging the nation out of the fiscal ditch.[29] They did not intend to let go of Reaganism, denying the president the crucial bipartisan support he would need to make lasting change possible. This meant that the newly elected president would need as much popular support as he could muster to get his stimulus package passed, because without Republican support, he would need to keep every Democrat he could in the fold. As such, Obama began his remarks by pointing to the gravity of the crisis and, as we saw with both Roosevelt and Reagan before him, working to enlist his viewers as participants in his cause. However, his task in uniting the audience looks, upon reflection, much more difficult than theirs turned out to be:

> We begin this year and this Administration in the midst of an unprecedented crisis that calls for unprecedented action. Just this week, we saw more people file for unemployment than at any time in the last twenty-six years, and experts agree that if nothing is done, the unemployment rate could reach double digits. Our economy could fall $1 trillion short of its full capacity, which translates into more than $12,000 in lost income for a family of four. And we could lose a generation of potential, as more young Americans are forced to forgo college dreams or the chance to train for the jobs of the future.[30]

The *we* at the heart of the president's remarks is somewhat nebulous —at least at first—and probably intentionally so. With the phrase, "*We* begin this . . . administration," did Obama mean to refer to himself and his team, or to himself and the American people? That is, does the president mean for the *we* to be narrowly tailored or broadly construed? It could go either way, and this slippage works to draw the viewer into Obama's remarks. As such, by the time the

next *we* is uttered, Obama is able to draw on the immediate and personal in order to make the viewer his coconspirator in passing his
stimulus plan. The viewer and the president must work together, he
suggests, to tackle the scourge of unemployment, which has reached
levels not seen for twenty-six years—and things could worsen still.
For those still working, the sputtering economy means money lost
from their pocket. Something must be done.

Having quickly laid out the recession's depth, and having rhetorically joined the viewer with himself in the cause of recovery, Obama
hit his next punchline. "In short," he said, "if we do not act boldly
and swiftly, a bad situation could become dramatically worse." The
president then spent the next 476 words, out of a mere 807 total for
the entire address, specifying the components of his stimulus act.
It was to include spending monies for progressive priorities such
as clean energy programs, computerizing medical records, investing
in federal Pell grants for low-income college students, and rebuild-
ing the nation's infrastructure. Obama closed by acknowledging
that "some [were] skeptical about the size and scale of this recovery
plan." He insisted that he should be held accountable for results, a
means for assuring the viewer he did not intend to simply "throw
money at our problems," but rather to "invest in what works."[31]
For the Democrats who supported him, Obama had programs they
would love. For Republicans who didn't, Obama was willing to be
put to the test. Without saying so, the president acknowledged in
these early remarks that his political success would require bipartisan appeal. Neither Roosevelt nor Reagan had to even mention the
opposition. Their audience was *already* the American people writ
large. And this made all the difference.

Like the first weekly addresses of both Roosevelt and Reagan before him, Obama's remarks were a call to action as much as they
were a description about what was happening. Whereas Roosevelt
needed people to trust that the banks were safe in the aftermath of
the bank holiday and the reopening of the nation's financial institutions, and Reagan needed people to stick with his plan in spite of
high unemployment and high inflation, Obama needed citizens to
understand the main components of his proposed stimulus package
and then to "act as citizens and not partisans and begin again the

work of remaking America."[32] He needed a country, a citizenry—something his predecessors *already* had. This, then, is what makes Roosevelt's and Reagan's use of new media so interesting. It further added to their gravitas. They did something new, which made their already appealing personas even more appealing. Obama's use of new technology, however, was but another media fragment in an already fragmented media world.

And indeed, there is little doubt that Obama had to exist in a deeply partisan political environment as well as in a deeply fractured media environment. This made it much harder for him to send a clear message that would unify the people. The weekly video messages might have been a good idea; the problem was, almost no one watched, and it no longer carried the same capacity to set the national news agenda as Reagan's addresses had. Through December 2014, 1.2 million people had watched the president's first video message, which seems like a lot. However, that is but a tiny percentage of the nearly 70 million people who voted for him, not to mention the Republicans he hoped to bring into the fold. When it came to actually governing, the Obama team struggled mightily to maintain much of the excitement that had surrounded the 2008 campaign.

This is hardly a novel insight. Moreover, I don't mean to argue that one weekly address about a proposed stimulus package *should* have been able to serve as a transformative piece of oratory. Rather, what I suggest is that even in this very first address one can already see the strands of the hoped for Obama transformation coming apart. In their first weekly addresses, Roosevelt and Reagan, alike, were both able to speak in terms that presumed the rightness of their position and the unity of the people. Their main work of persuasion was merely to reconvince—to remind—citizens to trust in the leader they had already chosen. Both Roosevelt and Reagan enjoyed support that turned out to be relatively wide and deep. Obama, on the other hand, had to work rhetorically to manufacture the "we" to whom he hoped to speak. Popular though he was when first elected, neither he nor his policies had the kind of staying power his predecessors enjoyed. It was not the right political time for economic reconstructive change to come, and that made all the difference.

Conclusion

In his 2016, and final, State of the Union address, President Obama gestured toward some of the limitations he had come up against during his years in office and demurred that among his "few regrets" was "that the rancor and suspicion between the parties [had] gotten worse instead of better." He also imagined that a president like Lincoln or FDR—reconstructive leaders both, under Skowronek's terms—would have done better. In part, as I have shown in this essay, Obama was right to point out that those other leaders might have had more success, but perhaps 2008 was simply not the right political time.

As I stated at the outset of this chapter, the main power presidents have when it comes to economic issues is to use speeches—and the technology through which these speeches are carried—to coax citizens toward economic confidence. But as media channels have fragmented and the nation has become more electorally polarized—which are related and unrelated developments at once—the president's ability to move the needle has shrunk. And so while citizens may still vote aspirationally—for example, for Obama's promises of hope and change—once the election has passed, these same constituents may tend to fall back on their previously held beliefs and so refuse their new leader the support he needs to execute his new programs and plans, even in moments of crisis. As such, it is unclear when or how transformation will come again to the American presidency or to American national politics in general.

Notes

1. Jennifer M. Mercieca and Justin S. Vaughn, eds., *The Rhetoric of Heroic Expectations: Establishing the Obama Presidency* (College Station: Texas A&M University Press, 2014), chapter 1.

2. Krugman is a Princeton professor and *New York Times* columnist and a noted supporter of Keynesian economic theory, which promotes government spending and stimulus as necessary for spurring economic growth and reducing unemployment. Wallison, on the other hand, holds the Arthur F. Burns Chair in Financial Policy Studies at the American Enterprise Institute, a long-standing conservative think tank. Peter J. Wallison, *Hidden in Plain Sight: What Really Caused the World's Worst Financial Crisis and Why It Could Happen Again* (New York: Encounter Books, 2015); Paul Krugman, *The Return of Depression Economics and the Crisis of 2008* (New York: W. W. Norton, 2009).

3. Jack M. Balkin, "What It Will Take for Barack Obama to Become the Next FDR," *Atlantic*, November 1, 2012, http://www.theatlantic.com/politics/archive/2012/11/

what-it-will-take-for-barack-obama-to-become-the-next-fdr/264195/. In the August 2016 RealClearPolitics.com average of presidential approval polls, 86.7 percent of Democrats approved of Obama's performance in office and only 9.9 percent disapproved, http://www.realclearpolitics.com/epolls/other/president_obama_job_ap proval_among_democrats-1046.html.

4. Stephen Skowronek, *The Politics Presidents Make: Leadership from John Adams to Bill Clinton*, rev. ed. (Cambridge: Harvard University Press, 1997), 30, 36.

5. Ibid., 31.

6. Michael Duffy and Michael Scherer, "The Role Model: What Obama Sees in Reagan," *Time*, January 27, 2011, http://content.time.com/time/magazine/article /0,9171,2044712,00.html.

7. Walter I. Trattner, *From Poor Law to Welfare State: A History of Social Welfare in America*, 6th ed. (New York: The Free Press, 1999), 277, 281.

8. Halford R. Ryan, *Franklin D. Roosevelt's Rhetorical Presidency* (New York: Greenwood Press, 1988), 1.

9. "David Brinkley," Emmy TV Legends, Archive of American Television, December 8, 1999, http://www.emmytvlegends.org/interviews/people/david-brinkley.

10. Jeffrey W. Coker, *Franklin D. Roosevelt: A Biography* (Westport, CT: Greenwood Press, 2005), 91.

11. Ibid.

12. Michael Hiltzik, *The New Deal: A Modern History* (New York: Free Press, 2011), 51; Amos Kiewe, *FDR's First Fireside Chat* (College Station: Texas A&M University Press, 2007), 92.

13. Judith Stein, *Pivotal Decade: How the United States Traded Factories for Finance in the 1970s* (New Haven, CT: Yale University Press, 2010). Prevalent in managerial theory during the 1950s was the idea of the so-called soulful corporation with equal responsibility to profit and to society (the community). The notion stemmed from Adolf A. Berle and Gardiner C. Means, *The Modern Corporation and Private Property*, rev. ed. (New York: Harcourt, Brace & World, 1968).

14. Rick Perlstein, *Before the Storm: Barry Goldwater and the Unmaking of the American Consensus* (New York: Nation Books, 2009); Robert Horwitz, *America's Right* (Cambridge: Polity Press, 2013).

15. Milton Friedman and Rose Friedman, *Free to Choose: A Personal Statement* (New York: Avon, 1979), 41.

16. "Of Neckties," *New York Times*, March 29, 1981.

17. Eric Louw, *The Media and Political Process* (Thousand Oaks: Sage Publications, 2010), 88. To wit, Reagan's administration was expert at using especially television to project a preferred "sunny" image that substantiated its message and rhetoric, whether those moving pictures in fact matched ongoing economic indicators or the truth of what was being said. In one famous example, Leslie Stahl of CBS News reported a story that was critical of Reagan but that included pictures of Reagan smiling and looking confident and presidential. The day after it aired, a member of Reagan's team called Stahl, she thought—at least, at first—to object to her story. Not quite. "You television people still don't get it," came the retort from the White House official. "No one heard what you said. Don't you people realize the picture is all that counts? A powerful picture drowns out all the words." James Fallows, *Breaking the News: How the Media Undermine American Democracy* (New York: Vintage Books, 1997), 62.

18. W. Eliott Brownlee, "Introduction: Revisiting the Reagan Revolution," in *The Reagan Presidency*, edited by W. Eliott Brownlee and Hugh Davis Graham (Lawrence: University Press of Kansas, 2003), 3.

19. Lori Cox Han, "New Strategies for an Old Medium: The Weekly Radio Addresses of Reagan and Clinton," *Congress and the Presidency* 33, no. 1 (2006).

20. Ronald Reagan, "Radio Address to the Nation on the Program for Economic Recovery," The American Presidency Project, April 3, 1982, http://www.presidency.ucsb.edu/ws/?pid=42359.

21. John W. Sloan, *FDR and Reagan: Transformative Presidents with Clashing Visions* (Lawrence: University Press of Kansas, 2008), 289.

22. Ibid., 292. Many scholars have suggested that Reagan was not ultimately as true to fiscal austerity and monetarism as he set out to be. For example, in early 1982 the administration pressured Federal Reserve chairman Paul Volker to end the monetarist experiment and expand the money supply to lower interest rates. Also, there is significant evidence that what really "maintained living standards during the 1980s was the increase in the number of women working outside the home," (ibid., 293).

23. US Bureau of Labor Statistics, "Databases, Tables & Calculators by Subject," United States Department of Labor, http://www.bls.gov/data/.

24. James E. Katz, Michael Barris, and Anshul Jain, *The Social Media President: Barack Obama and the Politics of Digital Engagement* (New York: Palgrave MacMillan, 2013), 3.

25. Rahaf Harfoush, *Yes We Did: An Inside Look at How Social Media Built the Obama Brand* (Berkeley: New Riders, 2009), 148, 151.

26. Katz, Barris, and Jain, *Social Media President*, 15; Matt Viser, "Obama Holds to Weekly Radio Tradition," *Boston Globe*, July 7, 2014. It should be noted that although Viser suggests in this quote that the making of these videos was an onerous task, the White House did upload and post thousands of videos and clips over the Obama tenure in Washington, DC. George Edwards in chapter 7 details this video effort in full, well beyond this first postinaugural YouTube video speech.

27. As George Edwards explains in chapter 7, almost as soon as he became president-elect, Obama and his team began making these official YouTube videos for supporters, as had also been their habit during the campaign. However, this was the first official video after his swearing in and is also listed as the first official video on the White House record. As such, it is my focus here.

28. Much has been written about presidential rhetoric in times of crisis, although most of this literature articulates to rhetoric about international affairs, not moments of economic calamity. However, the findings of these rhetorical studies largely match what I have argued in this chapter: that the rhetoric focuses on inclusive language (Murphy); that it is an important means for rallying public support (Zernicke); and that presidents use crisis rhetoric to construct and maintain shared meaning with audiences (Taylor). Chad Murphy, "The Evolution of the Modern Rhetorical Presidency: A Critical Response," *Presidential Studies Quarterly* 38, no. 2 (2008); Paul H. Zernicke, "Presidential Roles and Rhetoric," *Political Communication and Persuasion* 7, no. 4 (1990); Karen Taylor, "Telling the Story, Hearing the Story: Narrative Co-Construction and Crisis Research," *American Communication Journal* 9, no. 1 (2007).

29. Only eleven House Republicans would eventually vote for the American Recovery and Reinvestment Act of 2009, the stimulus bill Obama proposed upon taking office and that was passed 255–177. See https://www.govtrack.us/congress/votes/111-2009/h46.

30. Barack Obama, "The President's Weekly Address," US Government Publishing Office, https://www.gpo.gov/fdsys/pkg/PPP-2009-book1/pdf/PPP-2009-book1-Doc-pg13.pdf.

31. Ibid.

32. Ibid.

REALITY CHECK

Dinosaurs, Dimes, and the Digital Age

THOMAS DEFRANK

It is not true that I've been reporting from Washington since dinosaurs roamed the earth. It *is* true that my tenure as a White House correspondent is now in its sixth decade; my first presidential trip was with Lyndon B. Johnson in the summer of 1968 as a *Newsweek* intern. It is also true that from a communications perspective, I definitely date back to prehistoric times—pre-Internet, pre–cable TV, pre-iPhone, pre-Facebook, pre-Twitter, pre-Flickr, pre- pretty much everything.

In the almost half-century since my first White House briefing, the march of technology has made it easier for journalists to do their jobs; it's also made it easier for White House media-meisters to bypass reporters and spin their message unfiltered to the public while exercising more control over that message.

Everybody remembers FDR's fireside radio chats, but even with the advent of television, communicating remained a challenge for presidents. I remember being cleared into the White House in June of 1968 and being thrilled to walk through the West Wing entrance—the same spot where a Marine stands watch today. It's also where reporters arrived in those days and made their way to a cramped, stuffy press room with tiny cubicles and pay phones for calling stories in. If you look carefully at photos of that long-gone White House press area, you'll notice some interesting items: cigarettes, rotary-dial telephones, old-fashioned phone booths, and manual typewriters —not to mention, regrettably, very few women reporters.

This press area was there when I arrived for my first briefing, but there was no briefing room; actually, we just gathered in Press Secretary George Christian's office. Maybe two dozen reporters assembled to ask questions—no cameras, no photographers—with some sitting on the floor. Sometimes when President Johnson wanted to make some news, he'd stride unannounced into the West Wing reception area, where reporters were allowed to congregate. He'd quickly be surrounded by a captive audience eager to hear whatever he wanted them to hear.

My friend Peter Maer of CBS News retired at the end of 2014 after a quarter-century as a press corps stalwart. At his farewell salute by the White House Correspondents' Association, Peter told of being on an Obama trip a few months earlier. He was sitting a row behind a couple of White House staffers on the press bus and heard one of them say, "Can you imagine what it must have been like for these guys before cell phones?"

Peter leaned forward and said: "Yeah—dimes." As in, when you were traveling on assignment you needed to carry a roll of dimes and scope out the nearest pay phones so you could file in a hurry.

Dimes—contrast that with a presidential trip to Asia in the fall of 2014, where the press tab was ninety thousand dollars per journalist —nearly a million dimes. But that's another story.

Many of us from that era remember reporting a story somewhere in the heartland and pecking it out on a manual typewriter in a bar or hotel room. The next step was to dial a toll-free number in Omaha and dictate the story to a Western Union operator for forty-five minutes in the middle of the night. When presidents traveled, a Western Union representative went along on the press plane to punch out the stories. But it might still take hours for the copy to make it to the home office. Today, of course, a single keystroke sends a story instantaneously on its way.

It was slow and frustrating, and it wasn't much easier, and definitely not much faster, for presidents to get their story out. For example, on the evening of May 12, 1975, Washington time, Cambodian troops seized an American merchant tanker named the *Mayaguez* in international waters. The morning after this happened, I was in the White House at 6:45 in the morning for press secretary Ron Nessen's unusually early briefing. Nessen issued a statement on President

Ford's behalf making clear the United States considered the ship's seizure an act of piracy and demanded its return. Then he pointedly encouraged reporters to go file—twice.

"Now I am going to anticipate a couple of questions and then you can file," Nessen said.

A couple of minutes later, when reporters hadn't taken the hint, he was more direct: "Why don't you go file?"

The transcript doesn't record what happened next. Nessen went off the record to say the White House had reason to believe the hijackers were reading the wire services and listening to the hourly network radio newscasts and wanted them to see and hear the statement immediately. Specifically, the White House wanted them to know the United States already had military forces in the area and knew exactly where the ship was. The hope was that maybe the insurgents would think twice about squaring off with the Pentagon when faced with the reality of military action. That wasn't to be. Two days later, US forces recaptured the *Mayaguez* and freed the crew.

Can you imagine? The fastest way to get a message out to the bad guys was to send it out via the 7:00 a.m. network radio news. Talk about snail mail.

Television was a major leap forward, of course. Presidents could command the airwaves more or less whenever they wished; it was rare for the networks to deny a president precious prime-time minutes for an address to the nation. But presidents couldn't do that too often, lest they risk being charged with exploiting the media for political purposes, and other opportunities to disseminate their spin were limited. Except for the wire services, there were two news cycles—the so-called *Today Show* a.m. cycle and another for the evening network news shows.

The September 1974 morning when President Ford pardoned his disgraced predecessor, Richard Nixon, White House regulars received phone calls at home around nine o'clock saying there would be a rare Sunday briefing in a couple of hours and we would probably want to be there. Press office staffers divided up the roster of correspondents and laboriously went down their lists. It was slow and tedious. Today, of course, a single advisory would reach throughout the universe within seconds.

CNN changed everything forever; suddenly there was a twenty-four-hour news cycle demanding an insatiable amount of content. That presented presidents with more opportunities to reach the masses. Then the world as we old-timers knew it changed forever again on February 13, 2010, when Obama press secretary Robert Gibbs opened a Twitter account. It wasn't long before he was tweeting news.

There's no going back. In August 2014 Pentagon spokesman John Kirby used a tweet to announce the resumption of US air strikes in Iraq for the first time since American combat forces had left that troubled land. And three months later nobody was surprised to see President Obama preview his speech to the nation about his immigration executive order in a Facebook video. But these things are merely the tip of the iceberg in presidential communication via social media, a technique the Obama White House has embraced wholeheartedly to disseminate its agenda around the mainstream media—and aggressively monitor what we write and broadcast. For as long as I can remember, every president and his handlers have tried to bypass the mainstream media and use emerging technology to transmit their message unfiltered. The Obama operation was just more aggressive and sophisticated at this game than were its predecessors. The new Trump administration will likely go further.

Truthfully, every new president decides early on whether the White House press corps is an opportunity to be exploited or a pitfall to be avoided. Inevitably, it chooses the latter. George H. W. Bush was the last president whose handlers—at least for a while—saw value in genuinely engaging the media. New administrations examine the media policies of their predecessor, then look for ways to make *their* strategies more restrictive and controlling. For all its virtues, technology and social media have made this sobering trend far simpler to facilitate.

I recently ran across a picture of the way it used to be—a smiling Jerry Ford perched on the edge of his Oval Office desk, being peppered with queries from media legends like Helen Thomas of UPI, Fran Lewine of the Associated Press, and Al Sullivan of the US Information Agency. We'll not see that sort of engagement again, alas.

In fairness, President Obama was perched on the edge of *his* desk not that long ago, too. But he was doing a Facebook video. It was a metaphor for the ages.

PART THREE

Information and Its Discontents

5

Technological Transformations and Timeless Truths

The Press and the Presidency in a Social Media Age

STEPHEN A. SMITH

There is now more political information publicly available than at any time in history. Furthermore, this information comes to viewers, readers, and users through a previously unimaginable diversity of channels. Social media have created new public spaces, enlarged access to the public sphere, and provided vast and growing opportunities for political discourse. Citizens, once considered by so many in the press to be little more than passive recipients of mediated political messages, can now share their political opinions, seek and obtain public documents and information with unprecedented speed, and develop the perception of personal political efficacy as a result of unfiltered access.

The effects of our new digital reality on those who attempt to manage the communications of the president, to report on the presidency, or to provide scholarly analysis confirm that we are experiencing and confronting a brave new world. The Information Age has changed the business of political reporting as much as it has politics itself. Nonetheless, the White House did not go digital overnight. President Bill Clinton, reflecting on his first year in office in 1993, noted that there were only about fifty websites accessible then, and "the average cell phone weighed about five pounds."[1] When he gave his first State of the Union address on February 17, 1993, a record 66.9 million people watched it on either broadcast or cable

TV. There were no other options available. The White House did not have a Web page, and even if it had, fewer than 10 percent of Americans would have been able to watch it via a dial-up modem, the main purpose of which would have been sending email, not surfing the Web or viewing digital content, including presidential speeches.

The opportunity for the public to send email messages to the president became a possibility in June 1993, and more than a million messages would be sent in the next seven years. President Clinton was the first sitting president to send an email message, but that did not occur until November 7, 1998, and he personally sent only two emails during his time in office.[2]

The first White House Web page was launched in October 1994, and there were over 4 million hits on the White House website during the first year it was up. That number would triple every year thereafter during the Clinton administration. Hoping to enhance public access to government information, the administration launched the FirstGov.gov website in September 2000, making all public federal websites available and searchable from that page. By that time more than 56 million people were connected to the Internet, and websites had reached an astonishing (and still growing) number of 3.6 million.[3]

But even with all the growth in online communication during the Clinton term, not everyone was convinced the changes would prove wholly transformative. Some skeptics, such as Richard Davis, declared that "the internet [would] not lead to the social and political revolution so widely predicted" by its most optimistic advocates.[4] Yet others, such as Richard Wiggins, seemed to recognize how dramatically the Internet would change how the executive branch communicated, particularly the growth of the White House website and the advance of social media during the administrations to follow.

By the time Clinton handed off the Oval Office and its then nascent digital communications operation to George W. Bush, being online was expected, even for presidents. Nonetheless, Bush expressed regret that becoming president meant he would have to curtail his online activity. His 2002 State of the Union speech was the first to be broadcast online, but his administration remained cautious about engaging emergent social media platforms. Part of the problem was the uncertainty and limitations of the e-gov guidelines, privacy policies, security procedures, and restrictions that prevented the White House from linking to any sites besides .gov or .mil domains, but there were also failures of imagination. For example, explained David Almacy, who directed online projects for Bush, Facebook until 2007 was "locked down to only college students with .edu email addresses," YouTube appeared to be an irrelevant gimmick for posting videos of "sneezing pandas and dancing cats," and Twitter went live only in 2007. When Facebook did encourage President Bush to host a White House profile, the benefit wasn't immediately clear. After all, the administration was garnering seven million page views a week on the White House Web page. It didn't seem obvious that Facebook would be nearly as effective a vehicle for reaching the public.[5]

However, much as Clinton learned to leverage the Web to reach the public and Bush became the first truly digital president, with his entire term "captured online via WhiteHouse.gov in the form of transcripts, photos, video and audio,"[6] Barack Obama gained fame in 2008 as BlackBerry One, a commander in chief who was always online and ready to engage. His administration would oversee the White House launch accounts on Facebook, Twitter, and YouTube—to name just a few of the most obvious and popular applications—and, in so doing, make even more urgent concerns about how to maintain transparency among the president, the press, and the people. Obama's use of digital and social media has raised important questions about how best to preserve an ever-growing volume of electronic communication and information. Can citizens trust the White House to protect electronic communication and information and to do so with transparency? Or will administrations only save what they want to and delete the rest? That is, how much reason is there to be skeptical that presidential administrations might feel incentivized to create and save only those kinds of documents that present official policy and goals in the best light?

In the remainder of this chapter I examine these questions—transparency, creation, and preservation—especially as they relate to the nation's chief executive in the twenty-first century. As new technologies have allowed the president to communicate directly with the people, and the people with the government, and as the executive embraces this new relationship, some in media have asserted that their essential role in covering and explaining the making of public policy has been diminished. Understanding this tension requires unpacking differing assumptions about political communication, conflicting motives between the actors, and disagreement about the definition of transparency in democratic government. As I will show, there is little doubt that President Obama deployed new media in innovative ways that reached beyond those of traditional media. However, I argue that these changes were ultimately more in form than in substance, had to do with channels more than messages, and ultimately benefited both sources and audiences. Nonetheless, there are important issues to be considered, addressed, and resolved in this new and continually evolving electronic media ecology, with the White House press corps and contested perceptions of its role and value in national politics comprising the lynchpin of the conundrum.

The Social Media President

During the 2008 presidential campaign, the Obama team demonstrated innovative and unprecedented use of social networking sites, including Facebook, MySpace, and MyBarackObama.com, to recruit volunteers, announce events, rally supporters, and raise money. The effort included the development of a YouTube channel, where the campaign posted and shared more than eighteen hundred videos, several which garnered more than one million views.[7]

Then, on November 6, only two days after Obama's election, the campaign's social media team launched the website Change.gov, with the goal of communicating to the public complex policy proposals in order to continue the online conversation established during the campaign and to try to enhance public participation in government. Citizens were encouraged to share their opinions and ideas about important issues and comment on Obama's policy ideas as they were being crafted for the new administration. More than two million people responded and participated in the first month. This was part of a larger effort to "reboot democracy" that Obama and his team were putting forward and that emphasized deploying all the online and interactive means of communication available to foster dialogue between the government and the people.[8]

The political press corps, skeptical by nature, were cautious about embracing the promised changes. Some expressed concern that the White House meant to bypass traditional media and had taken to "manufacturing consent" for an unchallenged agenda—quite possibly a valid worry that other writers in this volume, most notably Jennifer Mercieca, take up at length. Bill Kovach, the chairman of the Committee of Concerned Journalists, worried, "They're beginning to create their own journalism, their own description of events of the day, but it's not an independent voice making that description. It's troublesome until we know how it's going to be used and the degree to which it can be used on behalf of the people, and not on behalf of only one point of view." Macon Phillips, the thirty-year-old new media director at the White House, acknowledged that it would provide a way for Obama to reach the American people without having to rely on the filter of the mainstream news media for choosing and characterizing information for the public. Even so, he argued, "there's a growing appetite from people to do it themselves."[9]

On Inauguration Day 2009, the White House signaled its intention to continue doing whatever it could to communicate directly with citizens and unveiled an interactive homepage at WhiteHouse .gov. In his first week in office, Obama turned the Saturday Radio Address into a video presentation posted on both the White House website and on YouTube. But even with these innovations, the anticipated transition to the full array of tools took some time to develop. The digital infrastructure inherited by the new administration was characterized by one media-savvy staff member as "kind of like going from an Xbox to an Atari."[10] Furthermore, the differences in campaigning and governing with social media quickly became clear to the White House Office of Digital Strategy, as George Edwards elucidates in his chapter about the administration's attempt to motivate citizen participation by engaging supporters via the group Organizing for Action. Not only did formal rules, regulations, and statutes slow down the direct release of information, but communication itself proved harder. Campaigns are often about simple slogans and easy messages. Governing demands more nuanced rhetorical choices that take into account not only public preferences, but also the realities of the existing institutional structure of the republic. Congress passes laws, and no matter how skilled a speaker Obama might have been, little could be accomplished without its consent.

Nonetheless, Obama made staying engaged with the public a priority. During his terms in office, President Obama received about one hundred thousand emails, one thousand faxes, and twenty-five hundred to thirty-five hundred phone calls per day, as well as sixty-five thousand paper letters every week. Every day, Mike Kelleher, director of the Office of Presidential Correspondence, chose a representative sample of ten letters or messages to share with the president, and Obama personally responded to three or four with a handwritten note. Regular electronic dispatches were also sent to supporters and subscribers, including "periodic updates from President Obama and senior Administration officials; a daily email with the photo of the day, highlights from the blog and the President's schedule; and weekly topic-based newsletters." The subscribers who received these email messages represented a different constituency from those reached by other social media channels. Individuals on the email list trended older and were more likely to visit traditional Web pages such as WhiteHouse.gov than they were to visit social networking sites such as Facebook or Twitter. All of those on the email list subscribed through the White House website. Nonetheless, the aggressive messaging to support administration policies quickly became a source of complaints from Republicans and the conservative media.[11]

Dave Boyer of the *Washington Times* complained that "the White House [was] increasingly waging a partisan-edged campaign funded by taxpayers through a flood of daily emails to the public in support of his [Obama's] agenda. Whether the topic [was] gun control or immigration reform, the White House [used] taxpayer dollars for staff and equipment to promote Mr. Obama's image and frequently to target his opponents in Congress for scorn through a series of e-newsletters." Pete Sepp, executive vice president of the National Taxpayers Union, suggested that the White House email operation presented "practical and political problems with making sure taxpayers are getting value from a robust debate between the branches of government rather than being forced to shell out for propaganda."[12]

Nonetheless, Obama used the new media to reach entirely new audiences and to foster a sense of civic engagement. Only two months after taking office, the White House hosted an online town hall meeting that used Web tabulators such as Google Moderator and AppEngine to manage the submission of questions from the public and decide which ones should be answered. By May 2008 the White House had a MySpace page. Of course there was a White House blog, and later came Pinterest. Eventually, the Social Hub portal on the White House website included an array of social networking and civic engagement tools, including Twitter, Facebook, a YouTube channel, a Google+ Fireside Hangout, Scribd, Flickr, Slideshare, LinkedIn, FourSquare, Instagram, and GitHub links. Finally, there was an official White House mobile app that offered to access the sites via iPhone, iPad, and Android—all available, of course, for free.[13]

This breadth of digital play led Fan Page List to rank Obama's social media presence as number one internationally among politicians, with a Klout influence rating of 99.0, based on activity of the 44.8 million Facebook fans and 53.97 million Twitter followers. (By contrast, Donald Trump entered the White House with 18.3 million Twitter followers and 16.9 million Facebook fans, although this number will likely grow.) In addition, Obama's official White House Facebook page garnered more than 3 million likes, and its primary Twitter account had at least 5.78 million followers. These numbers are important in light of the Pew Research Center's report in September 2014 that 64 percent of adults used Facebook, and 30 percent of the American people listed it as a source of news. Twitter was used by only 16 percent of adults, yet half of them considered it a news source. Overall, Obama's Twitter account ranked number three in the global top one hundred, while the *New York Times* ranked number fifty-one. The *Times* had only 28 percent as many followers as Obama did.[14]

There is no doubt that President Obama, his campaigns, and his administration developed an Internet and social media presence that reached far beyond that of any of his predecessors, if only because none of his predecessors possessed the technology to do the same thing. But numbers and statistics of use can offer only some sense of presence and volume—they can not delineate much about the messages themselves or what role the mainstream (traditional) press still played in arbitrating Obama's term. To get some sense of this, I will now unpack several specific examples of how Obama engaged digital media. As I do, it will become clear that the traditional media still had a role to play in mediating and explaining the president's message, and their complaints about being elided and avoided by the president in his communication effort were overblown. More specifically, what will become clear is that while it may be true that Obama and his administration did, indeed, omit the mainstream press in its media efforts, it does not necessarily follow that the president's messaging efforts were, therefore, self-serving and evasive on the one hand or without merit on the other, especially when taken in light of the administration's need to reach a disparate public, itself less engaged with the mainstream media.

Electronic Elaboration of the
Rhetorical Situation

President Obama's 2015 State of the Union address is an excellent example of how presidential communication has changed in the digital age. It was not unique in terms of a crafted text, but rather for how the speech was sent out through multiple channels in order to reach the most comprehensive and diverse audience possible.

Article II, Section 3 of the Constitution commands that the president "shall from time to time give to the Congress information of the state of the union, and recommend to their consideration such measures as he shall judge necessary and expedient." Up until the early 1900s, most presidents simply transmitted down Capitol Hill a document known as the Annual Message to Congress, which was then usually read into the record by a clerk in each chamber. However, since President Wilson personally delivered his remarks in a speech to a joint session of Congress in 1913, the State of the Union Address has become a familiar rhetorical ritual that allows the president to create and present discourse the president hopes will be successful in framing public issues for Congress and voters alike.[15]

In 2015 Barack Obama approached the constitutional mandate under significant constraints. First and foremost, he faced an audience comprised of a Republican majority in both chambers, emboldened by significant gains in the 2014 midterm elections, in which his policies and low job approval ratings were thought to have factored heavily into Democratic losses. Second, although the speech would be carried live on thirteen networks, Obama was certain to face a declining television audience. Historically, fewer viewers tune in for the annual message later in a president's tenure. Clinton had a record audience of 66.9 million for his first State of the Union and only about 31.5 million for his last; George Bush's numbers dropped from a high of just over 62 million in 2003 to 37.5 million in 2008. Obama's first in 2009 had a television audience of 52.4 million, while his 2014 address measured only 33.3 million.[16] Moreover, changes in the media environment have reflected a lower average number of television viewers for each president over the last two decades of the annual address.

Third, some were beginning to question the intrinsic value of the annual ritual. Before George W. Bush's 2006 address, an op-ed column in the *New York Times* predicted it would be an "exercise in forgettable dissembling." A *Pittsburgh Tribune-Review* columnist Bill Steigerwald predicted that "like most recent State of the Unions, it'll probably be 99 percent hot political air and instantly forgettable, not to mention a waste of prime network TV time. It's painfully clear that in our 24/7/52 News & Information Age, the State of the Union address has outlived its original civic usefulness. It's just another regularly scheduled presidential pseudo-event—a partisan infomercial. It's time for our presidents to resume sending their annual messages to Congress by letter. Or better yet, email."[17]

By the end of President Obama's first term, similarly dismissive comments were common. Brendan Nyhan, writing in the *Columbia Journalism Review*, suggested, "Despite what many reporters believe, the president can rarely change public opinion on domestic policy with this or any presidential address." Before the 2014 State of the Union, Elise Hu on NPR explained, "Viewership is declining. Washington seems increasingly dysfunctional and irrelevant to the daily lives of Americans. The presidency isn't the bully pulpit it used to be." She further added that "the annual, constitutionally mandated State of the Union speech is beginning to look like a stuffy relic from a bygone era." Reflecting on the television audience numbers from 2014, Ariel Edwards-Levy, writing for the *Huffington Post* before the 2015 State of the Union, agreed that it is "difficult to change minds when most people aren't tuning in."[18]

The message would be an even harder sell given the congressional opposition in 2015. Two months before the scheduled date for the 2015 State of the Union address, resenting that Obama did not appear appropriately humbled by the election results and was ready to exercise executive authority on several contentious issues, fringe elements in the GOP advocated refusing even to invite the president into the congressional chamber to make the speech. Republican leadership should "cancel the State of the Union address next year, so that the elected representatives of the people [would] not have to listen to, or applaud, a man who is violating his oath of office and governing as a tyrant," suggested an editor of the *Breitbart Report*. "Congress should indicate to President Obama that his presence [was] not welcome on Capitol Hill. . . . The gesture would, no doubt, be perceived as rude, but it [was] appropriate—and would be far less jarring or uncomfortable than the hostile reception Obama would likely receive in person. In lieu of an address, Congress would offer to read aloud whatever document Obama saw fit to send through." Rich Lowery, editor of the *National Review*, agreed: "If I were John Boehner, I'd say to the president: 'Send us your State of the Union in writing. You're not welcome in our chamber.'" As the speech approached, writers for both the *Chicago Tribune* and *Columbia Journalism Review*, among others, also forwarded doubts about the speech's utility. As much as these remarks may have seemed disrespectful to the president, they also make plain how the media— conservative and mainstream, alike—were still tussling with Obama and creating news and public discourse, even in the face of the president's large social media and direct-to-voter email activities.[19]

In spite of these criticisms and objections, President Obama and the White House communication team pushed forward with the speech and the agenda it implied. For them, the State of the Union address still mattered. As Dan Pfeiffer, assistant to the president and senior advisor, said, "It will be the largest audience we speak to in the year by far. We will talk directly to more people than probably every politician of note in America will do in all their speeches combined this year." It also presented an opportunity to reinvent the genre of the State of the Union, while also redefining some of the rules of civic engagement. The Obama team decided to reach for an audience beyond the one expected to gather in the chamber and on living room couches throughout America for two hours on a Tuesday evening in January. In so doing, the 2015 State of the Union address became "an extended, multimedia extravaganza that under-score[d] the dramatic evolution in political communication."[20]

First up in this "dramatic evolution" was a refusal on the White House's part to wait for the speech to happen before revealing its contents. Instead, explained Pfeiffer in a message posted online at Medium.com two weeks before the scheduled speech, "the President [would get] out of Washington and [take] his message on the road—straight to the people his policies . . . affect [the] most." The first of the promised SOTU spoilers was three events previewing issues in Michigan, Arizona, and Tennessee. Traditional press coverage accompanied Obama on these trips. The administration, however, augmented these stories by posting video segments on various social media platforms. These videos included footage of the president proposing free community college tuition posted on Facebook. That clip was viewed 8.3 million times, shared by viewers 145,000 times, and liked by 316,000 users.[21]

Moving beyond the teasers, the White House innovated again and publicly released the text of the State of the Union address on Medium.com. Before that, embargoed copies of the speech were released only to the Washington press corps in advance to allow reporters to review and prepare for coverage of the speech. The embargo had been breached in 2011 when the *National Journal* posted the entire text online before the speech, perhaps inadvertently marking "a turning point in which media delivery of the event was decisively channeled through the internet, not television." The White House's decision to post an advance copy of the entire text online in 2015 came with an explanation that putting out the speech would give regular citizens the same access as Washington insiders had. Like the elite reporter or congressperson, anyone with Internet access would be able to read the speech before it was presented or read along with Obama as he recited his words. More than four hundred thousand people viewed the text in advance.[22]

The White House also developed Twitter hashtags to drive the conversation and invited the public to join in, posting them on the White House Facebook page and Twitter account. As a result, there were more than 2.6 million tweets about the speech at #SOTU. Nielsen TV Twitter ratings ranked it the top program for the week, with an audience of 9,724,000 and with 295 million impressions,

681,000 authors, and 2.598 million tweets. In addition, 5.7 million people on Facebook contributed 13.8 million likes, posts, comments, and shares during the speech, and Google tracked and documented the related search traffic.[23]

But perhaps the most unique expansion of the audience occurred two days after the State of the Union address—and it was one of the most contentious moves, as well. The White House organized a live-stream interview between President Obama and three prominent vloggers, each with YouTube channels of their own. At the press briefing on January 15, CNN reporter Jim Acosta complained that the interviews were not even happening with *real* journalists, but with "people who post videos on YouTube." Press Secretary Josh Earnest replied that Acosta's complaint was, in some ways, the point. He said the president hoped to reach individuals the mainstream media usually missed, as "part of an integrated communication strategy to make sure that the American people [understood] exactly what the President [was] fighting for in Washington, D.C." The video chats with Bethany Mota, Hank Green, and GloZell Green also drew the ire of Howard Kurtz on Fox News, who said it "seemed beneath the dignity of the office to be hanging out with some of these YouTubers."[24]

Mota and the Greens, however, did not see themselves as political interlopers with no business on the presidential main stage. Instead, the vloggers insisted that they, too, were now part of the media and had just as much right to interact with the president as did any other journalist. They, too, could ask hard questions that put Obama on his toes. The most incisive rebuttal came from Hank Green, who protested that his work was essential because a "complete lack of objectivity and representation in cable news [had] degraded the legitimacy of news media as a whole. Young people have absolutely no faith in people sitting at desks on television anymore." As to Kurtz and others who offered rebukes, Green said, "Legacy media isn't mocking us because we aren't a legitimate source of information; they're mocking us because they're terrified. Their legitimacy came from the fact that they have access to distribution channels and that they get to be in the White House press pool because of some long-ago established procedures that assumed they would use that power in the public interest. In reality, those things are becoming less and less important and less and less true."[25] This put the lie to the complaint that Obama meant to cut the media out of his presidency. Actually, he meant to increase access, even if doing so angered the credentialed elite.

Anyone doubting the efficacy of using the YouTube interview to reach and engage an expanded and diverse citizen audience should ponder its reach: "The YouTube Interview with President Obama" posted on the White House YouTube channel has been viewed online more than 3 million times. The online subscriptions to the three celebrity YouTubers is more than 14 million: Hank Green has 2.4 million, GloZell Green has 3.5 million, and Bethany Mota has more than 8 million YouTube subscribers and more than 4 million Instagram followers. This almost certainly expanded the number of people who were familiar with Obama's proposals in the State of the Union, especially because viewership of the speech itself was down from previous years, as was predicted. In fact, the *Washington Times* headline proclaimed it "the least watched address in the last 15 years," and *Breitbart* concluded that "America just isn't into this president anymore."[26]

What the *Washington Times* and *Breitbart* missed were the ways Obama's speech found an audience beyond the night of its actual delivery. Because of that expansion, the 2015 State of the Union address was a marketing success, one that shifted the messaging and reached a more diverse spectrum of people. Thus, while President Obama's message met the constitutional requirements of the genre, it was far more than the required annual message. It was produced and presented to engage a younger demographic than previously possible, and future presidents will surely continue to employ all the available channels of communication, particularly digital ones. Obama's innovation did not work to limit media access and public conversation about his proposals, then, but rather expanded them.

Bypassing the Bylines

As evidenced by the mainstream media responses to Obama's communication strategy for diversifying the audience for the 2015 State of the Union speech, the president's efforts to alter and expand his press universe created tension between the White House and the press corps. As a result, conflicting conceptions about what role each institution should play in setting the nation's agenda, and differing assumptions about the nature of public communication in a modern republic, were brought into sharper contrast. On the one hand, the Obama administration—the executive branch—argued that that direct communication with citizens, unimpeded by the gatekeepers of the elite corporate media, enhanced civic engagement and so increased government transparency. On the other hand, the press saw its role being usurped, as its members argued they were being prevented from asking hard questions on behalf of the public and, in so doing, thwarting the possibility of government by propaganda. I suggest that neither has the upper hand in this argument. This is because, historically, both institutions have been complicit in manufacturing consent and assuring structural stability by marginalizing dissenting voices and so protecting the status quo. However, the rise of digital communication has indeed created a rift between the two about how power should work and how power should be challenged in this technologically advanced age.[27]

Attempts by public officials to bypass the press and speak directly with the public are nothing new. The current clash regarding the growing reliance on social media by the Obama administration is only the most recent manifestation of the electronic alternative channels that developed in the presidential campaign of 1992 and have continued to be employed as new media platforms emerged. Both the press and the politicians have contributed to those changes, and neither has been particularly consistent in articulating a general philosophy beyond one of privileging self-interested priorities and needs.

To wit, in July 2009 network news personnel objected that Obama's news conferences were an inconvenience. To put this point even more starkly: the media weren't upset that the president was refusing to go through them, but rather that he was using them too much or at times they didn't like. Paul Friedman, CBS senior vice president, complained about feeling pressured to cover the events on television. "It's an enormous financial cost when the president replaces one of those prime-time hours. The news divisions also have mixed feelings about whether they are being used," he said. Mark Whitaker, NBC Washington bureau chief, said the White House news conferences were seldom newsworthy but were more about the president wanting "to continue a dialogue with the American people. There are other ways of continuing that dialogue than taking up an hour of prime time."[28] But even as these complaints hung in the air, there were also sustained choruses from the national press corps that they were being ignored as the White House attempted to bypass the mainstream media and employ its elaborate social media arsenal to communicate directly with the American public. So which was it?

Maybe because of these ambivalent messages, and often with mixed results, presidents have long sought to speak directly with the people rather than rely strictly on the kindness of reporters and editors to reproduce their intended message. President Andrew Johnson took his battle with Congress and the Northern newspapers on the road in late summer of 1866, giving a series of speeches known as the Swing Around the Circle. It was a political disaster that led the press to question the dignity of such a performance. In fact, Johnson's September 3 speech at Cleveland became the basis of the tenth of the Articles of Impeachment adopted against him in 1868. President Woodrow Wilson undertook a national speaking tour on behalf of his effort to secure Senate ratification for the League of Nations, another unsuccessful exercise that ended when Wilson collapsed. And President Roosevelt's series of thirty radio broadcasts between 1933 and 1940, the famous Fireside Chats, are frankly acknowledged by the Roosevelt Library to have been used "to bypass Congress and the press and speak directly to the nation" on important issues. One need only read Stephanie Martin's chapter 4 in this book to get a strong sense of how—and how well—this worked.[29]

So presidents wanting to speak directly to the people, in part because they don't trust the press to fairly pass the message along, is hardly new. Moreover, the press has long grumbled over these presidential efforts. To that end Howard Kurtz labeled the 1992 presidential election as "the talk show campaign," because the "candidates, tired of having their words sliced and diced into a few sentences in the paper, or challenged by the Sunday-morning pontificators, would simply cut out the middleman." Bill Clinton made a record forty-seven talk show appearances, while his predecessor, President George H. W. Bush, did only sixteen. Reporters covering the campaign "complained that the campaign was losing dignity and substance. And they protested that the candidates were ducking hard questions from trained journalists in favor of softball questions from poorly informed voters." Making matters worse, as Jacob Weisberg noted, "was the Clinton camp's indifference to media complaints. During the campaign, they had bypassed the media—using satellite broadcasts, town meetings, and appearances on *Larry King Live* to get around the scrutiny of national correspondents." Increasing media outlets and expanded campaign coverage gave presidents more options. That led veteran Associated Press political reporter Walter Mears to observe, during the first year of Clinton's administration, that "times and technology have changed, and the president's message doesn't always have to pass through the White House press. . . . All presidents try to talk to the people as directly as they can, with messages that fit their aims, not topics chosen by the news media. And the direct lines to do it are more accessible than ever."[30]

By the time Barack Obama took up residence in the White House in 2009, the kinds of media Clinton had available for leveraging in 1993 probably seemed quaint. Obama had not only the cable news universe at his disposal, but the Internet and its social networking capabilities as well. And, much as Obama was able to use these digital capabilities to expand awareness of his 2015 proposals in his State of the Union address, he had also been able to use them in 2014 in an effort to drum up citizen backing for his signature health care reform.

Indeed, President Obama seemed willing to visit even the most distant corners of the talk show landscape in an effort to increase public support for the Affordable Care Act. As was highlighted in the introduction to this book, in March 2014 Obama invited the off-beat Internet comedy show *Between Two Ferns with Zach Galifianakis* to the White House diplomatic reception room to promote sign-up via HealthCare.gov. Once again, the effort proved worthwhile. A columnist for *Forbes* asked and answered the key question: "So why would Obama go on such a silly internet-only show? For the viral video possibilities." The program was viewed by more than ten million people the first day and has since been viewed twenty-eight million times online at FunnyorDie.com. More significantly, the segment was the top source of referrals to HealthCare.gov on March 11, which was the whole point of Obama's talk show "swing around the circle." As then secretary of Health and Human Services Kathleen Sebelius explained to HuffPost Live, "What we're trying to do is reach people in the language that they most understand. . . . As a mother of two 30-something sons, I know they're more likely to get their information on 'Funny or Die' than they are on network TV."[31]

It would be a mistake, however, to assume that because Funny or Die was a nontraditional format it was also low-quality media without distinction. To the contrary, the *Between Two Ferns* program segment was nominated for an Emmy for outstanding short-format live-action entertainment program, and it won the Adweek Gold Originator Award. Nonetheless, and probably predictably, Obama's appearance on the program was slammed by mainstream television hosts and other journalists as inappropriate. On *Fox & Friends* Elisabeth Hasselbeck said, "Some would argue that it's inappropriate for the president of the United States to be advertising a law, an insurance plan," to which Brian Kilmeade replied, "I think it's pretty tragic. Whoever recommended that he do that show should be fired." The *Washington Free Beacon* opined that it "was just dreadful," specifically the "utterly unbearable moment during which he hawks the failed social experiment that is HealthCare.gov. It's just gross." Kathleen Parker of the *Washington Post* "wondered whether this was an appropriate venue for the president, especially in consideration of current events." She further suggested the possibility that "this kind of display is beneath the dignity of the office, and the president should be more circumspect in choosing public appearances, virtual or otherwise."[32]

Obama, however, remained unbothered. He returned to cable with a December appearance on *The Colbert Report*, again with the goal of promoting the Affordable Care Act. In a self-effacing segment titled "To Health in a Handbasket," the president said the way to kill the program was to "make signing up for Obamacare unappealing to young people," as the on-screen graphic suggested "Send Request via LinkedIn," one of the social media tools used by the administration to reach the forty-and-up crowd. In the week following the broadcast, more than one million people signed up for Obamacare plans on HealthCare.gov, a record number for the year.[33]

However, while members of the mainstream press grumbled about the president's appearances on "nonserious" talk shows, their most vociferous complaints concerned the White House's unprecedented social media use. During the first months of Obama's term, reporters expressed concern that the president planned "to bypass the White House Press Corps and communicate directly with particular constituencies and with people who derive news and views from nontraditional sources."[34] The chorus of this complaint only grew over his time in office. The heart of the criticism had to do with concern that the Obama team used social media to hide information as much as it was using it to share news.

While some of the critiques about transparency in government were serious and profound, such as many of those enumerated in a 2013 special report from the Committee to Protect Journalists, more often the continuing struggle between the White House and the press had more of a ring of an argument among storytellers about who should control the narrative in a rapidly changing media environment. As former White House press secretary Jay Carney said, "What presidents try to do is focus on a policy issue that the president wants to advance. . . . [We're] trying to advance that agenda against the resistance of a whole world of news and events and opinions that want to take you in a different place generally." In short, Carney contended that Obama's efforts, like those of presidents before him, had to do with supplementing the media mix. This, in turn, required continuing to accommodate the demands of the Washington media covering the president while also augmenting their message with available social media platforms to reach an expanded audience. "It would be absolute malpractice for President Obama's team not to take advantage of the social media that's out there that everybody else is taking advantage of and to reach people where they are," Carney further explained. "If folks aren't watching the evening news in the numbers they used to watch it, which is definitively true, [then] they're getting their information in different ways. . . . [We] need to reach them there. And that's what we tried to do."[35]

Reporters sometimes contend that efforts such as the ones Carney described amount to little more than White House propaganda campaigns meant to strategically limit the traditional role of the press as a meaningful check on power. Perhaps some of the resentment stems from relative status deprivation as the national media environment has become more fragmented and the White House has devoted

considerable resources, including the availability of the president to social media and their audience over that of more traditional media forums. At other times reporters suggested that the Obama administration relied most heavily on nontraditional media outlets when it felt weakest or most unsure. For example, some expressed ire when the new president called "on a blogger at one of his early news conferences." Others claimed that the reason for Obama's negative job ratings with the public resulted from the public's being "put off by the President's failure to answer tough questions" from reporters. After the White House posted an informational video about the amount of mail it received and how Obama reads and responds to that correspondence, a *Newsweek* column objected, "It looks and sounds like a news story, no doubt to the chagrin of TV reporters at the White House. The only real giveaway . . . is a little logo identifying it as a WhiteHouse.gov video." And even with that identification marker, the columnist continued, "we [still] don't get the full story. For instance, does Obama actually get to see letters from Americans who dislike his policies and does he respond? That's a question the White House video doesn't really answer—and it should."[36]

Another tempest occurred when the White House press corps protested that it was barred from reporting on a golf outing President Obama took with Tiger Woods, even though the round was tweeted live by Tim Rosaforte, a writer for *Golf Digest* and *Golf World*. Although the story was not likely of much concern to most informed voters, Fox News reporter Ed Henry was upset: "Speaking on behalf of the White House Correspondents Association, I can say a broad cross section of our members from print, radio, online and TV have today expressed extreme frustration to me about having absolutely no access to the President of the United States this entire weekend. There is a very simple but important principle we will continue to fight for today and in the days ahead: transparency."[37]

Conclusion

Beyond any imaginary importance of access to a golf game, the ubiquitous media presence of President Obama shifted the agenda setting function of the media decidedly toward the White House. Does this mean that the press no longer requires or has any claim to direct access to the president? Should members of the public no longer look to the traditional, mainstream media as an important arbiter of news and poser of uncomfortable queries to the commander in chief? Absolutely not, on both counts. The Fourth Estate must have direct access and adequate time to question the president on issues of their own choosing. Our democracy depends on it. Nonetheless, it is worth remembering that the convention of a White House press conference began only in 1913 with President Wilson. Like Obama, Wilson also "was accused of being too professorial and aloof, and he loathed the news culture for its focus on the trivial and commercial." Since then, the press conference "has retained the shape of that first meeting—awkward, impersonal, and with little pleasure for the president. The moment legitimized the press corps and put the president and the press in an extended clutch—entwined and angling for advantage."[38]

Whether to demonstrate cleverness in a game of gotcha, to raise issues of interest to corporate media, to create controversy to drive ratings, or to act as surrogate for a curious public, the media's assumed role of creating or shifting the dialogue to other issues is quite different from reporting on official actions or policy proposals. As we have seen throughout this chapter, what the media wants to cover and what the president puts forward as an agenda are often not the same thing. The conflict is inherent and worth remembering. Presidents have an agenda they hope to enact and an interest in being perceived positively so that they have the best chance of achieving legislative success. Political reporters are skeptics, and they doubt the president's best intents. They claim to care little about image and a lot about truth and facts. But that truth and those facts are not always objective and straightforward, and therein lies the rub. Complaining about the positive pictures being produced and projected by "the Obama image machine, serving up a stream of words, images and videos that invariably cast the president as commanding, compassionate and on the ball," Nancy Benac of the Associated Press said that from now on dedicated reporters and readers would "have to look elsewhere for bloopers, bobbles or contrary points of view." Or, not satisfied with straight recitation of facts, CBS's White House correspondent Chip Reid averred how "important [it was] for us to hold the president's feet to the fire." NBC's Chuck Todd added that administrations (like Obama's) should not try to control the message, but rather step back and allow reporters to intervene and move the conversation in an "unscripted" direction determined by the media, with questions composed by them. Ron Fournier said that the informal question-and-answer sessions with reporters force presidents "to think on their feet and be accountable." And Santiago Lyon boldly asserted that "allowing the press independent access" to the activities of presidents was traditionally held to be "a necessary part of the social contract of trust and transparency that should exist between citizens and their leaders."[39]

Perhaps. But as Holly Yeager suggested in the *Columbia Journalism Review*, if the White House press corps "want to make a case that something's really at risk, they need to do a better job in showing off some recent examples of White House reporting we really couldn't do without." This fact is all the more important in the now always emergent digital age, when audiences neither simply nor passively consume texts but actively engage with and interpret them as they wish. There is no pretending that a magic media bullet, whether fired by the president or the press, will always be received as it was intended. The reader's role has become even more prominent in the world of reality television and Twitter. "This is not a couch-potato age," observed Simon Rosenberg. "Average people are expecting to be part of the process." It is this requirement of inclusion that has confounded political reporters in the commercial media. Resolution through disinterested dialogue about the press-state relationship is needed, and the press, the politicians, and the public are stakeholders in the ongoing redefinition of the role of each in the political conversation.[40]

Notes

1. "Wired for Change: A Special Address from President Clinton," YouTube, February 16, 2011, https://www.youtube.com/watch?v=kJ9SQjvHOPw.

2. John Burgess, "Clinton Goes Online with Email," *Washington Post*, June 2, 1993, F3; "The Clinton White House Web Site," About.com, US Government, http://us govinfo.about.com/library/weekly/aa012201a.htm; Leonora Epstein, "The Story of How Bill Clinton Sent the First Presidential Email," BuzzFeed, April 15, 2014, http://www.buzzfeed.com/leonoraepstein/the-story-of-how-bill-clinton-sent-the-first-presidential-em#.rlqnWJoVae.

3. Chad Catacchio, "The Political Start, Slow & Go of Whitehouse.gov," TNW, News, April 20, 2010, http://thenextweb.com/us/2010/04/20/political-start-slow-white-

housegov/; Elahe Izadi, "The White House's First Web Site Launched 20 Years Ago This Week: And It Was Amazing," *Washington Post*, The Fix (blog), October 21, 2014, http://www.washingtonpost.com/blogs/the-fix/wp/2014/10/21/the-white-houses -first-website-launched-20-years-ago-this-week-and-it-was-amazing/; Edwin Chen, "Clinton Holds Historic Online Chat," *Los Angeles Times*, November 9, 1999, http:// articles.latimes.com/1999/nov/09/news/mn-31597. A screenshot of the 1995 home page is archived at http://clinton1.nara.gov/.

4. Richard Davis, *The Web of Politics: The Internet's Impact on the American Political System* (New York: Oxford University Press, 1999): 168.

5. Linda Feldmann, "The Real West Wing, Coming to a Modem Near You: Wednesday's Web Event Exemplifies Efforts by the Bush Team to Reach the Public, Directly and Online," *Christian Science Monitor*, April 18, 2003, USA2; David Almacy, "WhiteHouse.gov, Drupal & CMS: A Little History," Capital Gig, October 29, 2009, http:// capitalgig.com/2009/10/29/whitehouse-gov-drupal-cms-history/; Frank Zeccola, "Presidential PR: Former White House Web Communications Director on Obama, Katrina, Twitter," Bulldog Reporter, May 7, 2009, http://www.bulldogreporter.com/ dailydog/article/presidential-pr-former-white-house-web-communications-director -obama-katrina-twitte/; Catacchio, "Political Start, Slow & Go."

6. Almacy, "WhiteHouse.gov, Drupal & CMS."

7. BarackObama.com, YouTube, https://www.youtube.com/barackobama.

8. Monte Lutz, *The Social Pulpit: Barack Obama's Social Media Toolkit*, Edelman, Digital Public Affairs, 2009, 4, http://cyber.law.harvard.edu/sites/cyber.law.harvard .edu/files/Social Pulpit - Barack Obamas Social Media Toolkit 1.09.pdf; Brandon Griggs, "Obama Poised to Be First 'Wired' President," CNN, January 15, 2009, http://www.cnn.com/2009/TECH/01/15/obama.internet.president/index.html. The term *reboot democracy* comes from Personal Democracy Forum's June 2008 conference "Rebooting the System."

9. Jim Rutenberg and Adam Nagourney, "Melding Obama's Web to a YouTube Presidency," *New York Times*, January 26, 2009, A1.

10. Bill Burton quoted in Scott Merrill, "New Job Challenges in the White House," TechCrunch, January 22, 2009, http://techcrunch.com/2009/01/22/new-job-chal lenges-in-the-white-house/.

11. Mike Kelleher, "Letters to the President," White House (blog), August 3, 2009, http://www.whitehouse.gov/blog/Letters-to-the-President; "Inside the White House: Letters to the President," YouTube, http://youtu.be/eG00mM8QEGk; Ashley Parker, "Picking Letters, 10 a Day, That Reach Obama," *New York Times*, April 20, 2009, A14; Katelyn Sabochik, "A Few Interesting Things About the White House's Email List," White House (blog), November 26, 2010, http://www.whitehouse.gov/blog /2010/11/26/a-few-interesting-things-about-white-houses-email-list; Jim Rutenberg and Adam Nagourney, "Melding Obama's Web to a YouTube Presidency," *New York Times*, January 26, 2009, A1.

An online survey taken during Obama's term found that 75 percent of respondents were over the age of fifty. Nearly half of the email list (45 percent) visited WhiteHouse.gov less than once a month, and only 3 percent visited the White House website every day. Subscribers also reported visiting social networking sites such as Facebook or Twitter more rarely than did other Internet users, with more than 43 percent visiting them less than once a month, and very few email list subscribers followed the White House on social networking sites such as Facebook, Twitter, or LinkedIn.

TRANSFORMATIONS AND TRUTHS

The thirteen million email contacts developed by the campaign could not be legally transferred to the White House government email list; they became part of the ongoing political operation renamed Organizing for Action and were housed at the Democratic National Committee.

12. Dave Boyer, "A Different Kind of Obamacare: White House's Daily Emails Use Tax Dollars to Boost Obama's Image," *Washington Times*, August 12, 2013, http://www.washingtontimes.com/news/2013/aug/12/white-houses-daily-emails-use-tax-dollars-to-boost/.

13. Michael Arrington, "White House Using Google Moderator for Town Hall Meeting. And AppEngine. And YouTube," TechCrunch, March 24, 2009, http://techcrunch.com/2009/03/24/white-house-using-google-moderator-for-town-hall-meeting/; Erick Schonfeld, "The White House Gets a MySpace Page to Show Off Obama's Hoop Skills," TechCrunch, May 1, 2009, http://techcrunch.com/2009/05/01/the-white-house-gets-a-myspace-page-to-show-off-obamas-hoop-skills/.

During the 2014 election, 28 percent of registered voters used their cell phones to follow political news, up from 13 percent in the 2010 election. Aaron Smith, "Cell Phones, Social Media and Campaign 2014," Pew Research Center, Internet, Science & Tech, November 3, 2014, http://www.pewinternet.org/2014/11/03/cell-phones-social-media-and-campaign-2014/.

14. "Most Influential Politicians on Twitter (Klout)," Fan Page List, http://fanpagelist.com/category/politicians/view/list/sort/influence/, accessed January 29, 2015; Monica Anderson and Andrea Caumont, "How Social Media Is Reshaping News," Pew Research Center, FactTank, September 24, 2014, http://www.pewresearch.org/fact-tank/2014/09/24/how-social-media-is-reshaping-news/; "TwitterCounter Global Top 100," Twitter Counter, http://twittercounter.com/pages/100. Katy Perry is ranked number 1 and Justin Bieber is number 2. Other news sources and their rankings are CNN, number 48; Stephen Colbert, number 171; *Economist*, number 177; *Time*, number 192; and the *Wall Street Journal*, number 266.

15. Lloyd Bitzer, "The Rhetorical Situation," *Philosophy & Rhetoric* 1, no. 1 (1968): 1–14.

16. "33.3 Million Tune In to Watch Pres. Obama's State of the Union Address," Nielsen Newswire, January 29, 2014, http://www.nielsen.com/us/en/insights/news/2014/33-3-million-tune-in-to-watch-pres-obamas-state-of-the-union-address.html.

17. Ted Widmer, "The State of the Union Is Unreal," *New York Times*, January 31, 2006, http://www.nytimes.com/2006/01/31/opinion/31widmer.html; Bill Steigerwald, "Expect Nothing New—State of the Union," Cagle Cartoons, January 28, 2006, http://www.caglecartoons.com/column.asp?columnID={9A214537-9AF2-4B1E-94AF-394F84EFBF22}.

18. Brendan Nyhan, "A State of the Union Media Prebuttal," *Columbia Journalism Review*, January 24, 2012, http://www.cjr.org/united_states_project/a_state_of_the_union_media_pre.php; Elise Hu, "Obama's State of the Union, Playing on a Second Screen Near You," NPR, It's All Politics, January 28, 2014, http://www.npr.org/blogs/itsallpolitics/2014/01/27/267139207/obamas-state-of-the-union-playing-on-a-second-screen-near-you; Ariel Edwards-Levy, "Here's Why the State of the Union Doesn't Usually Change Many Minds," *Huffington Post*, January 20, 2015, http://www.huffingtonpost.com/2015/01/20/state-of-the-union-poll_n_6508034.html.

19. Joel B. Pollak, "Congress Should Cancel the State of the Union Address in 2015," *Breitbart*, November 20, 2014, http://www.breitbart.com/big-government/2014/11/20/congress-should-cancel-the-state-of-the-union-2015/; Jeremy W. Peters,

"After Obama's Immigration Action, a Blast of Energy for the Tea Party," *New York Times*, November 25, 2014, http://www.nytimes.com/2014/11/26/us/obamas-immigration-action-reinvigorates-tea-party.html. See also Arit John, "Conservatives: Don't Let Obama Give State of the Union Address," *Bloomberg*, Politics, November 26, 2014, https://www.bloomberg.com/politics/articles/2014-11-26/conservatives-to-john-boehner-dont-let-obama-give-state-of-the-union-address.

Less than a week before the scheduled date for the State of the Union speech, *Chicago Tribune* columnist Steve Chapman questioned the value of the event and said, "Too bad he isn't canceling the whole exercise. . . . Whether this event is still worth their time, however, is doubtful. If there was ever a time that direct exposure to presidential eloquence could melt the hearts of hostile legislators, it has passed. Even the public seems to have acquired immunity." Likewise, some in the media appeared unenthusiastic about the 2015 State of the Union. "The annual speech no longer packs a punch, and the media is starting to notice," wrote David Uberti in the *Columbia Journalism Review* on the morning before Obama's remarks. "The State of the Union is antique. That's not what President Barack Obama will tell a joint session of Congress on Tuesday night, but it is how new media organizations have treated this year's annual address."

20. Olivier Knox, "Why Obama's State of the Union Still Matters in the Twitter Era," Yahoo! News, January 20, 2015, http://news.yahoo.com/why-obama-s-state-of-the-union-still-matters-in-the-twitter-era-160637081.html; Juliet Eilperin, "How 'State of the Union Night' became 'State of the Union Month,'" *Washington Post*, January 16, 2015, http://www.washingtonpost.com/blogs/post-politics/wp/2015/01/16/how-state-of-the-union-night-became-state-of-the-union-month/.

21. Dan Pfeiffer, "The Road to the State of the Union (Spoiler Alert)," Medium, January 7, 2015, https://medium.com/@pfeiffer44/the-road-to-the-state-of-the-union-spoiler-alert-cc45fd726dac; White House, Facebook, January 8, 2015, https://www.facebook.com/video.php?v=10153120229619238.

22. Alan Yuhas, "White House Breaks Own State of the Union Embargo for Online Audience," *Guardian*, January 20, 2015, http://www.theguardian.com/us-news/2015/jan/20/white-housebreaks-state-of-the-union-embargo-medium; Erik Wemple, "Medium Editor on SOTU Coup: 'People Are Already Here,'" *Washington Post*, January 21, 2015, http://www.washingtonpost.com/blogs/erik-wemple/wp/2015/01/21/medium-editor-on-sotu-coup-people-are-already-here/; Tommy Christopher, "National Journal Skirts Embargo, Posts Full Text of Obama's State of the Union Address," Mediaite, January 25, 2011, http://www.mediaite.com/online/national-journal-posts-full-text-of-president-obamas-state-of-the-union-address/; Dylan Stableford, "Analysis: The Internet Stole Obama's State of the Union from Cable News," TheWrap, January 25, 2011, http://www.thewrap.com/media/column-post/media-reaction-obama-state-union-24218/; White House, "President Obama's State of the Union Address: Remarks As Prepared for Delivery," January 20, 2015, https://medium.com/@WhiteHouse/president-obamas-state-of-the-union-address-remarks-as-prepared-for-delivery-55f9825449b2; Matthew Hilburn, "White House Pre-Speech Release Creates Social Media Storm," Voice of America, Silicon Valley and Technology, January 21, 2015, http://www.voanews.com/content/white-house-pre-speech-release-creates-social-media-storm/2607914.html.

23. Bridget Coyne, "Big Night for #SOTU on Twitter," *Twitter Blog*, January 21, 2015, https://blog.twitter.com/2015/big-night-for-sotu-on-twitter; "Nielsen Twitter TV Ratings (1/19–1/25)," Nielsen Social, http://www.nielsensocial.com/nielsen

twittertvratings/weekly/; Kelly Cohen, "What #Trended on Social Media during the State of the Union," *Washington Examiner*, January 21, 2015, http://www.wash ingtonexaminer.com/what-trended-on-social-media-during-the-state-of-the-union/ article/2559054; "2015 State of the Union Trends," Google+, https://plus.google.com/ photos/+GooglePolitics/albums/6106629398246725425; Catalina Camia, "Obama's State of the Union Goes Big on Social Media," *USA Today*, January 21, 2015, http:// www.usatoday.com/story/news/nation-now/2015/01/21/obama-sotu-twitter-facebook/22100811/.

The main hashtag was #SOTU, with a number of specific ones such as #FreeCom-munityCollege for the tuition plan, #LeadOnLeave and #FamiliesSucceed for more paid sick leave for private sector workers, #BetterBroadband for the push for improved Internet access in rural America, #CyberSecurity for new consumer cyber protections, and #ActOnClimate for new regulations to control industrial methane releases. Major Garrett, "Welcome to the First Premeditated Twitter State of the Union," CBS News, January 20, 2015, http://www.cbsnews.com/news/welcome-to-the-first-pre-meditated-twitter-state-of-the-union/.

24. "Daily Briefing by the Press Secretary Josh Earnest," WhiteHouse.gov, January 15, 2015, http://www.whitehouse.gov/the-press-office/2015/01/15/daily-briefing-press-secretary-josh-earnest-011515; "'The Kelly File' with Megyn Kelly," Fox News, January 22, 2015, https://www.youtube.com/watch?v=GIpL49bTsfM, accessed February 2015.

25. Hank Green, "Holy Shit, I Interviewed the President," Medium, The Message, January 24, 2015, https://medium.com/@hankgreen/holy-shit-i-interviewed-the-president-fa3e8fb44d16.

26. "The YouTube Interview with President Obama" January 22, 2015, https:// www.youtube.com/watch?v=GbR6iQ62v9k; Neha Prakash, "Everything You Need to Know About the YouTube Stars Interviewing Obama," Mashable, January 22, 2015, http://mashable.com/2015/01/22/youtube-stars-obama/.

The Nielsen television viewership totals do not include digital live streams. While the combined television audience was down 4.8 percent from 2014, traffic on the White House website was up roughly 50 percent. There have been 1.65 million views on the White House YouTube, and there were almost 1.5 million views of real-time clips on Facebook during the speech. By comparison, Fox News had its worst State of the Union ratings in total viewers since 2001, dropping 25 percent in total viewers (3.52 million vs. 4.72 million) and 29 percent in the age twenty-five to fifty-four demographic (856,000 vs. 1.198 million). Jennifer Harper, "31.7 Million Viewers: State of the Union Address Was Least Watched in 15 Years," *Washington Times*, January 21, 2015, http://www.washingtontimes.com/news/2015/jan/21/317-million-viewers-state-union-address-was-least-/; John Nolte, "Report: State of the Union Audience Hits 15 Year Low," *Breitbart*, January 21, 2015, http://www.breitbart.com/big-government/2015/01/21/report-state-of-the-union-audience-hits-15-year-low/; Nathaniel Lubin, "The Enhanced 2015 State of the Union: By the Numbers," White House, Blog, January 21, 2015, http://www.whitehouse.gov/blog/2015/01/21/enhanced-2015-state-union-numbers; Matt Wilstein, "SOTU Ratings: Fox Wins Total Viewers, CNN Wins Demo," Mediaite, January 21, 2015, http://www.mediaite.com/tv/sotu-ratings-fox-wins-total-viewers-cnn-wins-demo/.

27. Brandice Canes-Wrone, "A Theory of Presidents' Public Agenda Setting," *Journal of Theoretical Politics* 13, no. 2 (2001): 183–208; Everett M. Rogers, "The Anat-omy of Agenda-Setting Research," *Journal of Communication* 43, no. 2 (1993): 68–84;

Maxwell E. McCombs, Donald L. Shaw, and David H. Weaver, "New Directions in Agenda-Setting Theory and Research," *Mass Communication & Society* 17, no. 6 (2014): 781–802; David Manning White, "The 'Gate Keeper': A Case Study in the Selection of News," *Journalism Quarterly* 27 (1950): 383–91; Pamela Shoemaker, Jaime Riccio, and Philip Johnson, "Gatekeeping," Oxford Bibliographies, 2013, http://www.oxford-bibliographies.com/view/document/obo-9780199756841/obo-9780199756841-0011 .xml; Edward S. Herman and Noam Chomsky, *Manufacturing Consent* (New York: Pantheon Books, 1988); W. Lance Bennett, "Toward a Theory of Press-State Relations in the United States," *Journal of Communication* 40, no. 2 (2006):103–27.

28. Howard Kurtz, "Howard Kurtz Media Notes: Networks Grouse About Coverage of Obama's Conference," *Washington Post*, August 3, 2009, http://www.washingtonpost.com/wp-dyn/content/article/2009/08/02/AR2009080202045.html.

29. Proceedings of the Senate Sitting for the Trial of Andrew Johnson, President of the United States, on Articles of Impeachment Exhibited by the House of Representatives, Article X, http://law2.umkc.edu/faculty/projects/ftrials/impeach/articles.html; J. Michael Hogan, *Woodrow Wilson's Western Tour: Rhetoric, Public Opinion, and the League of Nations* (College Station: Texas A&M University Press, 2006); "FDR's First Fireside Chat—March 12, 1933," Franklin D. Roosevelt Presidential Library, http://fdrlibrary.tumblr.com/post/79357164537/fdrs-first-fireside-chat-march-12-1933.

30. Howard Kurtz, *Media Circus: The Trouble with America's Newspapers* (New York: Times Books, 1993): 283; Edward C. Pease, "'New' Media Voices Challenge the 'Old' Media Status Quo," in *The Homestretch: New Politics, New Media, New Voters? The Media and Campaign '92 Series* (New York: Freedom Forum Media Studies Center, 1992): 99–101; Susan Herbest, "On Electronic Public Space: Talk Shows in Theoretical Perspective," *Political Communication* 12, no. 3 (1995): 263–74; Kenneth Jost, "Talk Show Democracy," *CQ Researcher* 4 no. 16 (April 29, 1994): 361–84, http://library.cqpress.com/cqresearcher/cqresrre1994042900; Diana Owen, "Who's Talking? Who's Listening? The New Politics of Radio and Television Talk Shows," in *Broken Contract: Changing Relationships between Citizens and Their Government*, edited by Stephen C. Craig (Boulder, CO: Westview Press, 1995); Jacob Weisberg, "The White House Beast," *Vanity Fair*, September 1993, http://www.vanityfair.com/magazine/archive/1993/09/presscorps199309; Walter Mears, "Clinton Takes Talk Straight to People," *Lawrence Journal-World*, March 28, 1993, 5A.

31.http://www.funnyordie.com/videos/18e820ec3f/between-two-ferns-with-zach-galifianakis-president-barack-obama; Dorothy Pomerantz, "Obama on 'Between Two Ferns' Shows the Power of the Viral Video," *Forbes*, March 11, 2014, 21; T. L. Stanley, "How Between Two Ferns Landed Obama," *Adweek*, June 22, 2014, http://www.adweek.com/news-gallery/advertising-branding/how-between-two-ferns-landed-obama-158496; Tweet from White House Senior Communications Advisor Tata McGuinness, March 11, 2014, https://twitter.com/HealthCareTara/status/443421401903820800; Brian Fung, "Zach Galifianakis Is Now HealthCare.gov's Biggest Traffic Driver," *Washington Post, The Switch* (blog), March 11, 2014, http://www.washingtonpost.com/blogs/the-switch/wp/2014/03/11/zach-galifianakis-is-now-healthcare-govs-biggest-traffic-driver/; "Sebelius on Obamacare: 'We Definitely Saw The Galifianakis Bump,'" HuffPost Live, March 31, 2014, http://live.huffingtonpost.com/r/archive/segment/533981ce78c90a4a8e000035.

32. Olivia Kittel and Samantha Wyatt, "Right-Wing Media Indignant over President Obama's Funny or Die Interview," MediaMatters, March 11, 2014, http://

mediamatters.org/research/2014/03/11/right-wing-media-indignant-over-president-obama/198442; Elias Isquith, "Bill O'Reilly: Abraham Lincoln Wouldn't Have Done 'Between Two Ferns,'" *Salon*, March 12, 2014, http://www.salon.com/2014/03/12/bill_oreilly_abraham_lincoln_wouldnt_have_done_between_two_ferns/; Kathleen Parker, "President Obama's Unbecoming Appearance on 'Between Two Ferns,'" *Washington Post*, March 11, 2014, http://www.washingtonpost.com/opinions/kathleen-parker-president-obamas-unbecoming-appearance-on-between-two-ferns/2014/03/11/3546be92-a959-11e3-b61e-8051b8b52d06_story.html.

33. Jeffrey Gottfried and Monica Anderson, "For Some, the Satiric 'Colbert Report' Is a Trusted Source of Political News," Pew Research Center, "Fact Tank," December 12, 2014, http://www.pewresearch.org/fact-tank/2014/12/12/for-some-the-satiric-colbert-report-is-a-trusted-source-of-political-news/; *The Colbert Report*, Comedy Central, December 8, 2014, http://media.mtvnservices.com/embed/mgid:arc:video:colbertnation.com:683edc2a-e024–4168-be61–5a66dfaf23d2; Chris Matyszczyk, "Obama Jabs at HealthCare.gov on 'Colbert Report,'" *CNET Magazine*, December 9, 2014, http://www.cnet.com/news/on-colbert-report-obama-jokes-about-healthcare-web-site/; Alexis Simendinger, "Why Obama Wanted to Appear on 'Colbert,'" RealClearPolitics, December 9, 2014, http://www.realclearpolitics.com/articles/2014/12/09/why_obama_wanted_to_appear_on_colbert_124905.html; Alexander Wayne, "Obamacare's Best Week Yet Brings 1 Million New Sign-Ups," *Bloomberg*, December 16, 2014, http://www.bloomberg.com/news/articles/2014–12–16/obamacare-s-best-week-yet-brings-1-million-new-sign-ups.

The Colbert Report was likely an effective venue for Obama to use to generate awareness and positive political conversation, as the Pew Research Center found that 10 percent of online adults "said they got news from the show in the previous week, on par with such sources as the *Wall Street Journal* and *USA Today*."

34. Jonathan Martin, "Obama Seeks Filter-Free News," *Politico*, March 24, 2009, http://www.politico.com/news/stories/0309/20395.html; "Flooding the Zone," *Democratic Strategist*, March 24, 2009, http://thedemocraticstrategist.org/2009/03/flooding_the_zone/.

35. Leonard Downie Jr. with Sara Rafsky, "The Obama Administration and the Press: Leak Investigations and Surveillance in Post-9/11 America," Committee to Protect Journalists, Special Report, October 10, 2013, https://cpj.org/reports/2013/10/obama-and-the-press-us-leaks-surveillance-post-911.php; "An End to Kerfuffles and Questions: Former Press Secretary Reflects," NPR, *All Things Considered*, June 27, 2014, http://www.npr.org/2014/06/27/326205965/an-end-to-kerfuffles-and-questions-former-press-secretary-reflects.

36. James Rosen, "White House Cuts the Middle Man," Fox News, April 30, 2011, http://video.foxnews.com/v/4194583/white-house-cuts-the-middle-man/?#sp=-show-clips; "Obama's Bid to Control Narrative," editorial, *Lancaster New Era*, September 13, 2013, http://lancasteronline.com/opinion/editorials/obama-s-bid-to-control-narrative/article_9558dc46–3c29–5f31-a8c8–7c16df99a11a.html; Holly Bailey, "Does Obama Need the Traditional Media? Yes and No," *Newsweek*, August 3, 2009, http://www.newsweek.com/does-obama-need-traditional-media-yes-and-no-211464.

37. Jack Mirkinson, "White House Press Corps: 'Extreme Frustration' With Lack of Obama Access," *Huffington Post*, February 18, 2013, http://www.huffingtonpost.com/2013/02/18/white-house-press-corps-obama-extreme-frustration-access_n_2710028.html.

38. John Dickerson, "Meet the Press," *Slate*, March 14, 2013, http://www.slate
.com/articles/news_and_politics/politics/2013/03/woodrow_wilson_held_the_
first_presidential_press_conference_100_years_ago.html.

39. Nancy Benac, "Flattering Obama Images Flourish As White House Media
Access Narrows," Associated Press, April 2, 2013, http://washington.cbslocal
.com/2013/04/02/flattering-obama-images-flourish-as-white-house-media-access-
narrows/; Howard Kurtz, "White House Press Corps Feels Bypassed by Obama
in Favor of TV Shows, YouTube," *Washington Post*, Media Notes, February 8, 2010,
http://www.washingtonpost.com/wp-dyn/content/article/2010/02/07/AR2010
020702693.html; Ron Fournier, "From Lincoln to Obama, Presidents as Propagandists,"
National Journal, April 2, 2013, http://www.nationaljournal.com/politics/from-
lincoln-to-obama-presidents-as-propagandists-20130402; Santiago Lyon, "Obama's
Orwellian Image Control," *New York Times*, December 12, 2013, A39.

40. Holly Yeager, "Grove's Death Knell for White House Press Corps Skips a
Beat," *Columbia Journalism Review*, April 6, 2010, http://www.cjr.org/the_audit/
groves_death_knell_for_white_h.php#sthash.tha65zfZ.dpuf; Stuart Hall, *Encoding
and Decoding in the Television Discourse* (Birmingham, England: Centre for Cultural
Studies, University of Birmingham, 1973); Philip Elliott, "Obama Turns to Web to
Bypass News Media," *Daily Progress*, January 23, 2013, http://www.dailyprogress
.com/news/obama-turns-to-web-to-bypass-news-media/article_8b2c09fb-a698-5145-
890f-52efa7ad2d72.html.

6

Keeping It Classified?

Reportorial Privilege and Presidential
Stonewalling in a Time of Terror

TONY PEDERSON

Governments keep secrets on behalf of the nation's security. Journalists uncover secrets to protect democracy. But since the terrorist attacks on the United States in 2001, the underpinnings of this deal—this conflict—have changed dramatically. The concept of the press as a check on government has existed since the founding of the United States and has been a part of the give and take involving the government, the public, and the press. The USA Patriot Act, passed less than two months after the 2001 attacks, gave the government expanded authority for surveillance and intelligence gathering and also limited news media access to information in the name of national security. There were clear concerns raised by journalists and news media groups that the act would make it easier for government to subpoena information from reporters who were working on matters related to national security and terrorism. Particularly troubling was Section 215 of the Act, which expanded the ability of government to search the records of businesses, including, apparently, newsrooms.[1]

Even before 2001, tensions had been growing over the issue of reporter privilege and what rights journalists had to maintain confidential sources. Technology was a part of this discussion as more data were stored in computer databases, accessible to more people and much more easily distributed in mass quantities.

Amid these rising tensions over national security and general questions about what is reported in the mainstream press, two major disclosures of classified materials have complicated the issue and brought about new concerns about how the US government functions. In 2010, Julian Assange, an Australian journalist and founder of WikiLeaks, disclosed thousands of military and diplomatic documents on the WikiLeaks website. He was further able to disseminate this classified information by working with selected media organizations, among them the *New York Times*. In 2013 a former CIA employee and National Security Administration (NSA) contractor named Edward Snowden leaked massive amounts of information about how the NSA functioned and details about the agency's monitoring of public and private individuals worldwide.

The actions of both Assange and Snowden raised comparisons with Daniel Ellsberg, a former military analyst who worked for the RAND Corporation and in 1971 leaked the Pentagon Papers, a military, political, and diplomatic history of the Vietnam War. The seven thousand pages of documents disclosed, among other things, embarrassing and questionable decisions by the Kennedy, Johnson, and Nixon administrations. The papers also included what to many was a surprising vindication of the CIA. Unknown to the public, the agency argued that the so-called domino theory about Southeast Asia wasn't valid and that the tactics chosen by the government for prosecuting the war had little likelihood of success. Ellsberg's leaking of the Pentagon Papers to the *New York Times* and the *Washington Post* would lead to a landmark US Supreme Court decision on press freedom. After the *Times* had begun publishing reports based on the papers, the Nixon administration, citing national security, went to court to block publication. The Supreme Court affirmed the papers' right to publish, saying that government seeking a prior restraint against news media had a heavy burden that, in the case of the Pentagon Papers, had not been met. Separately, Ellsberg was charged under the Espionage Act, but in 1973 charges were dismissed in large part because of the disclosure of criminal activities that had been authorized by the White House.[2]

Among government whistle-blowers, Ellsberg remains a historic figure, certainly as the first to leak massive amounts of classified information. The Nixon administration claimed that disclosure of the

Pentagon Papers amounted to espionage and constituted a threat to national security. The same claims regarding national security are being made today against Assange and Snowden as well as traditional journalists such as James Risen of the *New York Times*. Risen has reported extensively on the NSA's monitoring of communications of private individuals as well as CIA activities. Opinions vary greatly on whether the actions of these individuals amount to whistle-blowing by which the government is held accountable or whether their actions are treasonous and disclose information that puts the United States at risk. In addition, the questions of reporter privilege are more complex than ever. Reporter privilege, simply defined, is the right of journalists to use and maintain confidential sources in gathering sensitive information. Especially in the case of Assange, the question of who is a journalist has emerged as a vexing part of the traitor-or-hero issue.[3] Indeed, in the aftermath of the election of Donald J. Trump, and with Assange's role in releasing hacked emails from operatives inside the campaign of Hillary Clinton as well as the Democratic National Committee, there is renewed debate about how to think about such leaks, and the ethics of reporting on them.

A Brief History of Reporter Privilege

Reportorial privilege is a relatively fraught constitutional issue. Reporters have long believed there is a compelling need to keep confidential certain sources of information, and many believe there is a legal right to do so. The question of reporter privilege is simply this: Do journalists have any right to withhold information about sources when questioned as a part of the legal process? Is there any protection, constitutional or otherwise, that enables journalists to protect the confidentiality of sources used in the reporting process?

Currently, the majority of states and the District of Columbia have specific statutes that establish at least some degree of protection for journalists. These laws are typically called shield laws, and they vary greatly from state to state. More than seventy major news organizations and media companies, including the *New York Times* and the *Washington Post*, back a federal shield law, but the effort has so far failed.[4]

The conflict over the right of journalists to keep sources of information confidential has a long history that goes back to colonial
times. In 1722 James Franklin, brother of Benjamin Franklin, pub-
lisher of the *New England Courant*, was taken before authorities who
sought information about criticism of government published in the
paper. James Franklin refused to cooperate and was ordered to jail.
Benjamin Franklin was also taken before authorities but received
only an admonishment.[5]

James Franklin was in many ways the early prototype of the feisty,
crusading newspaper editor. He had clashes with authority of all kinds,
including that of the Puritan establishment led by Increase Mather
and his son Cotton. But it was Franklin's criticism and perceived libel
of the government that landed him in jail. Though it was very literate and expressed many of the sentiments of the public against the
authorities, the *Courant* declined in popularity, and James Franklin
abandoned the paper several years later. After his release from jail, he
accepted a position as government printer in Rhode Island.[6]

As will become clear, the basic issue has changed little from James
Franklin's experience to that of James Risen. The idea of a press that
is independent and has extraordinary freedom to serve as a check
on government has roots from the Enlightenment. The American
Founders took it to be a democratic and constitutional essential.
Indeed, they held to the libertarian theory of the press, which holds
that self-government best flourishes through maximum press freedom, a free flow of information, and minimal government interference in reportorial efforts.[7]

Long before journalism schools or even the hint of any ethics or
standards for the press, the Founders envisioned a media system
with a rather special role in society. "Thus, the press, while comprised of ordinary citizens with no special office, has an extraordinary function, tied to the heart of the democratic process," wrote
North Carolina senator Sam Ervin Jr., who chaired the famed Watergate hearings. "And this peculiar obligation to the public reinforces
the reporter's determination to resist commands of the government
which interfere with that obligation."[8]

This special role without official government portfolio for the press
has been the starting point for many discussions and—no doubt—
much of the modern resentment toward the media expressed by

the public. While states typically license everything from doctors to barbers and from plumbers to chiropractors, any discussion of the licensing of journalists has historically been met with vigorous opposition and the notation of "make no law" firmly placed in the First Amendment. Journalists need no particular education—no specific training—and need pass no exam to work in any media position in the United States. Yet the modern media are widely perceived as being one of the most powerful institutions in the United States.

The Supreme Court's decision in *Branzburg v. Hayes* in 1972 was a watershed event in US journalism. Three separate cases were combined in the *Branzburg* decision. The cases all involved reporters' refusal to cooperate with authorities conducting investigations. Paul Branzburg, a reporter for the *Courier-Journal* of Louisville, Kentucky, refused to answer a grand jury's questions after he had witnessed hashish being synthesized from marijuana. The other two cases involved government investigations of the Black Panther Party. Earl Caldwell, a reporter for the *New York Times* in San Francisco who had covered Black Panther activities, refused to appear or testify before a federal grand jury. Milt Pappas, a television reporter in New Bedford, Massachusetts, who had visited Black Panthers' headquarters, refused to disclose to a grand jury what he had seen. Courts in Kentucky and Massachusetts refused to grant any protection to Branzburg or Pappas. Caldwell, on the other hand, had received a favorable ruling from the US Circuit Court of Appeals, 9th Circuit, affirming the existence of a qualified privilege.[9]

In a 5–4 decision, the US Supreme Court ruled that no reporter privilege existed that could protect the reporters from testifying. But the decision was sharply divided. In his often-quoted dissent, Justice Potter Stewart noted that the decision "invites state and federal authorities to undermine the historic independence of the press by attempting to annex the journalistic profession as an investigative arm of government." And even in his concurring opinion, Justice Lewis F. Powell Jr. noted that it was not the court's ruling that journalists were "without constitutional rights with respect to the gathering of news or in safe-guarding their sources." Powell said that a claim of reporter privilege "should be judged on its facts by the striking of a proper balance between freedom of the press and the obligation of all citizens to give relevant testimony."[10]

Despite other skirmishes over reporter privilege, out of *Branzburg v. Hayes* grew sentiment for a qualified reporter privilege that stressed striking the balance to which Powell referred. And several lower-court decisions reached favorable decisions in protecting reporters. Out of *Branzburg* also came what was called a gentleman's agreement involving Department of Justice guidelines that prosecutors would not abuse subpoena power against journalists. These guidelines became part of the Code of Federal Regulations.[11]

The guidelines, first proposed in a speech by Attorney General John Mitchell in August 1970, seem generous in recognition of the privilege. The guidelines state that "the approach in every case must be to strike the proper balance between the public's interest in the free dissemination of ideas and information and the public's interest in effective law enforcement and the fair administration of justice." And in the next part, "All reasonable attempts should be made to obtain information from alternative sources before considering issuing a subpoena to a member of the news media."[12]

But the recent cases and the public's increasing skepticism about the integrity of media call into question how ultimately the issue should be balanced. An unfortunate string of ethics scandals in recent years has been met with increasing anger and resentment by the public toward all media. One of the first media scandals to break was the case of Janet Cooke and the *Washington Post*. Cooke fabricated a story in 1981 about an eight-year-old addicted to heroin, for which the *Post* won a Pulitzer Prize. When it was discovered that Cooke made the story up, the paper was compelled to return the award. Stephen Glass was an up-and-coming reporter for the *New Republic* until it was discovered in 1998 that he had fabricated numerous stories published by the magazine. Then the *New York Times* was tainted by scandal when it was learned that Jayson Blair plagiarized and fabricated much of his work over a two-year period. A similar scandal was uncovered at *USA Today* involving reporter Jack Kelley, who reported fantastic stories about international events that never happened. The paper had nominated Kelley several times for a Pulitzer Prize. And CBS was embarrassed by a report on President Bush and his National Guard service that was based on documents whose authenticity ultimately could not be established. Four journalists were fired and longtime anchor Dan Rather resigned in the aftermath.[13]

In making any compelling ethics case for privilege to withhold information from the legal process, journalists need to establish that the potential good done by investigative and explanatory journalism clearly outweighs any harm done by withholding information. In arguing the need for a federal shield law, many news organizations have taken the approach that such a law protects the public as much as journalists. The editorial position of the *New York Times* is typical: "A shield law does protect journalists. But the real benefit for society is that it protects sources, allowing whistle-blowers or other insiders to expose wrongdoing in government and the private sector. The information they provide is vital to the public's ability to know what government and businesses are doing and to make informed judgments."[14]

Prosecutors are on the opposite end of the argument. Patrick Fitzgerald, appointed as special prosecutor in the Valerie Plame case, which will be detailed later in this chapter, has emphasized the government's position that a federal shield law would inhibit the government's ability to safeguard national security. He said:

> The proposed shield law poses real hazards to national security and law enforcement. The bipartisan Sept. 11 commission and the Robb-Silberman commission on prewar intelligence both found our national security at great risk because of the widespread leaking of classified information. The proposed law would have the unintended but profound effect of handcuffing investigations of such leaks. In many cases, authorities would face the Catch-22 of being required to prove specific criminal activity—in a hearing before a judge, often resulting in notice to the subjects of investigation or their associates—before they could take the investigative steps to determine whether criminal activity had occurred. In effect, the law would require "trial before investigation." Even worse, in cases involving leaks of classified information, the law would require the government to disclose in a hearing the specific damage caused by the leak—information often more sensitive than the leak itself.

Fitzgerald also argued that the overly broad definition of a journalist in the federal bill would protect a whole range of potential sources from "charity" organizations fraudulently raising money for groups affiliated with al-Qaeda to child pornographers who communicate over the Internet.[15]

In short, there is real tension over the need to protect reporters and the need to protect classified information, especially in the aftermath of September 11. It is in this complicated environment that the debate over the actions of Assange, Snowden, Risen, and others is best understood.

Assange and Wikileaks

WikiLeaks was founded in 2006 and published the first documents in December of that year. The website claims that it is a "secure and anonymous way for sources to leak information to . . . journalists" and is dedicated to free speech and media publishing based on Article 19 of the Universal Declaration of Human Rights.[16] In the early going the site was responsible for publishing information as diverse as operating manuals for Guantánamo Bay, Sarah Palin's Yahoo emails, and secret Scientology manuals.

In 2010, WikiLeaks began receiving a series of classified documents from US Army private Bradley Manning. Assange began working with the *New York Times*, the *Guardian* of London, and the German magazine *Der Spiegel*, all of which participated in the release of classified military and diplomatic cables involving the wars in Afghanistan and Iraq. The first contact between the *New York Times* and the *Guardian* involved a phone call from *Guardian* editor Alan Rusbridger to *Times* executive editor Bill Keller in June 2010. Keller discussed the relationship between the paper and Assange, one that became increasingly confrontational and in the end even hostile, in a lengthy *New York Times Magazine* piece published in 2011.[17]

Assange was born in 1961 in Australia. He is largely home-schooled and self-educated. Although journalist and editor seem to be frequent descriptions of his profession, he is more computer hacker and expert cryptologist. When he was twenty, criminal charges were brought against him for hacking into the system in Melbourne maintained by the Canadian telecommunications company Nortel. He eventually pleaded guilty and paid a small fine. The lead investigator in the case, Ken Day, told reporter Raffi Khatchadourian of the *New Yorker*, "He had some altruistic motive. I think he acted on the belief that everyone should have access to everything." While some have tried to make favorable comparisons between what Assange did with WikiLeaks and traditional journalism, there are obvious contrasts. Journalism historically has involved the gathering of information and the writing and editing of news that is relevant to the public. Standards of libel, decency, privacy, and not putting innocent people in danger have been an accepted part of the journalistic process. Assange, on the other hand, published thousands of documents online with seemingly little regard for editing or any concern over the consequences the release of the information would have. Sensitive and private information has been published on WikiLeaks, including, for example, documents that include the Social Security numbers of military personnel. Assange said that he couldn't weigh the impact of every document and that he preferred final judgment to be made in public and in the open. While the news organizations that published accounts based on the WikiLeaks documents said they were careful not to disclose information that might put people in danger, including the names and identities of government informants, it was easy for enemies of the United States, including the Taliban, to search directly on WikiLeaks for such details.[18]

Floyd Abrams, the noted First Amendment lawyer who represented the *New York Times* in the Pentagon Papers case, has been quick to draw distinctions between Assange and Ellsberg. Ellsberg kept secret four volumes of the Pentagon Papers that dealt with diplomatic efforts to resolve the war. "Not at all coincidentally, those were the volumes that the government most feared would be disclosed," Abrams wrote. "In a secret brief filed with the Supreme Court, the US government described the diplomatic volumes as including information about negotiations secretly conducted on its behalf by foreign nations including Canada, Poland, Italy and Norway. Included as well, according to the government, were 'derogatory comments about the perfidiousness of specific persons involved, and statements which might be offensive to nations or governments.'" Those volumes on the diplomatic efforts were not published until a dozen years later. When asked why they were withheld, Ellsberg said, "I didn't want to get in the way of the diplomacy. I wanted to get in the way of the bombing and killing."[19]

One of the most controversial parts of the WikiLeaks disclosures was a video showing an Apache helicopter attack on more than a dozen people walking on a Baghdad street. The video was shot from a helicopter camera on July 12, 2007, and released by WikiLeaks with the title "Collateral Murder." Two Reuters news employees were among those killed in the attack. Reuters had for three years unsuccessfully sought the video under the Federal Freedom of Information Act. The video includes conversation between soldiers that seems quite casual for what occurs. "Once you get on 'em, just open 'em up," is heard from one soldier. An eighteen-minute version of the video is available on YouTube and, as of this writing, has almost fifteen million views.[20] The full, unedited version of almost forty minutes is available at WikiLeaks.org.

Robert Gates, who was defense secretary at the time, said that the video was misleading. "These people can put out whatever they want and are never held accountable for it," he said. "There is no before and no after. It is only the present. That is the problem with these videos. You are looking at the war through a soda straw, and you have no context or perspective." The Pentagon said that no disciplinary action was taken against any personnel involved in the attack.[21]

Aside from the distinction drawn by Abrams, two other issues have likely marred the reputation of WikiLeaks. First is the volatile nature of Assange's personality and the fact that he was wanted for questioning in Sweden over allegations of sexual misconduct. "He could be charming, capable of deadpan humor and wit," wrote David Leigh and Luke Harding in their book about Assange and WikiLeaks, "but he could be waspish, flaring into anger and recrimination. Assange's mercurial temperament spawned groupies and enemies, supporters and ill-wishers, sometimes even in the same person. Information messiah or cyberterrorist? Freedom fighter or sociopath? Moral crusader or deluded narcissist?"[22]

Keller of the *New York Times* described the transformation that Assange underwent during the celebrity that came to surround WikiLeaks:

> The derelict with the backpack and the sagging socks now wore his hair dyed and styled, and he favored fashionably skinny suits and ties. He became a kind of cult figure for the European young and leftish and was evidently a magnet for women. Two Swedish

women filed police complaints claiming that Assange insisted on
having sex without a condom; Sweden's strict laws on nonconsen-
sual sex categorize such behavior as rape, and a prosecutor issued
a warrant to question Assange, who initially described it as a plot
concocted to silence or discredit WikiLeaks. I came to think of
Julian Assange as a character from a Stieg Larsson thriller—a man
who could figure either as hero or villain in one of the mega-selling
Swedish novels that mix hacker counterculture, high-level conspiracy and sex as both recreation and violation.[23]

Assange was in England when the complaints by the two women
became public, and his lawyers filed a series of appeals fighting the
extradition request from the Swedish government. But the British
courts ruled the extradition lawful. He took refuge in the embassy of
Ecuador in London in June 2012. He was granted asylum by Ecuador in August 2012 and has not left the embassy since. British police
maintain a twenty-four-hour guard at the embassy.[24]

Second, not only are there issues with the credibility of Assange,
himself, but there are questions about the motives of one of his main
informants, US Army private Bradley Manning. Manning, who identifies as gay—now transgender—and served in the military during
the don't-ask–don't-tell years, became disenchanted with a number of
army issues and the way in which war was being conducted while he
was serving as an intelligence analyst in Iraq in 2009. In his position
he had access to an extraordinary amount of classified information.[25]
The data disclosed by Manning included 250,000 State Department
cables, 500,000 pages of military reports, and videos of attacks in
Afghanistan and Iraq. While in the army, Manning was diagnosed
with gender identity disorder and later became known as Chelsea
Manning. She was dishonorably discharged, convicted of charges
under the Espionage Act, sentenced to thirty-five years in prison, and
served time at Fort Leavenworth, Kansas. Manning's sentence was
commuted by President Obama at the end of his term and she was
released in June 2017.

Edward Snowden

Edward Snowden fits just about anyone's definition of a computer
geek. Without a college degree, he ended up with extraordinary
access to classified information, raising serious questions about the

number of people who have access to high-level intelligence and how these individuals are granted such status. In 2006 he was hired by the CIA as a computer engineer. In early 2009 he resigned his position under circumstances that aren't entirely clear. Later that year he was hired by Dell Inc., a Texas-based computer and technology company. After leaving Dell, Snowden took a position with Booz Allen Hamilton, a consulting company, where he moved into cybersecurity. In Hawaii, Snowden eventually was given responsibility for copying millions of classified files from NSA computers located on the mainland onto backup servers in Hawaii. "In retrospect, it seems astounding that a single person—and an outside contractor at that—would be given such power to root through the country's national intelligence archives, but he was, according to the NSA itself," reported Suzanne Andrews, Bryan Burrough, and Sarah Ellison for *Vanity Fair* in 2014.[26]

Both Assange and Snowden appear by most accounts as eccentric, alienated, perhaps a bit naïve, and even self-absorbed. Both, for varying reasons, became disillusioned and even angry at what they perceived as the overreach of government in intelligence and military activities. By one account, Snowden originally had a completely unrealistic idea of how his leaking would be received, even believing that, over time, he would be regarded as a hero, not a traitor.[27]

And, indeed, prestigious awards have been given to Snowden and the journalists who reported his disclosures. The Ridenhour Prize for Truth-Telling was given to Snowden and filmmaker-journalist Laura Poitras. The Ridenhour Prizes are given by the Nation Institute and the Fertel Foundation in honor of Ron Ridenhour, the Vietnam veteran who disclosed details of the My Lai massacre. The Polk Award for National Security Reporting was given to Poitras, Glenn Greenwald, and Ewen MacAskill of the *Guardian* and Barton Gellman of the *Washington Post*. The *Washington Post* and the *Guardian* were awarded the Pulitzer Prize for Public Service, generally considered the most important newspaper award given in the United States.

After fleeing to Hong Kong to provide the NSA information to journalists, and after the first reports had been published, Snowden, at the time twenty-nine years old, identified himself publicly in a video in which he was questioned by Greenwald and filmed by Poitras.

In the video, posted by the *Guardian* on June 9, 2013, he discussed his motivations for releasing the documents and even talked about the potential consequences. He said that when he realized the extent of the abuses taking place, he decided that they should be judged by the public and not just by people who were hired by the government. When asked if he had come to Hong Kong because he intended to defect to China, identified by Greenwald in the questioning as "an enemy" of the United States, Snowden disputed the categorization of China as an enemy. He said that he had chosen to go to Hong Kong because of its long history of free speech.[28] Within weeks, his US passport was revoked, and he was charged with violation of the Espionage Act. He met with Russian representatives in Hong Kong and then flew to Moscow, where he remained in an airport transit zone for thirty-nine days. In August 2013 he was granted a one-year visa. The visa was renewed for three years in August 2014, and it is now considered likely that he will gain permanent citizenship in Russia.

The Snowden story took many twists and turns. It seems bizarre that a young man patriotically motivated by the US invasion of Iraq in 2003 to join the US Army would end up leaking some of the most highly secret data held by the government. Snowden joined the army in 2004, but his military career was brief. During infantry training he broke both legs, and he was soon discharged. Snowden's political leanings have been considered libertarian and most closely aligned with those of Ron Paul, a Republican and former member of Congress from Texas. In fact, it seems that Snowden made political contributions to Paul. Paul, in turn, has complimented Snowden and Greenwald. "We should be thankful for individuals like Edward Snowden and Glenn Greenwald who see injustice being carried out by their own government and speak out, despite the risk," Paul said in a statement released on the website of Campaign for Liberty, his nonprofit. "They have done a great service to the American people by exposing the truth about what our government is doing in secret."[29]

The irony of Snowden's claims that he acted in a desire for transparency and accountability and the fact that he has taken refuge in one of the most authoritarian countries in the world has not been lost. "Compromising US security isn't his sole achievement since going rogue at the NSA," stated an editorial in the *Wall Street Journal*. "Mr. Snowden has also sold himself as a noble whistle-blower to the more naïve in the West's media and political classes. And all while he has enjoyed the protection of one of the world's most dangerous tyrants, whose military assault on Ukraine may bring on a wider European war. Tightening the screws at home last week, Mr. Putin imposed regulations to stifle free expression on the Internet. We missed the protests from Mr. Snowden and his collaborator Glenn Greenwald."[30]

A number of critics have also noted that if Snowden truly believed what he did was right and that if he were a whistle-blower in the truest sense of following his ethical convictions, he would have remained in the United States, defended his actions vigorously, and, if he failed, taken the legal consequences.

Snowden's disclosures are by far the most extensive in history, particularly in the ways they detail the US government's technological reach in gathering intelligence. Also disclosed was specific information about the NSA itself, including the number of employees who work for the organization (35,000) and its annual budget ($10.5 billion). Retired general Michael Hayden, who served stints as director of the CIA and NSA, said, "He's not just revealing this report said that or this—that is like water dripping out. In Snowden's case, it's not just the buckets he's dumping—he's revealing the plumbing." The documents reveal agreements with major technology companies, including Apple, Google, and Yahoo, for the harvesting and cataloging of email and instant messages. Among the most embarrassing revelations was the monitoring of the phone conversations of world leaders, including German chancellor Angela Merkel. The revelation led to strained relations and continued questions as to what constraints the government might impose on NSA intelligence gathering.[31]

James Risen and the Obama Approach
to Prosecuting Leaks

If one could imagine an individual completely the opposite of both Assange and Snowden in terms of character, personality, and professional orientation, it would be James Risen, since 1998 a reporter for the *New York Times*. Everything about him is old school, including his tenacious, gumshoe reporting on national security issues.

In December 2005, Risen and Eric Lichtblau reported that the Bush administration had authorized monitoring of telephone and email communications of US citizens without court authorization. The article raised questions about whether the change in intelligence gathering had crossed constitutional barriers that protect individual privacy. The article also noted that the White House had asked the paper not to publish the piece and that the paper had waited more than a year to do so and had omitted some details that "could be useful to terrorists." Risen and Lichtblau shared the Pulitzer Prize for National Reporting in 2006. The Pulitzer citation said that the award was given for "carefully sourced stories on secret domestic eavesdropping that stirred a national debate on the boundary line between fighting terrorism and protecting civil liberty."[32]

Risen became the symbol of a protracted struggle between the government and the media in 2006 with publication of his book *State of War: The Secret History of the CIA and the Bush Administration*. The book detailed CIA and NSA involvement in fighting terrorism. Risen reported on the CIA's bungled attempt to thwart Iran's nuclear program, claiming that, in fact, what the CIA likely did was help the Iranians in the development of nuclear technology.[33] The Justice Department subpoenaed Risen to disclose his source. At the beginning of the book, in a note on sources, Risen wrote that his reporting included "the cooperation of many current and former officials from the Bush administration, the intelligence community, and other parts of the government." The Bush administration named former CIA agent Jeffrey Sterling as a possible source on the Iran story. Sterling was indicted on Espionage Act charges. The original subpoena on Risen expired in 2009, and the Justice Department under President Obama renewed it.

Risen steadfastly refused to disclose his sources, saying that he would go to jail if held in contempt. "A lot of people still think this is some kind of game or signal or spin," he said in August 2014. "They don't want to believe that Obama wants to crack down on the press and whistle-blowers. But he does. He's the greatest enemy to press freedom in a generation."[34]

In calling the Obama administration a threat to freedom of the press, Risen perhaps was thinking also of other major aggressions the Justice Department committed against journalists as well as the fact that the Obama administration prosecuted eight leakers, more than all previous administrations combined. In 2013 reports surfaced that the Justice Department seized two months of telephone records of the Associated Press in a leak investigation. The records gathered were cell, home, and office numbers of individual reporters and an editor, as well as the general office numbers in Washington, New York, and Hartford and the main number for AP reporters assigned to cover Congress. Associated Press CEO Gary Pruitt wrote to Attorney General Eric Holder that there was "no possible justification for such an overbroad collection of the telephone communications of the Associated Press and its reporters." Pruitt said that the records "provide a road map to AP's newsgathering operations and disclose information about AP's activities and operations that the government has no conceivable right to know." Other experts were even harsher in assessing the invasive nature of the government activity. Steven Aftergood, a government secrecy expert at the Federation of American Scientists, called the Justice Department action "an astonishing assault on core values of our society."[35]

Just a week after the reports about the AP phone records came a disclosure that the FBI had named James Rosen, the chief Washington correspondent for Fox News, as a coconspirator in a criminal investigation of another leak. The affidavit filed in federal court "made it clear that Mr. Rosen's comings and goings at the State Department were carefully monitored." The *New York Times* said in an editorial, "Obama administration officials often talk about the balance between protecting secrets and protecting the constitutional rights of a free press. Accusing a reporter of being a 'co-conspirator,' on top of other zealous and secretive investigations, shows a heavy tilt toward secrecy and insufficient concern about a free press."[36]

The relationship between candidate Obama and later President Obama and the news media had been considered quite cordial and even cozy. But that relationship somehow soured completely. Or, as Maureen Dowd, columnist for the *New York Times*, put it: "It's hard to fathom how the president who started with the press fluffing his pillows has ended up trying to suffocate the press with those pillows."[37]

In 2014 the Justice Department began to back off its aggressive behavior toward journalists. In May, Holder called a group of journalists together to discuss press freedom issues. A statement from the department after the meeting said: "The department officials declined to discuss any particular cases, but reiterated the attorney general's longtime assertion that, as long as he is in office, no journalist will be prosecuted or go to prison for performing ordinary news gathering activities."[38]

The description of Holder's position as "longtime" seems an exaggeration if not completely revisionist. For years the Justice Department of the Bush and Obama administrations had claimed that Risen's testimony was essential in the leak case. In hearings just before Sterling's trial, Justice Department lawyers changed their position and said that they would not be calling Risen to testify. The Justice Department was successful in getting a conviction of Sterling on all nine criminal counts. After the trial, Holder said, "It is possible to fully prosecute unauthorized disclosures that inflict harm upon our national security without interfering with journalists' ability to do their jobs."[39]

One can only speculate why the Justice Department changed its position so quickly and completely. Maybe federal officials felt some embarrassment about not knowing, understanding, or respecting federal guidelines regarding subpoenas of journalists that had been in place since the 1970s. Perhaps it was just surprised reaction to the unanimity and vigor of criticism expressed by virtually all news organizations, ranging from Fox News to the *New York Times*.

Before Obama was elected in 2008, a major security-related conflict involving the government and media ended with the release of Judith Miller, a reporter for the *New York Times*, who had been jailed for eighty-five days for refusing to disclose a source. The origin of the Miller case can be traced to a line in the State of the Union address by then-president George Bush in January 2003. Bush, in outlining his case for future action against Iraq, said that Saddam Hussein had sought significant quantities of uranium in Africa. The White House later said that the statement was based on faulty intelligence and should not have been included in the speech.[40]

The previous year, Vice President Dick Cheney's office had contacted former ambassador Joseph C. Wilson IV about the intelligence report on Iraq seeking nuclear technology. Wilson said the CIA then asked him to go to Niger to investigate. In a widely read piece in the *New York Times* published July 6, 2003, Wilson stated that he had found no evidence of Iraqi attempts to buy uranium in Niger.[41]

On July 14, 2003, the late syndicated columnist Robert Novak published a column claiming that Wilson's wife, who worked for the CIA, had asked that Wilson be sent to Niger. Wrote Novak: "Wilson never worked for the CIA, but his wife, Valerie Plame, is an agency operative on weapons of mass destruction. Two senior administration officials told me that Wilson's wife suggested sending him to Niger to investigate the Italian report." Miller and Matt Cooper, a reporter for *Time* magazine, also were told by White House officials that Plame worked for the CIA. Under federal law, identifying a CIA operative can be a crime. Wilson claimed that the White House identified his wife in retaliation for his criticisms of the Bush administration's claims linking Iraq to attempts to secure nuclear technology.[42]

This background set the stage for a messy debate over reporter privilege that was fraught with politics. Patrick Fitzgerald, US attorney for the Northern District of Illinois, was named special prosecutor to investigate the leak. Both Miller and Cooper were among the reporters subpoenaed to appear before a grand jury investigating the leak. Initially, both refused to testify, and the news organizations filed motions to quash the subpoenas. The motions failed, as did appeals to the US Court of Appeals for the District of Columbia Circuit.[43] The Supreme Court declined to hear the case. Ultimately, Cooper testified. Miller refused and spent eighty-five days in jail before reaching an agreement for limited testimony.

Many reporters felt little enthusiasm about supporting Miller because they believed that she and the *New York Times* had simply been wrong in the coverage of weapons of mass destruction that seemed to reinforce the Bush administration's argument for going to war in Iraq. In fact, on May 26, 2004, the *Times* published an extraordinary statement acknowledging that its reporting on the weapons of mass destruction had not been as rigorous as it should have been and had tended to rely on questionable sources that should have been subjected to more scrutiny.[44]

Miller eventually became the lightning rod for the controversy, obscuring what many felt should have been a sincere and needed discussion about the role reporter privilege plays in the journalistic process that allows the media to serve as a check on government.

Richard Cohen, a syndicated columnist for the *Washington Post*, came straight to the point: "The fury at Miller is ugly and does journalism no good. Whatever her politics, whatever her journalistic sins (if any), whatever the whatevers, she is in jail officially for keeping her pledge not to reveal the identity of a confidential source. . . . She's in jail, upholding a principle that has been an integral part of American journalism for years and years: You don't reveal confidential sources. At the moment, that—not her politics or her reporting or her tempestuousness—is what matters."[45]

Ultimately, after an investigation that lasted almost three years, no one was indicted for the leak of Valerie Plame's name, but Scooter Libby, Cheney's chief of staff, was indicted on charges of lying to federal prosecutors during the investigation. He was convicted and sentenced to thirty months in prison. President Bush commuted the sentence, even though he did not grant a full pardon.[46]

There can be little doubt that the Judith Miller–Matt Cooper case represented a fundamental change in the relationship between government and the media and indicated future problems for journalists. Norman Pearlstine, the former editor of Time Inc. directly involved in the case of *Time* magazine and Matt Cooper, leaves no doubt as to his belief that the government's aggressiveness in pursuing journalists as sources in investigations has hindered the media's ability to report news. "The indictment of Scooter Libby was a milestone in the Plame-Cooper-Miller story," Pearlstine wrote. "It exposed the Bush administration's efforts to manipulate the press while trying to destroy those who would criticize the President and his policies. But for those in the administration, battles with journalists were part of a broader effort to control leaks and to corral the press, which it had come to see as a part of the enemy forces it had to fight."[47]

The *New York Times*, in an analysis on the news pages published after the Libby conviction, made the point clearly that the general truce that had existed between government and media since the *Branzburg* decision by the Supreme Court in 1972 was over:

> The institution most transformed by the prosecution, and the one that took the most collateral damage from Patrick J. Fitzgerald's relentless pursuit of obstruction and perjury charges against Mr. Libby, may have been the press, forced in the end to play a major

role in his trial. After Mr. Libby's conviction . . . it is possible to
start assessing that damage to the legal protections available to
the news organizations, to relationships between journalists and
their sources and to the informal but longstanding understanding
in Washington, now shattered, that leak investigations should be
pressed only so hard. Ten out of 19 of the witnesses in Mr. Libby's
trial were journalists, a spectacle that would have been unthinkable only a few years ago.

The *Times* went on to quote Theodore J. Boutrous Jr., one of the lawyers
who represented *Time* magazine in the Cooper case: "Every tenet and
every pact that existed between the government and the press has
been broken."[48]

Conclusion

Many factors can be cited in the increased tensions involving government and the news media. The twenty-four-hour news cycle, the
ubiquitous nature of cable news, and, of course, national security
are all a part of the issue. Then there is technology and the Internet
itself, considered by Snowden "the most important invention in all
human history."[49] Add to this the highly partisan nature of government today, and there is reason to believe that the idea of media as a
check on government is endangered.

The issue of reporter privilege and the ability to keep sensitive
sources confidential can be separated as a legal concept from what
has occurred with Assange, WikiLeaks, and Snowden. Yet the disclosures by Assange and perhaps Snowden have had a negative
effect on the public perception of reporter privilege, as witnessed
by editorials and what now appears to be a very small chance of a
federal shield law passing Congress. "The disclosures by WikiLeaks
and Snowden are different, but no doubt because they both deal
with national security there's been an impact," said Bruce Sanford, a
well-known First Amendment and media lawyer at Baker Hostetler
in Washington, DC. "For sure, there's been a major transformation
since Ellsberg. I've said a number of times that the only surprising
thing about Snowden is that there aren't 50 more people like him.
More and more people are being given unfettered access to sensitive
material, and we're doing more and more things in the name of na-

tional security. I think you'll see more disclosures like Snowden['s] in the future."[50]

Sanford said he sees a clear difference in how Assange and Snowden are perceived by the public. "People [are] not impressed by someone hitting the button and releasing all sorts of information as in the case of WikiLeaks," he said. "Snowden is an interesting character. There are a lot of people who regard him as a hero and sort of a romantic figure. Part of the public thinks we really should know what he disclosed about the NSA. I'm not sure he's really hurt the image of the news media."[51]

While some in Washington, including former House speaker John Boehner and Senator Dianne Feinstein, former chair of the Senate Intelligence Committee, have described Snowden's actions as treason, some degree of public sympathy has emerged. In an editorial, the *New York Times* specifically said that what Snowden did wasn't treason, and that if he really wanted to damage the United States, he would have sold his data to an enemy. Daniel Ellsberg himself has praised Snowden's leaks. "Snowden believes that he has done nothing wrong. I agree wholeheartedly. More than 40 years after my unauthorized disclosure of the Pentagon Papers, such leaks remain the lifeblood of a free press and our republic. One lesson of the Pentagon Papers and Snowden's leaks is simple: secrecy corrupts, just as power corrupts."[52]

How reporter privilege continues to be recognized, whether in individual courts or in the form of a federal shield law, will determine to some extent if and how the media will be able to perform their function as a check on government. While most states have some level of confidentiality protection for journalists, Sanford sees little chance of a federal shield law being approved by Congress in the current environment. Presidents other than George Bush and Barack Obama have warred against the media. Leaks have been a part of the give and take between government and the media for years. The media serve as an integral part in the process of governance by being able to report on matters of trifling importance but also on issues of public concern ranging from Watergate to the Abu Ghraib prison scandal to the surveillance activities of the NSA.

The conscience of the mainstream media is also being tested in the debate over national security and the reporting on government activities. As Bill Keller wrote in the *New York Times*: "We are invested in the struggle against murderous extremism in another sense. The virulent hatred espoused by terrorists, judging by their literature, is directed not just against our people and our buildings but also at our values and at our faith in the self-government of an informed electorate. If the freedom of the press makes some Americans uneasy, it is anathema to the ideologists of terror. So we have no doubts about where our sympathies lie in this clash of values. And yet we cannot let those sympathies transform us into propagandists, even for a system we respect."[53]

Only time will tell if the aggressiveness of the Bush and Obama administrations becomes a pattern in seeking to "annex the journalistic profession as an investigative arm of government," as Justice Stewart wrote in *Branzburg* more than forty years ago. Surveillance on a level never before seen in US history will continue in the era of terrorism. Reporters such as James Risen will continue to report on activities about which the government doesn't want the public to know. Websites such as WikiLeaks and probably others can continue to operate on servers outside the reach of the US government. Leakers such as Edward Snowden will have access to sensitive data and, answering to personal conscience or simply some element of outrage, will inform news organizations of what they find.

Despite the public's misgivings about the media and all of the media's own failings, individually as journalists and collectively as an institution, a free press was at the heart of the Founders' intentions on establishing democracy. And democracy cannot—democracy will not—function without a free, robust, and independent media.

Notes

1. "Questions for Attorney General John Ashcroft on the USA Patriot Act and Its Effect on the News Media," Reporter's Committee for Freedom of the Press, August 20, 2003, http://www.rcfp.org/news/documents/20030820ashcroft.html.

2. Sanford J. Ungar, *The Papers & the Papers: An Account of the Legal and Political Battle over the Pentagon Papers* (New York: E. P. Dutton, 1972), 34–35; New York Times *v. the United States*, 403 U.S. 713 (1971); Martin Arnold, "Pentagon Papers Charges Are Dismissed," *New York Times*, May 11, 1971, http://www.nytimes.com/learning/general/onthisday/big/0511.html#article.

3. Margaret Sullivan, "Who's a Journalist? A Question with Many Facets and One Sure Answer," *New York Times Blogs*, June 29, 2013, http://publiceditor.blogs.nytimes.

com/2013/06/29/whos-a-journalist-a-question-with-many-facets-and-one-sure-answer/?_r=0.

For a detailed discussion of treason, legal protections afforded whistle-blowers, and whether leaks amount to First Amendment speech, see Mary-Rose Papandrea, "Leaker Traitor Whistleblower Spy: National Security Leaks and the First Amendment," *Boston University Law Review* 94, no. 2 (2014): 449–544.

4. Reporter's Privilege compendium on the Reporter's Committee for Freedom of the Press website, www.rcfp.org/privilege/index.php; Paul Farhi, "WikiLeaks Is Barrier to Shield Arguments," *Washington Post*, August 21, 2010, C1.

5. Sam J. Ervin Jr., "In Pursuit of a Press Privilege," *Harvard Journal on Legislation* 11 (1973–74): 233–34. This piece is an excellent summary of the history of reporter privilege and congressional response to the Supreme Court decision in *Branzburg v. Hayes* (1972). The author notes in the introduction that the article is "not primarily a legal analysis, but a political one."

6. Michael Emery, Edwin Emery, and Nancy L. Roberts, *The Press and America: An Interpretive History of the Mass Media*, 9th ed. (Boston: Allyn and Bacon, 2000), 25–29.

7. Fred S. Siebert, Theodore Peterson, and Wilbur Schramm, *Four Theories of the Press* (Urbana: University of Illinois Press, 1971), 40–44.

8. Ervin, "In Pursuit of a Press Privilege," 234–35.

9. *Branzburg v. Hayes*, 408 U.S. 665, 92 S. Ct. 2646 (1972).

10. Journalists and lawyers have pondered for more than four decades what Powell meant. The *New York Times* ("A Justice's Scribbles on Journalists' Rights," October 7, 2007, A4) reported on a document discovered among Powell's papers at Washington and Lee University. The document contained handwritten notes by Powell on the court's private conference after hearing oral arguments in *Branzburg*. "We should not establish a constitutional privilege," Powell wrote. He added that such a privilege would create problems "difficult to foresee," including "who are 'newsmen'—how to define?" But Powell was very clear in writing "there is a privilege analogous to an evidentiary one which courts should recognize and apply . . . to protect confidential informants." But even the notes leave disagreement over what Powell meant. The *Times* quoted noted First Amendment lawyer Floyd Abrams as saying the notes confirmed his position that there is a privilege. But former federal prosecutor Randall D. Eliason expressed doubt. "I'm not sure the notes clear up anything at all," he told the *Times*.

11. Dwight L. Teeter Jr. and Bill Loving, *Law of Mass Communications: Freedom and Control of Print and Broadcast Media*, 11th ed. (New York: Foundation Press, 2004), 648–51; Code of Federal Regulations, Title 28, Section 50.10.

12. Ervin, "In Pursuit of a Press Privilege," 252.

13. Ibid., 674; Robin Pogrebin, "Rechecking a Writer's Facts, a Magazine Uncovers Fiction," *New York Times*, June 12, 1998, A1; "The problems of Jack Kelley and *USA Today*," *USA Today*, April 22, 2004, http://www.usatoday.com/news/2004-04-22-report-one_x.htm; "CBS Ousts 4 for Bush Guard Story," CBS News, January 10, 2005, http://www.cbsnews.com/stories/2005/01/10/national/main665727.shtml.

The *New York Times* published a full account of the Blair scandal on May 11, 2003, beginning on A1 and written and reported by numerous staff members at the paper. The opening paragraph said, "A staff reporter for the *New York Times* committed frequent acts of journalistic fraud while covering significant news events in recent months, an investigation by *Times* journalists has found. The widespread fabrication and plagiarism represent a profound betrayal of trust and a low point in the 152-year history of the newspaper."

14. "Toward a Federal Shield Law," *New York Times*, May 3, 2007, A22.

15. Patrick Fitzgerald, "Shield Law Perils: Bill Would Wreak Havoc on a System That Isn't Broken," *Washington Post*, October 4, 2007, A25.

16. "About: What Is WikiLeaks?" WikiLeaks, http://wikileaks.org/About.html. Article 19 of the Universal Declaration of Human Rights states, "Everyone has the right to freedom of opinion and expression; this right includes freedom to hold opinions without interference and to seek, receive and impart information and ideas through any media and regardless of frontiers."

17. Bill Keller, "Dealing with Assange and the WikiLeaks Secrets," *New York Times Magazine*, January 26, 2011, http://www.nytimes.com/2011/01/30/maga-zine/30Wikileaks-t.html.

18. Raffi Khatchadourian, "No Secrets: Julian Assange's Mission for Total Trans-parency," *New Yorker*, June 7, 2010, 47, 50; Robert Mackey, "Taliban Study WikiLeaks to Hunt Informants," *New York Times*, The Lede, July 30, 2010, http://thelede.blogs.nytimes.com/2010/07/30/taliban-study-wikileaks-to-hunt-informants/.

19. Floyd Abrams, "Why WikiLeaks Is Unlike the Pentagon Papers," *Wall Street Journal*, December 29, 2010, A13; Ungar, *Papers & the Papers*, 85.

20. "Collateral Murder," video, YouTube, https://www.youtube.com/watch?v=5rX PrfnU3G0.

A detailed account of Assange's activities and work with a group of activists from Iceland during the spring of 2010 is available from Raffi Khatchadourian, a reporter for the *New Yorker*. This account describes the decryption, editing, and naming of the "Collateral Murder" video. Khatchadourian was embedded with the group and published his story in the June 7, 2010, issue of the magazine.

21. Julian E. Barnes, "Gates Says Video of U.S. Helicopter Attack in Iraq Out of Con-text," *Los Angeles Times*, April 14, 2010, http://articles.latimes.com/2010/apr/14/world/la-fg-gates-video14-2010apr14; Noam Cohen and Brian Stelter, "Airstrike Video Brings Attention to Whistle-Blower Site," *New York Times*, April 7, 2010, A8.

22. David Leigh and Luke Harding, *WikiLeaks: Inside Julian Assange's War on Secrecy* (New York: PublicAffairs, 2011), 14.

23. Keller, "Dealing with Assange."

24. Steven Erlanger, "Assange Says He'll Leave Embassy in London," *New York Times*, August 19, 2014, A8. For a detailed account of the accusations of sexual mis-conduct against Assange by two women in Sweden as well as what Assange sup-porters say, see Leigh and Harding, *WikiLeaks*, 145–63.

25. Leigh and Harding, *WikiLeaks*, 20–31.

26. Suzanne Andrews, Bryan Burrough, and Sarah Ellison, "The Snowden Saga," *Vanity Fair*, May 2014, 159, 163.

27. Ibid., 198.

28. "NSA Whistleblower Edward Snowden: 'I Don't Want to Live in a Society That Does These Sort of Things,'" video, *Guardian*, http://www.theguardian.com/world/video/2013/jun/09/nsa-whistleblower-edward-snowden-interview-video.

29. Luke Harding, *The Snowden Files* (New York: Vintage Books, 2014), 22–23, 29–30, 41; Rachel Weiner, "Ron Paul Praises Edward Snowden," *Washington Post*, June 10, 2013, http://www.washingtonpost.com/blogs/post-politics/wp/2013/06/10/ron-paul-praises-edward-snowden/.

30. "Safe in Putin's Arms," *Wall Street Journal*, Review & Outlook, August 8, 2014, A12.

31. Andrews, Burrough, and Ellison, "Snowden Saga," 155, 159; Mark Landler, "Merkel Signals Tension Persists over U.S. Spying," *New York Times*, May 3, 2014, A1.

32. James Risen and Eric Lichtblau, "Bush Lets U.S. Spy on Callers Without Courts," *New York Times*, December 16, 2005, A1; The Pulitzer Prizes, Journalism, http://www .pulitzer.org/citation/2006-National-Reporting.

33. James Risen, *State of War: The Secret History of the CIA and the Bush Administration* (New York: Free Press, 2006), 208–12.

34. Maureen Dowd, "Where's the Justice at Justice?" *New York Times*, August 16, 2014, SR11.

35. Jonathan Mahler, "Reporter's Case Poses Dilemma for Justice Dept.," *New York Times*, June 28, 2014, A1; Sari Horwitz, "Justice Department Obtained AP Phone Records in Leak Investigation," *Washington Post*, May 13, 2013, A1.

36. "Another Chilling Leak Investigation," *New York Times*, August 22, 2013, A26.

37. Dowd, "Where's the Justice at Justice?"

38. Charlie Savage, "Holder Hints Reporter May Be Spared Jail in Leak," *New York Times*, May 28, 2014, A13.

39. Matt Zapotosky, "Former CIA Officer Found Guilty in Leak Case," *Washington Post*, January 27, 2015, A1.

40. Eric Lichtblau, "Early Doubts about Uranium Sale to Iraq: '02 Memo Called Deal with Niger 'Unlikely,'" *International Herald Tribune*, January 18, 2006, News 3.

41. Joseph C. Wilson 4th, "What I Didn't Find in Africa," *New York Times*, July 6, 2003.

42. Robert Novak, "Mission to Niger," *Washington Post*, July 14, 2003, A21; Georgie Anne Geyer, "Wilson Sees Wife's 'Outing' as Retaliation," *Chicago Tribune*, October 3, 2003, http://articles.chicagotribune.com/2003-10-03/news/0310030137_1_cia-agent-iraq-war.

43. *In Re Grand Jury Subpoena, Judith Miller*, 365 U.S. App. D.C. 13; 397 F.3d 964.

44. "The Times and Iraq," *New York Times*, May 26, 2004, A10.

45. Richard Cohen, "Miller in Jail: Principle vs. Politics," *Washington Post*, August 2, 2005, A13.

46. Amy Goldstein, "Bush Commutes Libby's Prison Sentence," *Washington Post*, July 3, 2007, A1.

47. Norman Pearlstine, *Off the Record: The Press, the Government, and the War over Anonymous Sources* (New York: Farrar, Straus and Giroux, 2007), 195.

48. Adam Liptak, "After Libby Trial, New Era for Government and Press," *New York Times*, March 8, 2007, A18.

49. Harding, *Snowden Files*, 22.

50. Bruce Sanford, partner with Baker Hostetler, in Washington, DC, interview with the author, January 14, 2015.

51. Ibid.

52. "Surveillance: Snowden Doesn't Rise to Traitor," *New York Times*, June 11, 2013, http://www.nytimes.com/2013/06/12/opinion/surveillance-snowden-doesnt-rise-to-traitor.html; Daniel Ellsberg, "NSA Leaker Snowden Made the Right Call," *Washington Post*, July 7, 2013, http://www.washingtonpost.com/opinions/daniel-ellsberg-nsa-leaker-snowden-made-the-right-call/2013/07/07/0b46d96c-e5b7-11e2-aef3-339619eab080_story.html.

53. Keller, "Dealing with Assange."

REALITY CHECK

The Legacy Press—
Nobody Does It Better

ROBERT W. MONG

No serious journalist wants to be viewed as a two-dimensional figure in a three-dimensional world, but that's how legacy journalists are often positioned in any discussion of digital transformation. Journalists are viewed as a casualty in the rise of digital news because (or so it seems) everybody says twentieth-century reporters don't have what it takes to adapt. And without an ability to adapt, the outlook for journalism is said to be one of decline and stagnation. But although it is true that the digital age is shifting the sands of the field, I would like to suggest there is still more to the story. For one thing, legacy journalists *do* have what it takes to acclimate and use digital developments, maybe even better than the new players in the game. This is because journalism, even digital journalism, has a valuable and deeply rooted foundation in the offline past. As the managing editor of the *Dallas Morning News*, I have seen legacy journalism's continued success and importance in the current media environment. So while no one is immune to the effects of the digital revolution, most of the reporters I know and have spent my life working with are adapting quite well and doing the same good work they've always done, to the same high standards that are sure to stand up to the test of time.

It is because of these standards that legacy journalists will be able to adapt. The foundations of the craft have supported journalism for decades. A journalist's primary job does not change, even with digital advancements. Journalists still seek out and pursue important stories to share with the public. Some of their methods may change, and they may use technological innovations to help get the job done, but modern journalists are doomed if they merely practice the techniques of journalism without engaging the shoe-leather work that real reporting requires—no matter how digitally skilled they might be. Journalists must rely on essential skills that will never change if they desire to achieve journalism's long-standing purpose. I know how important it is for journalists to have the ability to research and think critically because I have seen time and time again that the truth is almost never simple or easy to discover. In order to find the truth in a story, journalists must be skilled in understanding people and be able to think past the obvious first, second, or even third question. Truth is beyond digital advancements, and if journalists are expected to discover it, they must be capable beyond digital advancements as well. A computer can't tell you when someone is obfuscating with a joke or sarcastic aside. A fancy graphic is no substitute for a keen insight or an incisive follow-up question.

One of the biggest playing fields on which legacy journalism has been tested is in the public sphere. Everybody seems convinced that digital advancements have drastically changed the world of politics, but I still have my doubts. Do we have a cyber democracy yet? I am not so sure. Yes, campaigns have discovered how to use the current digital environment to their advantage. Campaigns are able to reach voters by utilizing media that are familiar and preferred by them, like email, Facebook, and Twitter. Social media provide a platform for campaigns to target voters and donors on a personal and effective level. There is no question campaigns have figured out how to tap into social media trends to advance and defend their candidates' interests. But has any of this had an impact on the current political landscape? Despite these efforts, there doesn't yet seem to be a significant change in major political patterns such as the voting cycle. Except for presidential elections, voters are still withdrawn from the political process, and even then voters aren't completely engaged. Citizens have become highly engaged in other areas, from fantasy sports to celebrity news, but despite all the frenetic activity, I'm not sure we've seen a surge in interest or activity when it comes to politics.

There is no question that legacy journalists are fighting for survival. However, they are not already extinct, and it would be a mistake to assume they soon will be. Journalism is still needed—still demanded —in the current environment. I do not think that journalism will look completely the same in the future, but I do believe its foundation will stand the test of time. Disruption threatens existence, but it also points the way out. The changing media environment is giving journalism the chance to grow and develop new ways to seek out the truth and reach the people. Only time will tell how journalism will look in the decades to come, but I believe there is a very good chance that as the legacy press continues to adapt and emerge through the digital transformation, the public will find the institution stronger for the test—ready as ever to fulfill its mission of bringing a spotlight to dark places, asking tough questions, seeking truth, and writing stories that engage us all.

PART FOUR

Everything Old Is New Again

Organizing for (In)Action

The Obama Presidency and the
Vanishing Hope of an Online Vanguard

GEORGE C. EDWARDS III

Despite all their efforts to lead public opinion, presidents do not directly reach the American people on a day-to-day basis. For more than two centuries the primary intermediary between the president and the public has been the press, first newspapers and then radio and television. It was the traditional news media that provided people with most of what they knew about chief executives, their policies, and their policies' consequences. The press, in turn, found coverage of the president indispensable in satisfying its audience and reporting on the most significant political events.

With the advent of new media and online news services, the White House communications environment has undergone a sea of change. The president cannot depend on broadly focused newspapers, network television, and radio to reach the public. In response, the White House has embraced the latest technology to take its case to the people. As several writers in this book have suggested, including Stephanie Martin, Stephen Smith, and Jennifer Mercieca, new modes of communication offer an opportunity to bypass the press and communicate directly with the public.

These changes raise important questions: To what extent do a president's attempts to go around the traditional media change the relationship between the chief executive and the traditional press, and to what extent do these efforts influence the media's coverage of the president? For this chapter, however, the key question is whether advances in technology make it easier for the president to lead the public. I explore the challenges the new communications environment present for the White House, as well as the potential they open for the president to exploit the new media to rally likely supporters and reinforce their predispositions to back his initiatives.

The Nature of the Fragmented Audience

One of the most salient characteristics of the modern media environment is its fragmentation; audiences are able to choose from an abundance of media choices, select their preferred media, and determine an individual time to access their choice. Universal media coverage or delivery is no longer the norm. Reflecting on the presidency as recently as the tenure of Ronald Reagan, Barack Obama's press secretary, Jay Carney, observed, "You [could] reach almost every voter in the country. And that's not even remotely the case now. The only way you get that many eyeballs at one time is to have an enormous event, something like killing bin Laden."[1]

"Like any period of tumultuous change, it's not a happy one," added Obama's former communications director Anita Dunn. "This idea that somehow there's a bully pulpit that can be used effectively," Dunn said, "to communicate with everybody in this country at the same time and get them all wrapped around one issue—it's very much an idea whose time has passed." Carney said, "That's why we do all the unorthodox stuff, putting him [the president] in unusual places, just to try to reach people where they are. Because where they're not is watching the news or reading the newspapers."[2]

Wide viewership was common during the early decades of television. Presidential speeches routinely attracted more than 80 percent of those who were tuned in to TV. Things have changed, however. Audiences for presidential speeches and press conferences have declined steadily since the Nixon administration in the early 1970s. Only forty million viewers saw at least part of George W. Bush's first nationally televised address on February 27, 2001, compared with sixty-seven million viewers for Bill Clinton's first nationally televised address in 1993.[3] Barack Obama attracted more than fifty-two million viewers to his first nationally televised address in February 2009, during a severe economic crisis. The size of his audience dropped off substantially after that, however. When he spoke on behalf of his health care reform proposal the following September, for example, he drew only thirty-two million viewers, a typical audience for his national addresses (Table 7.1).

Table 7.1. Audiences for Obama's nationally televised speeches and press conferences

Date	Venue	Topic	Audience Size
Feb. 9, 2009	White House	Press conference	49.5 million
Feb. 24, 2009	Joint Session of Congress	Overview of administration	52.4 million
Mar. 24, 2009	White House	Press conference	40.4 million
Apr. 29, 2009	White House	Press conference	28.8 million
July 22, 2009	White House	Press conference	24.7 million
Sept. 9, 2009	Joint Session of Congress	Health care reform	32.1 million
Dec. 1, 2009	USMA, West Point	Afghanistan	40.8 million
Jan. 27, 2010	Joint Session of Congress	State of the Union message	48.0 million
June 15, 2010	Oval Office	Gulf of Mexico oil spill	32.1 million
Aug. 31, 2010	Oval Office	End of Iraq War	29.2 million
Jan. 12, 2011	Tucson, Arizona	Memorial for shooting victims	30.8 million
Jan. 25, 2011	Joint Session of Congress	State of the Union message	42.8 million

Date	Venue	Topic	Audience Size
Mar. 28, 2011	National Defense University	Libya	25.6 million
May 1, 2011	White House	Death of Osama bin Laden	56.7 million
June 22, 2011*	White House	Troop cuts in Afghanistan	25.4 million
July 25, 2011	White House	Debt limit	30.3 million
Sept. 8, 2011	Joint Session of Congress	Jobs proposals	31.4 million
Jan. 24, 2012	Joint Session of Congress	State of the Union message	37.8 million
May 1, 2012†	Afghanistan	War in Afghanistan	NA
Sept. 6, 2012	Charlotte, North Carolina	Acceptance of Democratic nomination	35.7 million
Jan. 21, 2013‡	Capitol	Inaugural address	20.6 million
Feb. 12, 2013	Joint Session of Congress	State of the Union message	33.5 million
Sept. 10, 2013	White House	Syria	32.3 million
Sept. 27, 2013†	White House	Budget	NA
Sept. 30, 2013†	White House	Budget	NA
Oct. 16, 2013	White House	Budget/ government shutdown	NA
Nov. 23, 2013†	White House	Iran nuclear capability	NA

Date	Venue	Topic	Audience Size
Jan. 28, 2014	Joint Session of Congress	State of the Union message	33.3 million
Sept. 10, 2014	White House	Islamic State of Iraq and the Levant	34.2 million
Nov. 20, 2014§	White House	Immigration	13.8 million

Source: Nielsen Company.
*Univision did not carry the speech.
†Not delivered in prime time; no audience ratings.
‡Not delivered in prime time.
§ABC, CBS, and NBC did not broadcast the speech.

An important cause of this drop in viewership is access to alternatives provided by cable, the Internet, and streaming television.[4] Almost all households receive cable service, and many also have access to digital video recording (DVR) packages as well (providing yet additional opportunities to avoid watching the president). Even more problematic for presidents and their administrations, television is a medium in which visual interest, action, and conflict are most effective. Unfortunately, presidential speeches are unlikely to contain these characteristics. Only a few addresses to the nation—such as President George W. Bush's address to a joint session of Congress on September 20, 2001, and so coming in the close aftermath of the September 11 attacks—occur at moments of high drama.

The public's general lack of interest in politics constrains the president's leadership of public opinion in the long run, as well as on any given day. Although they have unparalleled access to the American people, presidents cannot make much use of it. If they do, their speeches will become commonplace and lose any chance of inspiring drama and so, interest. That is one reason why presidents do not make formal speeches to the public on television very often—only four or five times a year, on average. Recent presidents, beginning with Richard Nixon, turned to radio and midday addresses to supplement their prime-time televised addresses, although media coverage of such addresses has diminished over the years.[5]

In addition to the challenge of attracting an audience for the president's television appearances, the White House faces the obstacle of obtaining television coverage in the first place. Traditionally, presidents could rely on full network coverage of any statement they wished to make directly to the American people or any press conference they wished to have televised. The networks began to rebel against providing airtime in the 1970s and 1980s when one or more of them occasionally refused to carry an address or a prime-time press conference held by President Ford, Carter, Reagan, or Bush. Bill Clinton encountered so much resistance from the networks to covering his speeches and press conferences that he held only four evening press conferences in his eight years in office (only one of which all the networks covered live) and made only six addresses on domestic policy, all of them in his first term.

In the two months following the terrorist attacks on the United States on September 11, 2001, George W. Bush received plenty of prime-time coverage for his speeches and press conferences. By November 8, however, most networks viewed the president's speech on the US response to terrorism as an event rather than news and did not carry it. Nearly a year later, on October 7, 2002, Bush made his most comprehensive address regarding his forthcoming decision to use force against Saddam Hussein's regime in Iraq. Nevertheless, ABC, CBS, NBC, and PBS chose not to carry the president's speech, arguing that it contained little that was new. The traditional broadcast networks also chose not to carry Barack Obama's address on immigration on November 20, 2014, which Jennifer Mercieca discusses in-depth in the next chapter.

In the contemporary media environment, the president even struggles to reach an audience through the traditional news format. The audience for the network evening news broadcasts declined to 22.6 million people in 2013, and the audience for prime-time cable news dropped to about 3 million.[6] Between 2003 and 2013, daily newspaper circulation dropped nearly 10 million to 46 million—a drop of 17 percent; Sunday circulation dropped 7 million to 50 million—a drop of 15 percent. Thus, the Obama White House had to innovate to reach the public and survive in this new communications environment.

Meeting the Audience Where They Are

Although technological change and corporate resistance have made it more difficult for the president to attract an audience on television, other changes may have increased the White House's prospects for reaching the public. Teddy Roosevelt gave prominence to the bully pulpit by exploiting the hunger of modern newspapers for national news. Franklin D. Roosevelt broadened the reach and immediacy of presidential communications with his use of radio. More recently, John F. Kennedy and Ronald Reagan mastered the use of television to speak directly to the American people. Now Barack Obama has positioned himself as the first Internet president.

And it is a good thing he has. The Pew Research Center reports that the vast majority of Americans now get news in some digital format. In 2013, 82 percent of Americans said they got news on a desktop or laptop, and 54 percent said they got news on a mobile device. Beyond that, 35 percent reported that they get news "frequently" on their desktop or laptop, and 21 percent "frequently" on a mobile device (cell phone or tablet).[7] The Internet, which emerged in 2008 as a leading source for campaign news, has now surpassed all other media except television as a main source for national and international news. More people say they rely mostly on the Internet for news than say they rely mostly on newspapers (although people often turn to the websites of traditional news sources for their news). Young people are even more likely to report that they rely on the Internet as a main source of national and international news.[8]

The 2008 Internet Campaign

Realizing that they could no longer depend on reaching the public through the traditional media, Obama's 2008 election campaign team made great efforts to send the candidate's messages directly to voters' inboxes, social media feeds, and television sets. Significant strategy announcements were often made in the form of videos, with campaign manager David Plouffe speaking straight into the camera, rather than through news releases or strategic interviews.[9] Similarly, Obama announced his intent to seek the presidency via Web video, revealed his vice presidential selection via text message, recruited about thirteen million online supporters during the campaign, and used the electronic medium to sidestep mainstream media and speak directly with voters throughout the primaries and campaign for the general election. This practice forged a firsthand connection and may have encouraged some supporters to feel they had a substantial, tangible stake in the campaign's success. Some Obama videos became YouTube phenomena: millions of people viewed his speech on Rev. Jeremiah A. Wright Jr. and race in America and his victory speech in Grant Park on November 4, 2008.

The new administration was oriented to exploiting advances in technology to communicate more effectively than ever with the public. For example, Bush State Department spokesman Sean McCormack had filed posts from far-flung regions during trips with his boss, Secretary of State Condoleezza Rice. On October 31, 2008, in the press briefing room of the State Department, McCormack unveiled "Briefing 2.0," in which he took questions from the public rather than the press and then put the session on YouTube.[10] The Obama White House wanted to do more. "It's really about reaching an extra person or a larger audience of people who wouldn't normally pay attention to policy," said Jen Psaki, a spokeswoman for Obama's transition team. "We have to think creatively about how we would do that in the White House, because promoting a speech in front of 100,000 people is certainly different than promoting energy legislation."[11]

Creating the Digital Presidency

On November 18, 2008, two weeks after election day, about ten million of Barack Obama's supporters found an email message from the president-elect's campaign manager, David Plouffe. In the message, labeled "Where we go from here," Plouffe asked backers to "help shape the future of this movement" by answering an online survey, which in turn asked them to rank four priorities in order of importance. First on the list was "Helping Barack's administration pass legislation through grassroots efforts."[12]

Plouffe's email message revealed much about Barack Obama's initial approach to governing. Even before taking office, the president-elect began making Saturday radio addresses—but with a twist. In addition to beaming his addresses to radio stations nation-wide, he recorded them for digital video and audio downloads for YouTube, iTunes, and the like. As a result, people could access them whenever and wherever they wanted. "Turning the weekly radio address from audio to video and making it on-demand has turned the radio address from a blip on the radar to something that can be a major news-making event any Saturday we choose," declared Dan Pfeiffer, the incoming White House deputy communications director. Videos are also easy to produce: a videographer can record Obama delivering the address in fewer than fifteen minutes.[13] After his inauguration, the White House put the president's Saturday videos on both the White House website and a White House channel on YouTube.

The Obama White House produced and distributed much more video than any past administration. To do so, it maintained a staff devoted to producing online videos for WhiteHouse.gov, Obama's YouTube channel, and other video depots. A search for "Barack Obama" revealed a bevy of videos approved and uploaded by the administration (which viewers may not realize). When filming a presidential speech, the production team tailored the video to the site, with titles, omissions, crowd cutaways, highlight footage, and a dozen other manipulations of sound and image that affected the impression they made, including applause that was difficult to edit out. The president's YouTube channel had more than 650 video uploads in its first year alone.[14]

In addition, the administration developed an extensive blog (*The White House Blog*) offering short stories accompanied by photos and videos. They also streamed live events and provided podcasts of speeches, remarks, events, and briefings. The administration also introduced *West Wing Week*, a video blog consisting of six- to seven-minute compilations that appeared each week on the White House's website and on such video sharing sites as YouTube. The items offered what a narrator on each segment called "your guide to everything that's happening at 1600 Pennsylvania Avenue."

The White House also adopted other strategies, such as hosting an animated page on Buzzfeed, letting Obama appear on the Internet show *Between Two Ferns with Zach Galifianakis*, and encouraging the president and others to pose for selfies and other funny pictures.

As Stephanie Martin noted in this book's introduction, the hope was that these items would go viral. As such, White House staff members promoted their content to popular sites such as Upworthy, which is known for its eye-catching headlines.

Staying on Top of the Message

"What's the first page on Google and Bing look like?" asked Dan Pfeiffer, the president's senior adviser and longtime communications strategist. "Let's take Benghazi," he continued, referring to the partisan battle over the administration's response to the attacks on US facilities in Libya in 2012. "Is it five things from *Free Beacon* and *Breitbart*? Or is it something from the *New York Times* or is it from the *New Republic*?" If the administration's perspective is not well represented in the Google search results, "we have to ask: Does it mean we need to do a better job of getting our message out?"[15]

Pfeiffer maintained that the White House is not bypassing traditional media such as news conferences and other events. But he emphasized that it was more important than ever to do late-night comedy and daytime talk shows, as well as ESPN and MTV. "It used to be that Ronald Reagan or, to a lesser extent, Bill Clinton could give a national address," he said. "We don't have that option. We have to go where the public is."[16]

The Obama White House tried to flood niche media markets via blogs, Twitter feeds, Facebook pages, and Flickr photostreams. To exploit more fully developments in communications technology, the White House established an Office of New Media. It regularly alerted its more than five million Twitter followers of the president's policy stances.[17] Indeed, Obama's Twitter feed, reached more people than all of the nightly news broadcasts combined and more than the total circulation of the seventy-five largest daily papers.

When he nominated Sonia Sotomayor to the Supreme Court, Obama sent a video appealing for support for his candidate to the huge email list that was accumulated during his campaign and to the Democratic Party's own lists. The email message included a directive from the president to share his views via Facebook, Twitter, and other Web connections. In addition, the White House tracked journalists' tweets for comments it might view as inaccurate, incomplete, or unfair as well as for clues about what the press was reporting and how it might portray the president or the administration. An aide then flagged the tweets it found objectionable in mass emails to more than eighty Obama aides, who then responded, sometimes with "obscenity-laced yelps of outrage."[18]

The Obama administration showed deftness at catering to a nonstop, Internet- and cable-television-driven news cycle. For example, the White House went to great lengths to project an image of competence in US relief efforts in Haiti, in implicit contrast to the way the Bush administration handled Hurricane Katrina and its aftermath. The administration and the military set up a busy communications operation with twenty-five people at the American embassy and in a cinder-block warehouse at the airport in Port-au-Prince, Haiti's capital. The public relations team released a torrent of news releases, briefings, fact sheets, and statements, including a ticktock (a newspaper term of art for a minute-by-minute reconstruction of how momentous events unfolded). It also issued a link to a Flickr photo of a meeting about Haiti in the Situation Room, presided over by the president; a video of American search teams rescuing a Haitian woman from a collapsed building; and a list of foreign leaders the president had telephoned.[19]

Politico.com, an online bulletin board of the stories on which the media are focused and what is happening in Washington on a given day, was a prominent face of the new media at the Obama White House. The White House started communicating with *Politico* early in the day to try to influence what others would view as important. It also used *Politico* as a forum to rebut its adversaries directly in front of the rest of the news media.[20]

The Matter of Those Internet Interviews

As Stephanie Martin details in chapter 4, Obama came to office in the midst of a serious economic recession. In response, the new president needed to promote to the public a new economic agenda. He did so on a variety of forums, including the *Tonight Show*, *60 Minutes*, and a prime-time news conference. On March 26, 2009, he added a new arrow to his quiver. The president held a town hall meeting in the East Room of the White House. Bill Clinton and George W. Bush answered questions over the Internet, but Obama was the first to do so in a live video format, streamed directly onto the White House website.

For more than an hour the president answered questions culled from 104,000 possibilities that had been sent over the Internet. On-line voters cast more than 3.5 million votes for their favorite queries, some of which an economic advisor, who served as a moderator, then posed to the president. The president took other inquiries from a live audience of about one hundred nurses, teachers, business-people, and others assembled at the White House. The questions covered topics such as health care, education, the economy, the auto industry, and housing. In most cases Obama used his answers to ad-vocate his policies. Although the questions from the audience in the East Room were mostly from campaign backers, the White House was not in complete control of the session. One of the questions that drew the most votes online was whether legalizing marijuana might stimulate the economy by allowing the government to regulate and tax the drug. (The White House listed the question on its website un-der the topics "green jobs and energy" and "budget." White House officials later indicated that interest groups drove the spiked interest in the topic.)[21]

On February 1, 2010, the president sat for a first-of-its-kind group interview with YouTube viewers, who submitted thousands of ques-tions and heard the president answer some in a live Webcast. You-Tube viewers voted for their favorite questions, and Steve Grove, the head of news and politics at YouTube, selected the ones to ask in the half-hour session.

On April 21, 2011, Obama sat down with Facebook founder Mark Zuckerberg and answered questions from Zuckerberg and Facebook users. Next, the president turned to Twitter. On July 6, 2011, he held the first Twitter town hall meeting, live from the East Room of the White House. The hour-long session involved the president answer-ing questions submitted by Twitter users, and selected in part by ten Twitter users around the country, who had been picked by Twitter. Twitter's chief executive, Jack Dorsey, moderated the session. The president also answered questions in a town hall meeting on LinkedIn on September 26, 2011.

All the News is Niche

The fragmentation of the media has provided the White House opportunities to tap into the market for specialized news. For example, the Obama administration held regular question-and-answer Webcasts, "Open for Questions," with policy officials on White House. gov. In addition, the president granted interviews to websites that many in Washington largely ignore but that provide large, niche, online audiences, such as Zillow for housing or WebMD for health care news.

In early May 2014, Obama and his staff spent hours giving top weather forecasters the royal treatment—a briefing in the Roosevelt Room with multiple cabinet secretaries and senior officials. The subject was a major new report on climate change. The forecasters were even treated to Rose Garden interviews with the president. The White House's explanation for this outreach effort was that Americans have more trust in meteorologists than in political figures or the mainstream media when it comes climate change, so they hoped they could raise awareness and promote action through this kind of media event instead of a more traditional, mainstream, press affair.[22]

The White House also made special efforts to speak directly to the huge and politically powerful audience of Latinos. A multimedia public relations campaign pushing for an overhaul of the nation's immigration system—delivered in Spanish and in English daily—reached millions of Hispanics across the country. The president sat for six lengthy interviews on Telemundo and Univision in January, March, and May 2013. In addition, Cecilia Muñoz, the director of the White House domestic policy council, appeared on the networks regularly, and the president's weekly Internet address was matched each Saturday by a corresponding one in Spanish by an administration official. Online, the White House office of Hispanic media posted messages on Twitter in both English and Spanish from @lacasablanca, which attracted more than forty thousand followers.[23]

Localizing News Content

Local television news provided another opportunity for the Obama White House to reach the public. Nearly three-quarters of Americans watch local television news at least once a month, more than watch the network news.[24] Once the Washington press reports an issue, it tends to drop it and move on to the next one; however, repetition is necessary to convey the president's views to the generally inattentive public. Moreover, the Washington press tends to place more emphasis on support for, or opposition to, a program than on its substance, although the White House usually wants to communicate the latter. The Washington- and New York–based national media also have substantial resources to challenge White House versions of events and policies and to investigate areas of government not covered by briefings or press releases. To ameliorate these challenges, and to try to get their substance-based message through, modern White Houses are incentivized to cater to the local as well as the national media.

During the rollout for the Affordable Care Act in the autumn of 2013, Obama and members of his cabinet visited nine of the top ten cities with the highest concentration of the uninsured, while senior administration officials held almost daily conference calls with reporters in nearly a dozen states to challenge Republican governors who refused to expand Medicaid. They pointed out the consequences of such actions for the citizens of those states. Organizing for Action took a similar approach, holding protests—some attended by only a dozen or so people—that won coverage on the local pages of the nation's small-town newspapers.[25]

The Obama White House invited local editors, reporters, and news executives to Washington for exclusive interviews and briefings by the president and senior administration officials. Recent presidents have also arranged to be interviewed from the White House by television and radio stations through satellite hookups, and the White House provides briefings for the local press using the same technology. It also sends administration briefing teams around the country to discuss the president's policies with local media representatives and provides press releases, speeches, other documents, and audio clips for local media.

Contemporary presidents also meet frequently with journalists representing local media during their trips around the country. These efforts enable the White House to tailor unedited messages for specific groups and reach directly into the constituencies of members of Congress while reinforcing its policy message. Naturally, presidents hope to create goodwill and to receive a sympathetic hearing from journalists who are grateful for contact with the White House and, perhaps, susceptible to presidential charm. After all, unlike the White House press corps, which may be jaded by daily access to the president, local media who get the chance to interview the nation's commander in chief may very well see it as a once-in-a-lifetime experience.

There are limits to the utility of such efforts, however. Bill Clinton took office with an antagonistic attitude toward the national media, which he planned to bypass rather than use as part of his political strategy. As he told an audience of journalists shortly after taking office: "You know why I can stiff you on press conferences? Because [talk-show host] Larry King liberated me by giving me to the American people directly." After a rocky start in his press relations, Clinton's orientation changed. He found that he could not avoid the national press, which remains the primary source of news about the federal government. "I did not realize the importance of communications," he confessed, "and the overriding importance of what is on the evening television news. If I am not on there with a message, someone else is, with their message."[26]

Another problem is the diminishing number of local news outlets. The Pew Research Center reported in 2014 that one-fourth of the 952 US television stations that air newscasts do not produce their news programs. Additional stations have sharing arrangements wherein much of their content is produced outside their own newsroom, and such arrangements are increasing.[27]

The Insulated Audience

Although technology provides the theoretical potential for the White House to communicate more effectively to greater numbers of people, other features of that same environment create obstacles to successfully realizing that potential. According to Obama press official Reid Cherlin, "People are increasingly getting information from an atomized, partisan, choose-your-news smorgasbord, where you're as likely to process the State of the Union through your brother-in-law's Facebook rants, the tweets of a few favorite reporters, and the top 17 GIFs of Nancy Pelosi blinking as curated by BuzzFeed."[28]

Cherlin makes an important point. Americans increasingly read and view material that matches their political beliefs. Newspaper editorial pages always offered different takes on the news, but now cable news networks and an extraordinary range of websites do this as well. Moreover, the algorithms of search engines and social media guide people toward material that is likely to reinforce their views. Ideological insulation poses a new challenge for White House communications, a challenge that cannot be overcome by simply communicating in different venues.

The Web was an enormous asset for reaching young people in the 2008 campaign. By his second term, Obama was faced with an ideologically fragmented media that made it more difficult to reach the public. "In every year, this project gets harder, the media gets more disaggregated, people get more options to choose from, and they self-select outlets that speak to their preconceived notions," said Pfeiffer.[29]

Reaching the Base

On the positive side were those most committed to the president's programs. When the Obama White House texted to reach its supporters, it was preaching to the choir. Such communications are useful because, perhaps, the first rule in the politics of coalition building is solidifying the core. Moreover, committed congregants can be very helpful evangelists. The explosion of social media, the fragmentation of news, and the erosion of the institutional press not only provide ample opportunity for the expression of partisan views, but they also actively encourage it. As Rita Kirk so helpfully explains in chapter 2, backing your friends and belittling your enemies is a healthy business model, one rewarded by a torrent of clicks, retweets, likes, and links.

In early May 2014, Republicans used a newly released email to criticize the president on the administration's handling of the attack on the US diplomatic mission in Benghazi, Libya. However, the White House had plenty of help in answering critics. The *New Republic*'s Brian Beutler dismissed Benghazi as "nonsense." *Slate*'s David Weigel, along with the *Washington Post*'s *Plum Line* blog, debunked any claim that the new email was a smoking gun. *Media Matters for America* labeled Benghazi a hoax. *Salon* wrote that the GOP had a "demented Benghazi disease." Daily Kos featured the headline: "Here's Why the GOP Is Fired Up about Benghazi—and Here's Why They're Wrong." The *Huffington Post* offered "Three Reasons Why Reviving Benghazi Is Stupid—for the GOP."[30]

On issues ranging from health care reform to Syria, such aid was typical for Obama during his administration and likely will be for future administrations, as well. When critics attacked the president, progressive bloggers jumped to his defense. Moreover, they employed sharper arguments than did the White House. Although presidential administrations have relied on friendly opinion shapers since 1789, no other White House ever enjoyed the luxury of having its arguments and talking points advanced on a day-by-day, minute-by-minute basis. Obama did not have to wait for evening news or the morning op-ed page to make his case and answer his critics.

Naturally, the Obama White House was attentive to its blogging supporters. Although many in the White House press corps objected, it should not be surprising that the administration held off-the-record briefings, sometimes with Obama in the room, for select progressive bloggers from outlets such as *Talking Points Memo* and *ThinkProgress*. Moreover, the press pool that took turns covering the president up close included Web-only publications such as *Talking Points Memo*, the *Huffington Post*, BuzzFeed, and the *Daily Caller*.

Encountering Resistance

Widespread home broadband and mobile access to the Internet has created the potential for people to communicate easily with each other as well as to receive communications from leaders. Conservatives exploited this technology to reinforce their and Republicans' opposition to the Obama administration. Indeed, nothing served conservative organizers better than Barack Obama, whom they vilified as the devil incarnate. The fragmented news audience allowed Fox News and conservative radio hosts to dominate the cable and radio airwaves; in fact, since the 1990s the political right has been a much stronger force on radio than the political left. This ideological segmentation of the audience has allowed conservative discourse to go largely unanswered in many venues, which will not feature the president's responses. Moreover, conservatives employ the same range of videos, emails, tweets, and blogs as the White House and its supporters do. All of these developments make leading the public more difficult for the president.

Also important has been the potential for liberals to use the new technologies to oppose the president's pragmatism and tendencies toward moderation. Americans glory in the freedom to dissent that is at the heart of blogging. Even during the transition period in 2008, there were hints of conflict within the base. Candidate Obama allowed his supporters to wage an online revolt—on his own My-BarackObama.com website—over his vote in favor of legislation granting legal immunity to telecommunications firms that participated in the Bush administration's domestic wiretapping program. President-elect Obama, however, did not provide a forum for comments on his YouTube radio addresses, prompting grumbling among some that YouTube without comments was no different from radio.[31]

Internet users are unfailingly creative, however. The day after Obama announced that Rev. Rick Warren would deliver the opening prayer at his inauguration, a discussion forum focused on community service was filled with pages of comments from people opposing the choice rather than promoting its usual community service messages. In early January visitors to Change.gov, the transition website, voted a question about whether Obama would appoint a special prosecutor to investigate possible Bush administration war crimes to the top of the questions submitted to the new administration. Progressive websites blasted the new administration's efforts to dodge the issue. Within a day, MSNBC's Keith Olbermann picked up the story. A day later, Obama was compelled to answer the question in an interview with ABC's George Stephanopoulos, who quoted it and pressed Obama with two follow-ups. Obama's answer, which prioritized moving forward but did not rule out a special prosecutor, made the front page of the January 12 issue of the *New York Times*.

Dissent among progressives did not end with the transition. For example, MoveOn.org, one of Obama's staunchest supporters during the 2008 campaign, called on its members in April 2010 to telephone the White House and demand that Obama reinstate the ban on off-shore oil drilling that he had lifted.[32] And neither was MoveOn.org supportive of the president's more aggressive foreign policy actions; it also criticized him on everything from immigration to net neutrality.

Missing the Congregation

The Democratic choir is composed of true believers. However, they do not represent most of the Democratic congregation, and, as we have seen, sometimes the flock contains skeptics. Most of those pre-disposed to support the president rarely, if ever, view a White House video or watch a presidential interview on the Internet. A perusal of the official White House Channel on YouTube tells the story. Most videos have no more than a few thousand page views, and this in a nation of 320 million people. A study found that between May 2009 and November 2010, no video of the president's radio addresses had more than 100,000 views, and most had closer to 20,000.[33] Many more people receive White House emails and tweets, of course, but we know little about the effects of these messages. There is reason to be skeptical about their impact.

Mobilizing Supporters

Reaching people is useful for political leaders, but mobilizing them is better. David Plouffe's emphasis on helping the Obama adminis-tration pass legislation through grassroots efforts indicates a desire to use public backing to move Congress to support the president's program. According to Andrew Rasiej, cofounder of the Personal Democracy Forum, a nonpartisan website focused on the intersec-tion of politics and technology, Obama "created his own special interest group because the same people that made phone calls on behalf of him [in the campaign were] going to be calling or emailing their congressman." A Pew study during the transition found that among those who voted for Obama, 62 percent expected to ask oth-ers to support at least some of the new administration's policies.[34]

Plouffe did not take a formal role in the White House until 2011.

He did, however, remain as an advisor and began overseeing the president's sprawling grass roots political operation, which at the time boasted thirteen million email addresses, four million cell phone contacts, and two million active volunteers. More than half a million people completed surveys following the election to express their vision for the administration; another forty-two hundred hosted house parties in their communities. On January 17, 2009, Obama sent a YouTube video to supporters to announce plans to establish Organizing for America (OFA). The goal of OFA was to enlist community organizers throughout the country to support local candidates, lobby for the president's agenda, and remain connected to other supporters from the campaign. There was speculation that the organization could have an annual budget of seventy-five million dollars in privately raised funds and deploy hundreds of paid staff members. It was to operate from the Democratic National Committee headquarters, but with an independent structure, budget, and priorities. (By 2010, OFA had virtually supplanted the party structure. It sent about three hundred paid organizers to the states, several times the number the national party hired for the 2006 midterms.)[35]

During the transition, the Obama team drew on high-tech organizational tools to lay the groundwork for an attempt to restructure the US health care system. On December 3, 2008, former Democratic Senate majority leader Thomas Daschle, Obama's designee as secretary of Health and Human Resources and point person on health care, launched an effort to create political momentum when he held a conference call with one thousand invited supporters who had expressed interest in health issues, promising it would be the first of many opportunities for Americans to weigh in. In addition, there were online videos, blogs, and email alerts as well as traditional public forums. Thousands of people posted comments on health on Change.gov, the Obama transition website, which encouraged bloggers to share their concerns and offer their solutions regarding health care policy.[36]

According to Rasiej, "It will be a lot easier to get the American public to adopt any new health-care system if they were a part of the process of crafting it." Simon Rosenberg, president of the center-left think tank NDN, was more expansive: "This is the beginning of the reinvention of what the presidency in the 21st century could be. This will reinvent the relationship of the president to the American people in a way we probably haven't seen since FDR's use of radio in the 1930s."[37]

Democratic political consultant Joe Trippi took the argument a step further. He said, "Obama will be more directly connected to millions of Americans than any president who has come before him, and he will be able to communicate directly to people using the social networking and Web-based tools such as YouTube that his campaign mastered." He then added, "Obama's could become the most powerful presidency that we have ever seen." Ed Rollins, Republican strategist and the head of White House political operations under Ronald Reagan, agreed. "No one's ever had these kinds of resources. This would be the greatest political organization ever put together, *if it works.*"[38]

Organizing for America

Whether it would work was indeed the question. The Organizing for America (OFA) team held several dry runs to test the efficacy of their volunteer apparatus, including a call for supporters to hold "economic recovery house meetings" in February to highlight challenges presented by the recession. The house parties were designed to coincide with the congressional debate over Obama's stimulus package and had mixed results. Although OFA touted the thirty thousand responses the email drew from the volunteer community and the more than three thousand house parties thrown in support of the stimulus package, a report in McClatchy Company newspapers indicated that many events were sparsely attended.[39]

The first major engagement of OFA in the legislative process began on March 16, 2009. An email message was sent to volunteers, asking them to go door-to-door on March 21 to urge their neighbors to sign a pledge in support of Obama's budget plan. A follow-up message to the mailing list a few days later asked volunteers to call the Hill. A new online tool on the DNC/OFA website aided constituents in finding contact information for their congressional representatives so they could call the lawmakers' offices to voice approval of the proposal.

OFA reported that its door-to-door canvass netted about 100,000 pledge signatures, while another 114,000 signatures came in through its email network. Republicans scoffed at the effort, arguing that this proved that even the most die-hard Obama supporters were uncertain about the wisdom of the president's budget plan. Several GOP aides noted that the number of pledges gathered online amounted to less than 1 percent of the names on Obama's vaunted email list. The *Washington Post* reported that interviews with congressional aides from both parties found the signatures swayed few, if any, members of Congress.[40]

By June, OFA was the Democratic National Committee's largest department, with paid staff members in thirty-one states and control of the heavily trafficked campaign website. Public discourse on health care reform was focusing on the high costs and uncertain results of various proposals. Remembering the "Harry and Louise" television ads that served as the public face of the successful challenge to Bill Clinton's health reform efforts, the White House knew it had to regain momentum. Thus, the president emailed millions of campaign supporters, asking for donations to help them launch the White House's largest ever issues campaign. They also urged these same individuals to get ready to participate in "a coast-to-coast operation [and to be] ready to knock on doors, deploy volunteers, get out the facts," and to show Congress people wanted change. The DNC deployed dozens of staff members and hundreds of volunteers to thirty-one states to gather personal stories and build support.[41]

In late June, the DNC reported roughly three-quarters of a million people had signed a pledge in support of the president's core principles of reducing cost, ensuring quality, and providing choice, including a public insurance option; another half-million volunteered to help; and several hundred thousand provided their own story for the campaign's use. OFA posted thousands of personal stories online to humanize the debate and overcome criticism of the president's plan. It also trained hundreds of summer volunteers and released its first Internet advertisement: a Virginia man explaining that he lost his insurance when he lost his job. As the health care debate intensified in August, the president again turned to the OFA for support. Obama sent an email to OFA members: "This is the moment our movement was built for," he wrote. He also spent an hour providing bullet points for the health care debate during an Internet video. OFA asked its volunteers to visit congressional offices and flood town hall meetings in a massive show of support. There is no evidence that this show of strength ever materialized.[42]

By August, OFA reported paid political directors in forty-four states. Nevertheless, it had to moderate its strategy. In response to Democratic complaints to the White House about television commercials on health care, climate change, and other issues broadcast in an effort to pressure moderates to support the president's proposals, the group started running advertisements of appreciation. It also found that its events around the country were largely filled with party stalwarts rather than the army of volunteers mobilized by the 2008 campaign.[43]

Despite some success in generating letters, text messages, and phone calls on behalf of health care reform, OFA was not a prominent presence in 2009. In response to the lack of action, in 2010 organizers held hundreds of sessions across the nation intended to reengage the base from 2008.[44]

In a video to members of OFA in April 2010, Obama delivered an appeal. He urged his supporters to realize that the Democratic majority in Congress—and his agenda—depended on the role they would play in that year's midterm elections. The recorded message was part of a new effort by the Democratic National Committee to impress upon Democrats—particularly those occasional voters who were likely to cast ballots only in presidential races—the importance of the midterm elections for the House and Senate. However, the enthusiasm Obama hoped to generate mostly failed to materialize. The Democratic party went on to suffer historic congressional losses that November.

At the end of 2010, OFA launched a public relations offensive to demonstrate support for repealing the don't ask, don't tell policy. The group ran online advertisements and staged events in the home states of moderate Republican senators inclined to support the repeal bill. OFA volunteers delivered petitions with tens of thousands of signatures to wavering senators in an effort to build momentum for repeal—and to try to show them that they were safe politically if they voted to overturn the ban.[45]

Overall, however, OFA had to have been a disappointment to the White House. In the midterm elections, OFA tried to rally its network of millions of Obama supporters to help Democratic candidates across the country, but the group was not very successful. Aside from a handful of victories, such as Senate majority leader Harry Reid's reelection in Nevada, most OFA-backed candidates lost. The president also received help from an array of interest groups, such as Health Care for America Now, a progressive coalition that deployed 120 paid organizers to forty-three states, staged events, and launched ads in a number of states. So even where it seemed like OFA had been effective, its strength was moderate at best, part of a larger group effort.[46]

Organizing for Action

In 2013 the administration tried again. It named its grassroots operation Organizing for Action (also called OFA, for short. For clarity in this chapter we will call it OFA II.) and did not turn it over to the DNC. The president's campaign manager in 2012, Jim Messina, chaired the operation, and a small group of former campaign advisers oversaw it. The aim of the group was to promote the president's policies and give Democratic activists and other allies a way to rally behind his agenda.

OFA II had access to the Obama campaign's data on voters, including email addresses and social network information. In theory, OFA II had a grassroots army of 2.2 million volunteers and social media assets that included 33 million Facebook friends, 26 million Twitter followers, and 17 million email subscribers. As an outside group, OFA II could raise money, broadcast television ads, and otherwise run a political campaign on issues without running afoul of government guidelines that prohibit directly advocating for legislation. The president put it to work right away, running ads in the constituencies of thirteen Republican members of Congress on behalf of his proposal for background checks for gun purchasers.

On June 14, 2013, Organizing for Action mobilized more than a thousand people to attend nearly eighty public events around the country to commemorate the six-month anniversary of the December 2012 Newtown shooting incident. The group hosted scores of "action planning sessions" and celebrated events that earned local news coverage. It also hosted informational phone banks and collected 1.4 million signatures for a pro–gun control petition with the intent of pressuring Congress.[47]

On the day after the Senate voted down all efforts to strengthen gun control laws, OFA II executive director Jon Carson sent an email to the group's members vowing, "Those senators who decided that not crossing the gun lobby was more important than making our kids and communities safer—OFA II supporters will call them out and hold them accountable to their constituents."[48]

OFA II's pledge to punish senators presented a difficult test, given that many of the senators voting no were in deep-red states where Obama had lost badly. Nevertheless, there is little evidence of any success at all. As one reporter put it, "The group did not sway a single vote for the background check proposal, and was not able to make any of those who voted against it feel any heat." Even in states Obama carried handily, such as Ohio and New Hampshire, the group could not hold big rallies, blanket the airwaves with TV ads, or motivate enough supporters to match the volume of phone calls from progun advocates.[49]

More broadly, OFA II focused on promoting legislation on climate change, gun control, economic policy, and immigration in six states that Obama had won in 2012 but that were represented by at least one GOP senator: Illinois, Maine, Pennsylvania, New Hampshire, Ohio, and Nevada. It also targeted the red states of Arizona and Georgia, whose senators could be persuaded to back parts of the president's agenda, group officials said. OFA II planned to hold five hundred events focused on immigration by the end of May, and it also emphasized defending the Affordable Care Act and claimed to have held over three thousand community events in support of enrollment in the new health insurance exchanges.[50]

A study of January 30, 2009, to August 7, 2014, found that OFA II sent its members emails 180 times spanning that period, encouraging them to contact representatives regarding presidential priorities and engage in mass persuasion campaigns in their neighborhoods. There is little evidence that these emails led to any notable effect or consequence, although such impact is inherently difficult to measure. Most of the activity appeared to be in Democratic areas, and the scale of nearly all the activities appeared to be small. Even ardent Obama fans could not make a strong push for him on the off time from their regular jobs, and they lacked the resources to mount the kind of field or messaging operation that made the 2012 campaign effort so successful.[51]

By mid-2014, OFA II was telling its donors that it would stop requesting large contributions and began shedding much of its staff.[52] The promise of exploiting technology to mobilize supporters behind White House initiatives had yet to be realized.

Conclusion

Technological developments such as email, the ease of uploading videos and photos via YouTube and Flickr, and the growth of social media sites such as Facebook and Twitter have fundamentally changed the relationships among the president, the media, and the public. Reporters are no longer the only—or even necessarily the main—conduit through which news flows. Now the White House has the potential to bypass the press and communicate directly and appealingly with the public. Indeed, many of the authors in this book have made precisely this point.

These technological advancements offer the president opportunities to compensate for the declining audience for presidential messages over the traditional media. They also better position presidents to reinforce the views of those predisposed to support their policies. Reinforcing copartisans' views can be an advantage to the president, albeit a modest one.[53] Given available information, it is not possible to determine the contribution, if any, of the new media to the reinforcement of supporters' views. It is likely to be small, however. When a president reaches the public through media, most of that reach is to the most ardent and true believers, not to the broader pool of potential supporters. The most balanced conclusion is that the impact of the new media on the president's ability to govern is marginal.

To make matters worse for the president, audience fragmentation and ideological insulation make it difficult to reach the bulk of the population. Moreover, the opposition is able to exploit the same tools and audience characteristics to challenge the White House and reinforce the tendencies of its adherents. And in the unkindest cut of all, true believers among Democrats—those even further to the left of Obama in the cases I have presented in this chapter—often pushed back against the president's moderate tendencies. This made it even harder for the president to mobilize his supporters to pressure Congress for change.

Notes

1. Quoted in Reid Cherlin, "The Presidency and the Press," *Rolling Stone*, August 4, 2014.

2. Ibid.

3. Joe S. Foote, "Ratings Decline of Presidential Television," *Journal of Broadcasting and Electronic Media* 32 (Spring 1988): 225; Matthew A. Baum and Samuel Kernell, "Has Cable Ended the Golden Age of Presidential Television?" *American Political Science Review* 93 (March 1999): 99–114; Jeffrey E. Cohen, *The Presidency in the Era of 24-Hour News* (Princeton, NJ: Princeton University Press, 2008); *Washington Post*, March 1, 2001, C1.

4. Baum and Kernell, "Has Cable Ended the Golden Age?"; Markus Prior, "News vs. Entertainment: How Increasing Media Choice Widens Gaps in Political Knowledge and Turnout," *American Journal of Political Science* 49 (July 2005): 577–92.

5. Paul Brace and Barbara Hinckley, "Presidential Activities from Truman through Reagan: Timing and Impact," *Journal of Politics* 55 (May 1993): 387; Lori Cox Han, "New Strategies for an Old Medium: The Weekly Radio Addresses of Reagan and Clinton," *Congress & the Presidency* 33 (Spring 2006): 25–45; Beverly Horvit, Adam J. Schiffer, and Mark Wright, "The Limits of Presidential Coverage of the Weekly Radio Address," *Press/Politics* 13, no. 1 (2008): 8–28.

6. "The State of the News Media 2014," Pew Research Center, Journalism and Media, March 26, 2014, http://www.journalism.org/packages/state-of-the-news-media-2014/.

7. Ibid.

8. Nielsen, Newswire, November 14, 2008, http://www.nielsen.com/us/en/insights/news/2008/election-gives-online-news-sites-major-traffic-boost.html; "State of the News Media 2014"; "News Use Across Social Media Platforms," Pew Research Center, Journalism and Media, November 14, 2013, http://www.journalism.org/2013/11/14/news-use-across-social-media-platforms/; "In Changing News Landscape, Even Television is Vulnerable," Pew Research Center, US Politics and Policy, September 27, 2012, http://www.people-press.org/2012/09/27/in-changing-news-landscape-even-television-is-vulnerable/.

9. Cherlin, "Presidency and the Press."

10. Helene Cooper, "The Direct Approach," *New York Times*, December 18, 2008.

11. Quoted in Sheryl Gay Stolberg, "A Rewired Bully Pulpit: Big, Bold and Unproven," *New York Times*, November 22, 2008.

12. Ibid.

13. Chris Cillizza, "Obama Makes a Point of Speaking of the People, to the People," *Washington Post*, December 14, 2008, A5.

14. Virginia Heffernan, "The YouTube Presidency—Why the Obama Administration Uploads So Much Video," *New York Times*, April 12, 2009; Brian Stelter, "Obama

to Field Questions Posted by YouTube Users," *New York Times*, February 1, 2010.

15. Quoted in Zachary A. Goldfarb and Juliet Eilperin, "White House Looking for New Ways to Penetrate Polarized Media," *Washington Post*, May 6, 2014.

16. Ibid.

17. Jonathan Alter, *The Promise: President Obama, Year One* (New York: Simon & Schuster, 2010), 278; "Celebrating 5 Million @WhiteHouse Twitter Followers," White House, Blog, July 11, 2014, www.whitehouse.gov/blog/2014/07/11/celebrating-5-million-whitehouse-twitter-followers.

18. Kate Phillips, "Obama Rallies the Base on His Supreme Court Choice," *CQ Today*, May 27, 2009; Oliver Knox, "When the White House Hates Your Tweet," *Yahoo! News*, May 1, 2014.

19. Mark Landler and Helene Cooper, "White House Eager to Project Image of Competence in Relief Efforts," *New York Times*, January 22, 2010.

20. See, for example, Ken Auletta, "Non-Stop News," *New Yorker*, January 25, 2010, 44.

21. Michael A. Fletcher and Jose Antonio Vargas, "The White House, Open for Questions," *Washington Post*, March 27, 2009, A2; Sheryl Gay Stolberg, "Obama Makes History in Live Internet Video Chat," *New York Times*, March 27, 2009.

22. Goldfarb and Eilperin, "White House Looking for New Ways."

23. Michael D. Shear, "White House Focuses on Reaching Latino Viewers," *New York Times*, July 16, 2013.

24. "State of the News Media 2014."

25. Carrie Budoff Brown and Reid J. Epstein, "White House Targets Local Media on Obamacare," *Politico*, November 26, 2013.

26. Quoted in Bob Woodward, *The Agenda: Inside the Clinton White House* (New York: Simon and Schuster, 1994), 313.

27. "State of the News Media 2014."

28. Cherlin, "Presidency and the Press."

29. Quoted in Goldfarb and Eilperin, "White House Looking for New Ways."

30. James Oliphant, "Progressive Bloggers Are Doing the White House's Job," *National Journal*, May 9, 2014.

31. Stolberg, "Rewired Bully Pulpit."

32. Michael D. Shear, "Campaign Urges Reinstating Ban on Offshore Oil Drilling," *Washington Post*, April 30, 2010.

33. Elham Khatami, "Who Listens to Obama's Addresses?" Congress.org, November 8, 2010, accessed August 2, 2015.

34. Rasiej quoted in Stolberg, "Rewired Bully Pulpit"; Aaron Smith, "Post-Election Voter Engagement," Pew Internet and American Life Project, 2008 Post-Election Survey, December 8, 2008, http://www.pewinternet.org/2008/12/30/post-election-voter-engagement/.

35. Lois Romano, "'08 Campaign Guru Focuses on Grass Roots," *Washington Post*, January 13, 2009, A13; Peter Wallsten, "Retooling Obama's Campaign Machine for the Long Haul," *Los Angeles Times*, January 14, 2009; Associated Press, "Obama Launches Grass-Roots Campaign," January 17, 2009; Matt Bai, "Democrat in Chief?" *New York Times Sunday Magazine*, June 13, 2010.

36. Ceci Connolly, "Obama Policymakers Turn to Campaign Tools; Network of Supporters Tapped on Health-Care Issues," *Washington Post*, December 4, 2008, A1.

37. Rosenberg quoted in ibid.

38. Trippi quoted in Cillizza, "Obama Makes a Point"; Rollins quoted in Wallsten, "Retooling Obama's Campaign Machine" (emphasis added).

39. Chris Cillizza, "Obama Enlists Campaign Army in Budget Fight," *Washington Post*, March 16, 2009, A1.

40. Dan Eggen, "Obama's Machine Sputters in Effort to Push Budget: Grass-Roots Campaign Has Little Effect," *Washington Post*, April 6, 2009, A3.

41. Peter Slevin, "Obama Turns to Grass Roots to Push Health Reform," *Washington Post*, June 24, 2009.

42. Ibid.; Eli Saslow, "Grass-Roots Battle Tests the Obama Movement," *Washington Post*, August 23, 2009.

43. Jeff Zeleny, "Health Debate Fails to Ignite Obama's Grass Roots," *New York Times*, August 15, 2009.

44. Alter, *The Promise*, 252, 398; Amy Gardner, "Midterms Pose Major Challenge for Obama's Grass-Roots Political Organization," *Washington Post*, March 28, 2010.

45. Philip Rucker, "Obama Mobilizes Volunteers to Urge Repeal of 'Don't Ask, Don't Tell'," *Washington Post*, December 17, 2009.

46. Ibid.; Slevin, "Obama Turns to Grass Roots."

47. Adam Aigner-Treworgy, "First on CNN: OFA Collects 1.4 Million Signatures for Gun Control," CNN, PoliticalTicker (blog), May 7, 2013, http://politicalticker.blogs.cnn.com/2013/05/07/first-on-cnn-ofa-collects-1-4-million-signatures-for-gun-control/.

48. Jon Carson, "What Do You Have to Say to Congress?" *Organizing for Action*, April 18, 2013.

49. Reid J. Epstein, "OFA's First Foray Falls Short," *Politico*, May 3, 2013.

50. Juliet Eilperin, "Organizing for Action Struggles to Move the Needle on Obama's Agenda," *Washington Post*, May 11, 2013; Philip Bump, "How Much Longer Will Organizing for Action Survive?" *Washington Post*, May 20, 2014.

51. Jonathan Kingler, "Going Private: Presidential Grassroots Lobbying Organizations, Targeted Appeals, and Neighborhood Persuasion Campaigns," paper presented at the annual meeting of the American Political Science Association, Washington, DC, August 27–31, 2014; Philip Bump, "Organizing for Action Wanted Us to Evaluate Them on Their Work. So We Did," *Washington Post*, July 30, 2014; Epstein, "OFA's First Foray Falls Short."

52. Bump, "How Much Longer?"

53. George C. Edwards III, "Presidential Influence on Partisans' Opinion," paper presented at the annual meeting of the Midwest Political Science Association, Chicago, April 18, 2015.

Ignoring the President

Barack Obama and the Postrhetorical Presidency

JENNIFER R. MERCIECA

On November 20, 2014, President Barack Obama addressed the nation about the controversial new immigration policy that one commentator called, "the biggest piece of immigration reform since Obama took office and . . . the boldest use of his executive power to date." Immigration policy had been on the nation's agenda for the past several years, and opinion polls repeatedly showed that Americans considered immigration reform to be a pressing issue facing the nation. With a presidential address scheduled announcing a key policy change on an issue requiring urgent action, we would expect that television network news organizations, in their role as watchdogs over the government, would be poised to offer their viewers not only the address, but also insightful commentary from their veteran political correspondents as well as rebuttals and extensions from the two major parties. But they did not. That night, the Americans who were eager to see news about the president's reforms turned their televisions to the Spanish-language channel Univision and to all-news channels such as Fox News and CNN, because ABC, NBC, and CBS chose to show their viewers not the president's address, but *Grey's Anatomy*, *The Biggest Loser*, and, of course, *The Big Bang Theory*.[1]

Why would television networks choose to ignore a major policy announcement made by the president of the United States? Several explanations are possible. For example, some have explained that the decision was based upon economic considerations: the networks couldn't afford to give their precious airtime to the president during November Sweeps Week. Some believed more conspiratorial explanations: the Obama administration prevented the networks from carrying the president's speech because Obama's new immigration plan is part of a plot to destroy America. Still others may believe that the decision was simply prudent: since presidential rhetoric doesn't matter much, networks can easily, and perhaps wisely, ignore presidential speech making, especially when such speeches interfere with popular programming.[2]

I argue that the decision to ignore the president on November 20, 2014, is an artifact of the postrhetorical presidency and signals a major shift in the relationship between the presidency and the press. Scholars of presidential leadership have traditionally worked within the paradigm of the rhetorical presidency, which is an institutional argument about the way that presidents have sought to lead the public by "going over the heads of Congress" to speak directly to the people. The rhetorical presidency model made good sense within the traditional media market of the twentieth century, but it makes little sense within the new media market of the new millennium. If during the era of the rhetorical presidency presidents upset the balance and separation of powers by using traditional news media to speak directly to the people in an effort to get the people to put pressure on Congress to enact the president's agenda, then during the era of the postrhetorical presidency presidents use social media to go over the heads of Congress and around the news filter to speak directly to supporters. The era of the rhetorical presidency was characterized by a relationship between the presidency and the press that was reciprocal, mutually beneficial, and stable; the era of the postrhetorical presidency is characterized by a relationship between the presidency and the press that is independent, competitive, and unstable. Like the rhetorical presidency model of presidential leadership, the postrhetorical presidency model is grounded in an institutional argument: the relationship between the press and the president that characterized the era of the rhetorical presidency has fundamentally changed. In this chapter, I attempt to make sense of that institutional change. While, as Stephen Hartnett and I have argued, the postrhetorical presidency began with the Bush administration, I believe that it flourished with the Obama administration's expert use of social and new media.[3]

Understanding the postrhetorical presidency helps us to make sense of the shift from columns to characters. In considering the implications of this shift I argue that while the postrhetorical presidency enabled the Obama administration to disseminate and control its message, it likely also prevented the press from acting as a watchdog over the government. In pursuit of this thesis, I first describe the reciprocally dependent relationship between the press and the president that characterized the rhetorical presidency (a context within which the networks could not have ignored the president's speech) before describing how the Obama administration managed the rollout of the immigration speech announcement, and finally, I analyze the features of the postrhetorical presidency. The immigration speech thus provides us with an excellent example of the way the relationship between the press and the president has changed with the shift from columns to characters.

The Reciprocal Relationship between the Press and the President

Perhaps the dirtiest insult in the early republic was to accuse a statesman of ambition. Ambition meant being self-serving, conniving, and most certainly not fit for leadership.[4] Rather than risk the semblance of ambition, leaders of the founding generation sought to cultivate, like Cincinnatus, disinterest in governing: one governed because one was called to serve his fellows by his fellows; one risked reputation and financial status to govern; one never sought power, but only begrudgingly accepted it because one's primary concern was the public good; and one gave power away as quickly as one could. Such a one never made speeches to gain office. To do so would be to give the lie to one's performance in emulation of Cincinnatus. Rather, one's friends wrote letters to other friends, urging them to urge you to lead; political power was thus left to be a negotiation among the nation's wealthy elite. And so after serving, one would occasionally retire to one's estate to rest until called again to serve.

The twin pressures of soldiers returning home at the conclusion of the War of 1812 and westward expansion forced states to remove their restrictive property qualifications for voting and extend the right of suffrage to all white males in the 1820s. One effect of the new voters was the rise of political parties to organize political opinion through party newspapers such as the *United States Telegraph* and the *Washington Globe* between 1824 and 1828. A second effect of the increase in voters was that politicians no longer aspired to Cincinnatus-like disinterest, but instead actively courted voters with election-day barbecues, promises of political spoils, and well-organized political campaigns. Political candidates even occasionally made speeches to the public in the nineteenth century. However, political scientists such as Jeffrey Tulis do not detect the emergence of the rhetorical presidency until Teddy Roosevelt or perhaps Woodrow Wilson. By the turn of the twentieth century, presidents used then-emergent mass media in the form of newspapers, phonograph records, and radio to go over the heads of Congress to speak directly to the people. According to Tulis, the rhetorical presidency was a "second constitution" that forever changed the relationship between the branches of government as well as the relationship between the president and the people. Mass media helped to elevate the president to the center of America's political system, which, of course, was never the intention of constitutional architect James Madison.[5]

The era of the rhetorical presidency, roughly the entirety of the twentieth century, was the halcyon days of the relationship between the press and the president. By that I do not mean that the press and the president had a happy relationship, or that either side of the relationship was perfectly satisfied. I mean that each side needed the other and, as such, the relationship between the press and the presidency was reciprocal, mutually beneficial, and stable. Without the cooperation of the press there would be no rhetorical presidency; likewise, without the cooperation of the White House there would be little news of the president for the press to cover. The press generally acted as an information conduit between presidents and the public, and presidents generally gave the press information, access, and interviews in return for the press's disseminating information on their behalf.

We can say that the relationship between the presidency and the press during the era of the rhetorical presidency was reciprocal, mutually beneficial, and stable without approaching it uncritically.

Indeed, there is much to criticize in the partnership that resulted in what Daniel Boorstin famously described as news reporting dominated by the pseudoevent in American politics. A pseudoevent, according to Boorstin, was an event like an interview or photo opportunity or press conference that was "planted primarily (not always exclusively) for the immediate purpose of being reported or reproduced. Therefore, its occurrence [was] arranged for the convenience of the reporting or reproducing media." News reporting dominated by pseudoevents required an immense amount of cooperation—and trust—between the presidency and the press. The president and his staff cooperated to provide the pseudoevents for media consumption, and the media, in turn, provided the conduit to the mass public for the pseudoevents to be broadcast. Indeed, according to Jeffrey Tulis, "The modern mass media . . . facilitated the development of the rhetorical presidency by giving the president the means to communicate directly and instantaneously to a large national audience, and by reinforcing the shift from written message to verbal dramatic performance." To understand the rhetorical presidency, therefore, is to understand how the press and the president cooperated to produce the news. During the era of the rhetorical presidency the press elevated the president to the center of the nation's political imagination by ceaselessly covering presidential pseudoevents and allowing the president to speak to the nation largely unfiltered. In return, the press gained access to the president and content for its news reports.[6]

The rhetorical presidency was beneficial for the president because the relationship enabled the media, and particularly the White House press corps, to elevate the president to the center of the nation's political imagination, decentering Congress in the process. There is, of course, a chicken-and-egg problem in arguing whether the press caused the president to decenter Congress or whether the press's paying more attention to the president and less attention to Congress was an effect of the rising importance of the president relative to Congress. Nevertheless, it is clear, as Tulis notes, "no other institution or personality is given as much attention by television or newspapers. In the nineteenth century, on the other hand, newspaper coverage of Congress exceeded that of the president."[7]

For example, "no ruler or chief executive of any country in the world is as thoroughly and consistently covered by the press as the

President of the US," reported *Life* magazine in 1951. "About a dozen reporters do full-time duty at the White House and often more than 200 show up for his weekly press conference. Harry Truman keeps the regulars very busy, starting to make news at 7:00 a.m. when he goes for his walk, and keeps at it until well past midnight."[8]

In the mid-twentieth century President Truman found the press useful and so gave it information and access. Indeed, how could a president not give the press access? By 1969 "at the height of their dominance, the combined audience for the three [network] newscasts accounted for three-fourths of all American households."[9] During the twentieth century the power of the press matched the power of the president, which led to a reciprocal, mutually beneficial, and stable partnership between the two. In short, the two needed one another, and this relationship was thought to benefit the public good. For example, in April 1961, just after the Bay of Pigs invasion of Cuba, President John F. Kennedy argued that "without debate, without criticism, no Administration and no country can succeed—and no republic can survive. That . . . is why our press was protected by the First Amendment—the only business in America specifically protected by the Constitution—not primarily to amuse and entertain, not to emphasize the trivial and the sentimental, not to simply "give the public what it wants"—but to inform, to arouse, to reflect, to state our dangers and our opportunities, to indicate our crises and our choices, to lead, mold, educate and sometimes even anger public opinion." And so the press did.[10]

The press enlarged the power of the president's bully pulpit to be sure, but post-Watergate–era media became increasingly antagonistic toward presidential candidates and presidents. The beginning of the end of the rhetorical presidency was first, perhaps, cable's twenty-four-hour news cycle, which required new news every thirty minutes, even if there was nothing new to say. Then, in addition to "horserace reporting"—in which the press focused more on who is ahead and who is behind than it did on policy platforms and issues—in 1992 we saw the rise of fact-check journalism, in which reporters took nothing candidates or presidents said as true, which threatened the positive working relationship between the press and the president. And then finally, the emergence of the Internet, with its bottom up information dissemination, meant that anyone and everyone could be a reporter and a news network (so long as they had an audience), which threatened the press's exclusive power to disseminate the news.[11] At the close of the twentieth century the president could no longer count on the press to help him disseminate his message. For example, in 1968 the average duration of a candidate's sound bite on network news broadcasts was over sixty seconds long; by 2004 the average sound bite was a mere 7.7 seconds. "Like any period of tumultuous change," President Obama's former communications director Anita Dunn explained to Reid Cherlin in Rolling Stone, "it's not a happy one. . . . This idea that somehow there's a bully pulpit that can be used effectively to communicate with everybody in this country at the same time and get them all wrapped around one issue—it's very much an idea whose time has passed."[12]

Today we are in the era of the postrhetorical presidency. If the rhetorical presidency was characterized by a reciprocal, mutually beneficial, and stable relationship between the press and the president, then the postrhetorical presidency is characterized by an independent, competitive, and unstable relationship. For example, let's consider how the press and the president handled the news of President Obama's November 20, 2014, immigration speech.

The Immigration Speech Roll-Out, November 19, 2014

President Obama's new immigration policy was controversial: the president planned to announce on November 20, 2014, that he was going to act unilaterally to protect five million undocumented immigrants from deportation. It was a bold step to resolve a seemingly intractable impasse between Obama and a Republican-controlled Congress. The White House sought to manage the news of President Obama's upcoming immigration speech carefully in order to present its case for immigration reform in as unfiltered a way as possible: on November 19, 2014, at 11:59 a.m. eastern time, the White House posted a one-minute video of President Obama with a caption that read, "It's time to fix our broken immigration system. Tomorrow night, President Obama will address the nation on new common sense steps he's taking to fix as much of it as he can. Tune in tomorrow at 8 p.m. ET."[13] Almost an hour later, at 12:51 p.m., Barack Obama's personal Facebook page (run by Organizing for Action) shared the White House's video. At the time this book went to press, the video had been viewed 4,366,904 times and shared more than 58,000 times from Barack Obama's two Facebook accounts alone.

At 12:04 p.m. the White House tweeted President Obama's video and speech announcement, linking to the White House Facebook post. The White House tweet was retweeted 1,064 times. At 1:00 p.m., in addition to a page explaining the history of immigration reform, data infographics, a petition and pledge to watch the speech, and so on linked by the original Facebook post, the White House blog also posted Obama's video along with content that readers could use to learn more about Obama's positions, stay informed of future action, and commit to watching the speech and spreading the news to their friends and followers on their social networks. At 1:08 p.m. Barack Obama's personal Twitter account (also run by Organizing for Action) tweeted a link to the White House blog post. It was retweeted 1,261 times. The hashtags #immigration and #immigrationaction trended on Twitter throughout the next twenty-four hours, and there was a massive spike in Google searches for the phrase *immigration reform*.[14]

At 1:03 p.m. the Democratic Senatorial Campaign Committee sent via its email list a "breaking news alert" to its supporters informing them of President Obama's planned speech and urging them to sign a petition or donate to help the cause.[15] Emails issued forth from Organizing for Action, the White House, Moveon.org, and Democratic National Committee headquarters and were signed by Jim Messina, Abby Witt, Astrid Silva, Eden James, Jon Carson, Helen Chavez, and even Barack Obama himself. The emails continued throughout the next forty-eight hours, reminding supporters to watch the speech, tell their friends, and take action.

And finally, at 1:12 p.m., White House Press Secretary Josh Earnest held a press briefing with members of the White House press corps. Earnest began, "As you saw just a little over an hour ago, the White House posted a video to the White House Facebook page, where the President announced that he is going to deliver an address to the nation tomorrow night where he will be laying out the details of his executive action to repair our broken immigration system."

Fox News White House correspondent Wendell Goler interrupted Earnest by asking, "Is that a thank-you to Zuckerberg? Was that a thank-you to Zuckerberg, announcing it [on Facebook]?" Earnest responded that announcing the speech thus gave President Obama the opportunity "to reach hundreds of thousands, if not millions of people. In under an hour, the video reached more than 1.2 million users on Facebook; 227,000 people have viewed it and another 12,000 people have shared it. So this is a pretty effective way of the President communicating with the American public." At the conclusion of the press briefing, *National Journal* White House correspondent George Condon followed up on the method of announcement: "You said, announcing this on Facebook was effective because he reached 1.5 million people. You believe that . . . you reached more people than if you had announced it to the wires, the networks and the press corps?" Press Secretary Earnest responded, "In the first hour. Pretty impressive, George, right? The good news is that the wires and the networks and the press corps are all on Facebook. And I noticed that even one of the networks, shortly after the video was posted to Facebook, actually broadcast it on their network. So the good news, George, is that we don't have to choose." Indeed, the first to tweet the news of Obama's speech with the #immigrationaction hashtag was *Roll Call* managing editor Cameron Easley, who tweeted the news just six minutes after the Facebook post, at 12:05 p.m. Easley confirmed that he had learned of President Obama's planned speech from the White House Facebook page.[16]

Perhaps the White House did not "have to choose" between breaking the news of the president's speech on social media or through traditional media, but broadcasters did have a choice about whether to preempt their prime-time programming to show the speech. At 8:00 p.m. on November 20, 2014, President Obama addressed the nation on immigration reform to a television viewing audience of about 12.4 million, which was about a third of the size of his State of the Union address of the previous January. CNN, MSNBC, Fox News, and Univision carried the speech, but the traditional broadcast networks did not (although some local affiliates did). Over on social media President Obama's speech caused the hashtags #immigration and #immigrationaction to trend on Twitter and elicited as many as 9,580 tweets per minute by the conclusion of the speech, which means that discussion of the speech dominated Twitter for that period of time.[17]

The Independent Relationship between the Press and the Presidency

While some decried the "Network News' Shameful Decision to Snub Obama's Immigration Address," as it turns out the Obama administration did not actually make a formal request to the networks to preempt their scheduled programming, although it did ask Univision to do so.[18] One version of the story of what transpired on November 19 is that the Obama administration "put out feelers" to the networks to see if they would run his speech and, finding little interest, decided to announce the speech via social media and not request the network airtime. Another version of the story is that the networks feared that the speech was "too political" to warrant disrupting scheduled programming and so refused.[19]

Whether the Obama administration snubbed the press by making its own announcement or whether the press snubbed the Obama administration by refusing to preempt their popular programming matters little. What matters is that the story of the immigration speech rollout demonstrates the independent, competitive, and unstable relationship between the press and the president that characterizes the postrhetorical presidency. Rather than cooperate to disseminate information to the public, it is clear that the White House and the press now compete for audience attention. It is clear, in other words, that the institutional relationship that facilitated the rhetorical presidency is broken and that the rhetorical presidency is dead.

Scholars such as Susan Herbst and Stephen Heidt have recently argued that the rhetorical presidency model has not withstood the test of time and that, in particular, the model suffers from changes wrought by new media. As I explain below, and as we saw with the example of the immigration speech rollout, new media have transformed how presidential rhetoric functions. According to Herbst, media "now wreak havoc with the text of a presidential speech" by endlessly slicing it up into sounds bites and by reconstructing and recirculating texts in ways that are beyond the control of the president. Herbst argues that presidents can no longer count on a stable audience, or even knowing "where the audience might be located. . . . [Jeffrey] Tulis has us sitting still, listening to the president speak from the back of a train car long ago, or on our couches in rapt attention, half a century back. These days, however, few are rapt." Further, in today's media environment it is difficult to tell who is speaking; indeed, "statements on behalf of the president can be made by anyone (whether they are legitimate and approved is another story), [and] presidential rhetoric can be hacked up and revised."[20]

Likewise, Stephen Heidt argues that the new media environment means that presidents now face the "utter fragmentation" of the electorate: "this altered scene poses a challenge for presidents and critics because presidential messages are more fragmented than ever, audience reception more partial, and the persuasive task of presidential speech near impossible."[21] We can think of these critiques of how the rhetorical presidency functions within the new media environment of the twenty-first century as being characterized by fragmented texts, unstable audiences, and phantom authors. If these critiques are accurate, and it appears that they are, then any president would have difficulty reaching the public, especially if media no longer willingly help the president to disseminate his (or someday her) messages.

The postrhetorical presidency emerged within this new media context in an attempt to overcome the obstacles of fragmentation and the impossibility of presidential leadership. As George Edwards noted in the previous chapter, "Technological developments such as email, the ease of uploading videos and photos via YouTube and Flickr, and the growth of social media sites such as Facebook and Twitter have fundamentally changed the relationship among the president, the media, and the public. Reporters are no longer the only—or even necessarily the main—conduit through which news flows. Now the White House has the potential to bypass the press and communicate directly and appealingly with the public."[22] President Obama admitted as much in July 2015, when he told Jon Stewart, "It's tough to get everybody's attention focused in the same way [as it used to be] and so, what that means is that on big tough issues, sometimes it's hard to get the entire nation's attention focused on it and we've been operating on soundbites, but look, part of my job and part of the job of everybody in the White House is, how do we adapt to this new environment? How are we more nimble? How are we dealing with social media? How do we deal more effectively?"

From Obama's perspective then, the postrhetorical presidency emerged as a way to address the problem of fragmented media audiences of the twenty-first century. Of course there is more to the story of the emergence of the postrhetorical presidency than Obama's neutral characterization would suggest. In fact, the postrhetorical presidency is a fundamental part of the permanent campaign and the hyperrhetorical practices of presidential public relations.[23] We can better understand the postrhetorical presidency by examining how Obama's campaign team handled media during the 2008 and 2012 election campaign cycles. I argue that we can trace Obama's enactment of the postrhetorical presidency in the case of the immigration speech to his presidential campaign communications practices, which were characterized by (1) strict message control, (2) going around the news filter by speaking directly to supporters, and (3) using social media to create intimacy between the president and his followers and counting on them to spread messages virally, knowing that messages that spread from friends are more persuasive than messages that come from campaigns, media, or the administration.

The increasing antagonism between the media and political candidates in the post-Watergate era was characterized by decreasing airtime for candidates, increased attention to the election horserace, process stories over substance stories, and feeding frenzies about private issues. In response, postrhetorical candidates have sought ever greater control over their campaign messages. "It was like the Wild West out there," explained Obama's 2008 chief communications officer Anita Dunn on the media's failure to report on substantive issues: "Part of the reputation we got for being such control freaks was because we simply were trying to control the things we could control." Obama's strategy for dealing with the media in the 2008 election campaign was "to force the media to actually cover the campaign on our terms. We had a reputation, to some extent deserved, for a level of discipline. . . . Part of that was the decision we made that we would force the coverage to our campaign events, to the things the campaign did, and we would not talk about anything else." Such campaign discipline, as Dunn noted, "was a source of great conflict between us and our press corps. They complained continually about accessibility."[24]

In the 2012 reelection campaign, according to Deputy Campaign Manager Stephanie Cutter, Obama likewise "used every communication tool on the campaign to communicate our message in a very disciplined way. We weren't out to win a news cycle, unless it fit into our message. If it didn't fit into our message, we were going to communicate what we wanted to communicate in different modes of communication." The Obama campaign refused to allow the press to dictate the tempo of the news and denied it the framing and priming functions that have made it so powerful by essentially ignoring and sidestepping traditional news media. By the 2012 election Obama's communications team had perfected the direct communication strategies that they had begun to develop during the 2008 campaign. By 2012, as Cutter noted, the Obama campaign attempted to control its message by using "different modes of communication" to go around the news filter entirely. The need for strict message control is, of course, not limited to the 2008 and 2012 elections. Indeed, the Obama administration's use of postrhetorical communication techniques is a direct consequence of its continued desire "to control the things we could control."[25]

One of the most noteworthy aspects of Obama's 2008 campaign was its massive scale and its ability to use its size to create its own communication network, which it used to control its message. Not only did Obama hire "by far the largest full-time paid staff in presidential campaign history," but his estimated six million unpaid volunteers, his five million social media followers, and his "13-million member" email list not only dwarfed that of opponent Senator John McCain, but also easily made candidate Barack Obama the most connected person in the world in 2008. As Chief Communications Officer Anita Dunn explained, the campaign used its massive reach to communicate its most important news announcements—withdrawing from the public finance system, selecting Joe Biden as the vice-presidential nominee, and choosing Invesco Field for Obama's nomination acceptance speech—directly to supporters who had signed up for text and email messages—before releasing the information through traditional news media. Obama perfected the direct communication strategy that would become the signature technique

of the postrhetorical presidency during the 2008 campaign by sending out "1 billion emails, including 10,000 unique messages targeted
at specific segments of their 13-million member list."[26]

By 2012, President Obama had expanded his network with thirty
million more Facebook followers and twenty-two million more twitter followers than he had in 2008. "Given our challenges in dealing with the [traditional news] media," recalled Deputy Campaign
Manager Stephanie Cutter, "we saw an opportunity to go around
that filter and directly to our supporters and those that we needed
to persuade, which was a much more valuable communication to
them than reading something in a newspaper." Yet, according to
Reid Cherlin in *Rolling Stone*, while Obama's direct communication
strategies were "a clever ploy to get the supporters to sign up for
text alerts," they were "also a clear 'fuck you' to the press, a very
public way of cutting them out of the relationship between Obama
and the voters." Indeed, according to Anita Dunn, "the campaign
went out of its way to let the press know we were communicating
around them."[27]

Once in office, Obama converted "the President's bully pulpit
into a social pulpit," according to public relations specialist Monte
Lutz. Obama's communications team crafted messages that were
"designed to be taken up and spread by others . . . harnessing the
power of public engagement to influence the conversation across
various spheres of cross-influence." Obama had learned of the power
of his increasingly massive social media network during the 2012
campaign, and, according to Stephanie Cutter, one of the key strategies of the reelection campaign was to count on that network to
spread messages virally. "We had 33 million people on Facebook
following Barack Obama," explained Cutter: "Those 33 million were
friends with 90 percent of Facebook users in the United States, more
than 90 percent. So we could communicate with 90 percent of Facebook users in this country, which in sum total is more than the people
that voted for us." The campaign had found that supporters trusted
messages that they received from their friends via social networks
more than they trusted messages coming from campaigns directly,
from traditional media, or from other sources. Cutter explained that
the networking power of social media enabled the campaign to run
"ward races online among Facebook friends, online followers, [and]

YouTube." Essentially, the massive Obama reelection campaign used social networking to run a "very localized, personalized" campaign, which "proved to be very effective, not just in getting people to vote for us but getting people to work for us to get that vote out."[28]

Cultivating intimacy, rather than mere information dissemination, between the president and the people is the third key strategy of the postrhetorical presidency. Obama's reelection networking strategy worked because "people really want to feel like they're part of a community," explained 2008 Democratic National Committee director of communications Karen Finney; "engaging people, and making them feel like they're getting a little bit of an inside look into the campaign or they're really a part of something bigger will make you far more successful." Obama's supporters felt more connected to Obama through social media and so were willing to pass along their "friend" Barack Obama's news and information to their other friends, which, of course, enabled Obama's campaign to spread virally rather than relying on traditional news streams. Obama's postrhetorical media strategies take advantage of voters' expectations for online content "to be delivered in an unprecedented niche, tailored, authentic, and interactive format. A format in which their favorite stars share every aspect of their life," according to political consultant Vincent Harris. Social media audiences, says Harris, have an "expectation of transparency in the highest form," and the postrhetorical presidency cultivates parasocial relationships between the president and the people, circumventing traditional media in the process. Did President Obama gain from cultivating intimate relationships with Americans through social media? Perhaps. Did traditional media lose from Obama's cultivating intimate relationships with Americans through social media? Most certainly.[29]

Conclusion

In considering how the relationship between the press and the presidency has changed with the shift from columns to characters, I have argued that we have entered into the era of the postrhetorical presidency. Like the rhetorical presidency, the postrhetorical presidency is a historical condition, an artifact of the evolution of media technology. Whereas the rhetorical presidency was characterized by a reciprocal, mutually beneficial, and stable relationship between the press and the president, the postrhetorical presidency is an independent, competitive, and unstable relationship. As we saw with the example of President Obama's November 20, 2014, immigration speech rollout, his enactment of the postrhetorical presidency relied upon strict message control, speaking directly to supporters, and counting on the president's "friends" and "followers" to circulate his messages throughout their networks. Obama's postrhetorical media strategies developed during his successful 2008 presidential campaign and were perfected through, as he admitted in 2015, his more "nimble" use of social media to get his message out to the public once he was in office.

Traditional media have repeatedly complained that the Obama administration's media tactics were so restrictive as to border on pathology and have sought to bring the executive branch back into its previous reciprocal relationship by expressing outrage over what some call a war on journalism and by disruptive strategies such as not making airtime available for President Obama's immigration speech. In November 2013 the Associated Press, ABC News, Fox News, the *New York Times*, and thirty-four other news organizations delivered a letter to the White House accusing the Obama administration of "arbitrary restraint and unwarranted interference on legitimate newsgathering activities." Obama's postrhetorical presidency prevented "government transparency," they argued, and was a "major break from how previous administrations have worked with the press." That major break, of course, was the shift from the rhetorical to the postrhetorical presidency. "The theme that emerges from these clashes between the White House and the press corps is powerlessness," wrote Erik Wemple. "When talking about loss of access, reporters commonly cite tradition and how things operated under previous administrations. They mention precedents and courtesies and the public's right to know. It's all another way of saying that the White House is obligated to do essentially whatever it pleases when it comes to media access. Don't want to answer questions, Mr. President? Okay." Indeed, the good news for the Obama administration—as Press Secretary Josh Earnest pointed out during his November 19, 2014, press briefing—was that it was no longer reliant upon traditional news media. In fact, Obama's executive branch had a larger share of the media audience than the traditional media did.[30] By my count President Obama had a potential audience of about 119 million viewers on Thursday, November 20, 2014, at 8:00 p.m., compared to the networks' potential audience of about 51 million viewers. Furthermore, as Earnest so earnestly explained, the press watches the White House Facebook page and reports what is posted there, so there seemed to be little incentive for the Obama administration to have cooperated more fully with the press.

This means, ultimately, that traditional news media can no longer count on being the first to know, which threatens their ability to provide news to their audiences. Whither the watchdog function of the press described by JFK? It does not look good for traditional news media. Perhaps there will be millions of watchdogs who will post information about politics, but who will have direct access to question leaders? Politicians may increasingly speak to supporters or targeted groups rather than the entire nation—as President Obama did when he asked Univision to preempt its programming on November 20, 2014, but not the US networks.[31] "Whenever I get together with former White House reporters to discuss old times," explained veteran

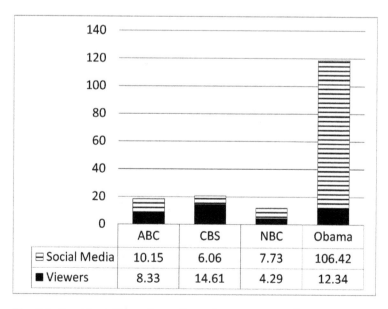

	ABC	CBS	NBC	Obama
⊟ Social Media	10.15	6.06	7.73	106.42
■ Viewers	8.33	14.61	4.29	12.34

Fig. 8.1. President Obama's media audience compared to network media audience, 8:00 p.m., November 20, 2014.

White House correspondent Helen Thomas, "we realize that we had the advantage of close proximity to the president that may never happen again. It seems unlikely that the White House will return to the days when President Harry S. Truman took his morning strolls down Pennsylvania Avenue at dawn with a couple of reporters and photographers in tow." Despite Thomas's pessimism, it is difficult to predict if the postrhetorical presidency is unique to this moment or if every president will have the same (or more) direct access to supporters through social media.[32]

Certainly some politicians will have the capability to "go around the filter," but not all. The incumbent advantage is now not just dollars raised and name recognition, but also email databases and Facebook and Twitter followers; the incumbent advantage is audience. At the same time, there is the potential for nonestablishment candidates to break through into the public conversation in the same way that YouTube videos or memes go viral. And, finally, social media corporations largely cooperated with the Obama administration, but they may also decide that they want more access to the executive branch in the future and begin to ask for a more balanced, reciprocal relationship.[33]

The shift from columns to characters is thus the shift from the rhetorical presidency to the postrhetorical presidency. It is a historical condition in which the president has used social media to build as large a network audience as the traditional news media (or larger), which means that the relationship between the press and the president is no longer reciprocal and cooperative. The postrhetorical relationship between the press and the president means that media may no longer have the privileged ability "to inform, to arouse, to reflect, to state our dangers and our opportunities, to indicate our crises and our choices, to lead, mold, educate and sometimes even anger public opinion."

Postscript

Many writers in this book, including me, have suggested that Obama was the nation's first social media president. Many also argued that Obama used social media and digital technology to go around the media and communicate directly with the people, much to reporters' dismay. Following him into office, of course, is Donald Trump, who is likely to take Obama's "go around the filter" impulse even further. While President Obama did stage many events and make his own news sometimes, such as in the announcement of proposed immigration reform that I described in this chapter, he still had a mostly viable relationship with the media that included more or less regular press conferences and a willingness to sit for interviews with both national and local media outlets. Indeed, Martha Kumar's first chapter in this book details the Obama press relationship in full. Subsequent writers, especially Martin, Smith, Edwards, and me, have demonstrated how the forty-fourth president used digital technology to engage the rhetorical presidency in ways that were quite different from those of his predecessors in office.

However, Donald Trump's postrhetorical impulses seem even stronger than were President Obama's, at least if Trump governs as he tended to campaign. Obama went around the press, but his rhetoric did not tend to disparage reporters in any kind of overt way. Trump, on the other hand, ran for president by naming media, especially the so-called mainstream media, as corrupt—part of the system of Washington elites who deserved to be disbelieved and distrusted. This, in turn, suggested that there was no need to use the filter because it was dishonest anyway. This gave Trump cover for using his own Twitter feed and speeches as vehicles for saying things other candidates couldn't get away with while advancing a discourse with the media that was uncooperative and combative. Whether Trump will continue with this postrhetorical strategy of media disengagement and disparagement will be telling in terms of how transparent his administration is as well as what kind of relationship he has with the press, the people, and the office of the presidency itself.[34]

Notes

1. Quotation from Lauren Walker, "Where Can I Watch Obama's Immigration Speech," *Newsweek*, November 20, 2014, http://www.newsweek.com/where-can-i-watch-obamas-immigration-speech-285890; Zachary M. Seward, "What the Major US Networks Put on TV Instead of Obama's Immigration Speech," *Quartz*, November 20, 2014, http://qz.com/300357/what-the-major-us-networks-put-on-tv-instead-of-obamas-immigration-speech/. In July 2014, Gallup found that 17 percent of Americans thought that immigration was the most important issue facing the nation: "One

in Six Say Immigration Most Important US Problem," Gallup, Politics, July 16, 2014, http://www.gallup.com/poll/173306/one-six-say-immigration-important-problem.aspx.

2. "The major broadcast networks generally carry presidential speeches on matters of national security and other important issues. But there can be a reluctance in executive suites if an anticipated address is seen as heavily political in nature. It is not clear if that's the reasoning here. CBS News, through a spokeswoman, said it declined to comment on editorial decisions. ABC News also declined comment, and NBC News did not have an immediate response to a query." David Bauder, "Major American TV Networks Did Not Air Obama Speech on Immigration," Global News, National, November 21, 2014, http://globalnews.ca/news/1685269/major-american-tv-networks-did-not-air-obama-speech-on-immigration/.

Why did the networks ignore Obama's speech? "In part because the White House did not give them advanced notice, and in part because the major news networks are in the business of making money. . . . As a business decision, this seems like a no-brainer. Ratings will be much higher carrying 'popular shows' than another groan-inducing and 'prime time' presidential address." Daniel Doherty, "Wow: Four Networks to Pass on Obama's Historic Amnesty Address," Townhall, Tipsheet, November 20, 2014, http://townhall.com/tipsheet/danieldoherty/2014/11/20/wow-four-networks-to-ignore-obamas-prime-time-address-n1921508.

For an example of a conspiracy explanation, consider: "Combine this with the Ferguson decision and you have not only cover for Obama's illegal activities, but a continued effort by this administration to engage in inciting insurrection among the people of America." Tim Brown, "Media Blackout & Ferguson Converge on Obama's Amnesty for Illegals Address," Freedom Outpost, November 20, 2014, http://freedomoutpost.com/2014/11/media-blackout-ferguson-converge-obamas-amnesty-illegals-address/#Gaak8qQBzCu0trPd.99. Consider also: "They're acting like it was the networks's [sic] decision, but we all know that they would only do whatever Obama wants them to do on such an important announcement, so we all know he told them not to air it because most Americans are opposed to it." Darby Crash, "STATE-RUN MEDIA: Obama Tells Networks Not to Air Amnesty Announcement," PatDollard.com, November 19, 2014, http://patdollard.com/2014/11/state-run-media-obama-tells-networks-not-to-air-amnesty-announcement/#QUCuH4XzYeTXM6b1.99, accessed August 12, 2015.

I imagine, though I did not ask, that interference with programming is what George Edwards III might say is the reason that the networks didn't air the speech. According to Jaime Fuller: "As the White House is very aware of, Americans stopped paying attention to presidential primetime addresses long before the glut of options provided by Netflix, HBOGo and Hulu arrived on the scene. By 2006, back when cable was the only competitor that network television truly had to worry about, the viewership of presidential addresses had plummeted." Jaime Fuller, "Why the Major Networks Didn't Give President Obama Primetime Real Estate for His Immigration Speech," *Washington Post*, November 21, 2014, http://www.washingtonpost.com/news/the-fix/wp/2014/11/20/why-the-networks-arent-giving-president-obama-primetime-real-estate-for-his-immigration-speech/.

3. The postrhetorical presidency, first theorized by Stephen Hartnett and Jennifer Mercieca in their 2007 analysis of President George W. Bush, is "marked by a president who, like all presidents before him, seeks to define the bounds of political discourse, but who does not do so through the traditional means of eloquence, logic,

pathos, or narrative storytelling, but by marshaling ubiquitous public chatter, waves of disinformation, and cascades of confusion-causing misdirection. Post-rhetorical presidential discourse attempts to confuse public opinion, prevent citizen action, and frustrate citizen deliberation." Stephen John Hartnett and Jennifer Rose Mercieca, "'A Discovered Dissembler Can Achieve Nothing Great'; or, Four Theses on the Death of Presidential Rhetoric in an Age of Empire," *Presidential Studies Quarterly* 37, no. 4 (December 2007): 600.

In ibid., Stephen Hartnett and I concluded that Bush's postrhetorical discourse attempted to "confuse public opinion, prevent citizen action, and frustrate citizen deliberation," which may have been true in the case of the Bush administration's Iraq War discourse, but I now think does not accurately describe all aspects of postrhetorical political discourse.

4. Alexander Hamilton wrote: "A dangerous ambition more often lurks behind the specious mask of zeal for the rights of the people than under the forbidden appearance of zeal for the firmness and efficiency of government. History will teach us that the former has been found a much more certain road to the introduction of despotism than the latter, and that of those men who have overturned the liberties of republics, the greatest number have begun their career by paying an obsequious court to the people; commencing demagogues, and ending tyrants." Publius, *The Federalist Papers*, No. 1.

5. Alexander Keyssar, *The Right to Vote: The Contested History of Democracy in the United States* (New York: Basic Books, 2000); Jennifer Rose Mercieca, *Founding Fictions* (Tuscaloosa: University of Alabama Press, 2010), especially 147–202; Jeffery K. Tulis, *The Rhetorical Presidency* (Princeton, NJ: Princeton University Press, 1987), 4.

6. Daniel Boorstin, *The Image: A Guide to Pseudo-events in America* (New York: Harper & Row, 1964), 11; Tulis, *Rhetorical Presidency*, 186.

7. Tulis, *Rhetorical Presidency*, 186.

8. "Season in the Sun," *Life*, April 9, 1951, 59, regarding Harry Truman and a trip to Key West with "29 reporters, photographers and radio men."

9. Shanto Iyengar, *Media Politics: A Citizen's Guide*, 2nd ed. (New York: W. W. Norton & Company, 2011), 51. Earlier, Iyengar wrote: "The preoccupation with media imagery is hardly surprising, given that, for most Americans, the [mass] media are their only contact with the world of public affairs. On the flip side, from the perspective of the public, events not covered by the news media make no greater impression than the proverbial tree falling in the forest. For the public, what's covered in the news is all there is to know" (ibid., 2).

10. President John F. Kennedy, "Address before the American Newspaper Publishers Association, April 27, 1961," John F. Kennedy Presidential Library and Museum, John F. Kennedy Speeches, http://www.jfklibrary.org/Research/Research-Aids/JFK-Speeches/American-Newspaper-Publishers-Association_19610427.aspx.

11. "In the 2004 campaign, we witnessed the advent of blogs and their impact on [both] how voters got and shared information and how the press got their information about candidates. That was the beginning of the journalism paradigm being somewhat reversed. [In the past] the big media folks set the pace and tempo of the coverage and the discussion and the debate. And campaigns played along with that with full recognition of it. [Then] a very top-heavy system started to crumble. A lot of power began to come from the bottom up." Kevin Madden, senior advisor to Mitt Romney's 2012 campaign, in *Electing the President, 2012: The Insiders' View*, edited by Kathleen Hall Jamieson (Philadelphia: University of Pennsylvania Press, 2013), 55.

Indeed, according to Todd Purdum, "It's easy to see why Obama wants to pick his own shots. He faces the most hyperkinetic, souped-up, tricked-out, trivialized, and combative media environment any president has ever experienced. The long-building trend toward coverage of the presidency and politics as pure sport has reached absurd levels." Todd Purdum, "Washington, We Have a Problem," *Vanity Fair*, Hive, September 1, 2010, http://www.vanityfair.com/news/2010/09/broken-washington-201009.

12. Iyengar, *Media Politics*, 76; Reid Cherlin, "The Presidency and the Press," *Rolling Stone*, August 4, 2014, http://www.rollingstone.com/politics/news/the-presidency-and-the-press-20140804#ixzz30MRfqP2y.

13. The White House, video, Facebook, November 19, 2014, https://www.facebook.com/video.php?v=10152967942944238&set=vb.63811549237.

14. "Google Trends—Web Search Interest—Worldwide, 2004–Present," Google Trends, https://www.google.com/trends/explore?date=2014-01-01%202014-12-31&q=immigration%20reform.

15. I'm grateful to Robin Bedenbaugh, Zoë Hess Carney, Pamela Matthews, Rita Shah, and Barbara Sharf for their research support.

16. "Press Briefing by Press Secretary Josh Earnest, 11/19/2014," White House, Briefing Room, November 19, 2014, https://www.whitehouse.gov/the-press-office/2014/11/19/press-briefing-press-secretary-josh-earnest-11192014; Cameron Easley, "Obama to Announce #immigrationaction Thursday at 8 p.m. ET," Twitter, November 19, 2014, https://twitter.com/CamRollCall/status/535131870204526592. Thank you, Olivier Knox, for helping me to identify George Condon as the person asking the question.

17. Univision (4.8 million viewers), Fox (4.153 million), MSNBC (1.763 million), CNN (1.652 million). Believing that Obama's speech was important for its audience to see, Univision delayed its broadcast of the Latin Grammy Awards, a large ratings draw for the network (about 10 million viewers for the previous several years). Matt Wilstein, "Univision Dominates Obama Immigration Speech Ratings," Mediaite, November 21, 2014, http://www.mediaite.com/tv/univision-dominates-obama-immigration-speech-ratings/. Obama's largest ratings to date were the 56.5 million people who watched his speech on the targeted killing of Osama Bin Laden. Brian Stelter, "Obama's TV Audience Was His Largest," *New York Times*, Television, May 3, 2011, http://www.nytimes.com/2011/05/04/arts/television/bin-laden-speech-drew-obamas-largest-audience-as-president.html?_r=0.

Visual of the number #immigration hashtag tweets: "#Immigration: Mentions of Pres. Obama's Speech, EST," Twitter Reverb, November 21, 2014, http://reverb.guru/view/781664283926065652. Archived tweets using #immigrationaction: Twitter Search for #immigrationaction, https://twitter.com/search?f=tweets&vertical=default&q=#immigrationaction since:2014-11-19 until:2014-11-21&src=typd, accessed August 12, 2015. Geotagged #immigration tweets globally: "#Immigration: The President's Speech," CartoDB, http://srogers.cartodb.com/viz/aef7d30e-7120–11e4-a4d7–0e9d821ea90d/embed_map, accessed August 12, 2015.

18. "Is the new network standard that if a president announces a primetime address but the opposing party doesn't agree with the contents of the speech, networks won't air the event because it's too "political"? That's absurd and reeks of a cop-out. In exchange for using the public airwaves for free, and generating enormous profits off them, television broadcast networks in America agree to set aside time to fulfill their public interest obligation. Tonight's brief, 10 to 15 minute address about immigration

reform ought to be one of those times." Eric Boehlert, "Network News' Shameful Decision to Snub Obama's Immigration Address," Media Matters for America, Blog, November 20, 2014, http://mediamatters.org/blog/2014/11/20/network-news-shameful-decision-to-snub-obamas-i/201649.

19. Brian Stelter, "Broadcast Networks Opt Out of Obama Immigration Speech—Except for Univision," CNN, Media, November 19, 2014, http://money.cnn.com/2014/11/19/media/networks-and-obama-speech/index.html.

"A network insider tells Playbook, 'There was agreement among the broadcast networks that this was overtly political. The White House has tried to make a comparison to a time that all the networks carried President Bush in prime time, also related to immigration [2006]. But that was a bipartisan announcement, and this is an overtly political move by the White House." Mike Allen, "Why the Nets Stiffed Obama . . . ," Politico, Playbook, November 20, 2014, http://www.politico.com/playbook/1114/playbook16177.html.

20. Susan Herbst, "The Rhetorical Presidency and the Contemporary Media Environment," Critical Review: A Journal of Politics and Society 19 (2007): 2–3, 335–43, 440.

21. Stephen Heidt, "The Presidency as Pastiche: Atomization, Circulation, and Rhetorical Instability," Rhetoric & Public Affairs 15, no. 4 (2012): 623–34.

22. George C. Edwards III, "Organizing for (In)action: The Obama Presidency and the Vanishing Online Vanguard," chapter 7, this volume.

23. Sid Blumenthal, The Permanent Campaign: Inside the World of Elite Political Operations (Boston: Beacon Press, 1980); John J. DiIulio Jr., "The Hyper-Rhetorical Presidency," Critical Review: A Journal of Politics and Society 19, nos. 2–3 (2007): 315–24.

24. Anita Dunn, in Kathleen Hall Jamieson, ed., Electing the President, 2008: The Insiders' View (Philadelphia: University of Pennsylvania Press, 2009), 141, 146.

25. Stephanie Cutter. See Kathleen Hall Jamieson, ed., Electing the President, 2012: The Insiders' View (Philadelphia: University of Pennsylvania Press, 2013), 67.

26. Brian Mooney, "Obama's Paid Staff Dwarfing McCain's: Democrat Targets 50 States as Rival Focuses on Tossups," Boston.com, July 20, 2008, http://www.boston.com/news/nation/articles/2008/07/20/obamas_paid_staff_dwarfing_mccains/?page=1; Victoria Chang, "Obama and the Power of Social Media and Technology," European Business Review, May–June 2010, 16; Monte Lutz, The Social Pulpit: Barack Obama's Social Media Toolkit (Chicago: Edelman—Digital Public Affairs, 2009) 5, http://http://cyber.harvard.edu/sites/cyber.harvard.edu/files/Social%20Pulpit%20-%20Barack%20Obamas%20Social%20Media%20Toolkit%201.09.pdf. Anita Dunn commented: "One of the things that we did was communicate, by and large, most of our news to our supporters," as quoted in Jamieson, Electing the President, 2008, 141.

27. Micah L. Sifry, "Presidential Campaign 2012, by the Numbers," Personal Democracy Media, TechPresident, November 26, 2012, http://techpresident.com/news/23178/presidential-campaign-2012-numbers; Stephanie Cutter, in Jamieson, Electing the President, 2012, 66. Dunn is quoted in Cherlin, "Presidency and the Press."

28. Lutz, Social Pulpit, 3–4; Cutter, in Jamieson, Electing the President, 2012, 66–67 Stephanie Cutter also remarked: "People trust their information when it's coming from a Facebook friend much more than if it's me on TV saying something" (Jamieson, Electing the President, 2012, 67).

29. Karen Finney, in Jamieson, Electing the President, 2008, 164; Vincent Harris, "TV-ing the Web: The GOP's Coming Problem Is More Than Ethnic Diversity," Medium,

July 28, 2015, https://medium.com/@vincentrharris/tv-ing-the-web-the-gop-s-com ing-problem-is-more-than-ethnic-diversity-a29d30186f75#.txr0fi9f6.

According to Bruce Gronbeck, "If 'instrumental functions' are thought of as ways in which additional behaviors (voting, legislating, thinking) are generated by pieces of communication, then 'consummatory functions' are embodied in those communication processes which produce end-states or 'products' that go beyond (or stop short of) voting and electing per se. That is, campaigning creates second-level or metapolitical images, personae, myths, associations, and social-psychological reactions which may even be detached or at least distinct from particular candidates, issues, and offices. Simply put, one may (and most probably do) 'use' a presidential campaign for some things other than selecting Presidents and ordering priorities." Bruce E. Gronbeck, "The Functions of Presidential Campaigning," *Communication Monographs* 45, no. 4:271. Gronbeck defines "Para-social Interaction" as "providing persons with 'messages' and 'sources'—via radio, television, newspapers, brochures— with which to 'interact,' as when people 'argue' with their television sets' projected personae" (272).

According to Susan Herbst, at the close of the twentieth century lack of intimacy between the president and the people had become a problem for the rhetorical presidency: "But the truth is that even the 'rhetorical president' who has left the ceremonial isolation of George Washington behind remains distant from the audience. Conversation, intimacy, and friendship with the president are simply not possible. I am not sure how presidents might insinuate themselves with more power into our households; the likes of Dr. Phil do it through the topics they pursue. But presidents are doomed to failure, in the contemporary arena of speech and persuasion, unless they adapt to the intimate nature of contemporary media. So far, we see little creativity from presidents in this area, most likely because they feel it will compromise their dignity as leaders. Regardless of their triumphs or failures, there is a culture clash between what presidents can offer and what audiences seem to desire. Until a president can both understand this desire for intimacy and figure out how—in normal times, not crises—to use the media to achieve it, presidential speech will not be a compelling form of American public rhetoric." Herbst, "Rhetorical Presidency," 341.

"That's a good thing," Democratic strategist Joe Trippi said in the November 11, 2008, *New York Times*. "This medium demands authenticity, and television for the most part demanded fake. Authenticity is something politicians haven't been used to." Joe Trippi, "How Obama's Internet Campaign Changed Politics," *New York Times*, Bits, November 11, 2008, http://bits.blogs.nytimes.com/2008/11/07/how-obamas-internet-campaign-changed-politics/.

30. Catherine Taibi, "Journalists Protest Restrictions on Photographing Obama, Compare White House to Soviet Union," *Huffington Post*, Media, November 21, 2013, http://www.huffingtonpost.com/2013/11/21/white-house-photographers-protest-restrictions_n_4317284.html?utm_hp_ref=media; Erik Wemple, "White House Press Corps, Please Keep the Complaints Coming," *Washington Post*, February 20, 2013, http://www.washingtonpost.com/blogs/erik-wemple/wp/2013/02/20/white-house-press-corps-please-keep-the-complaints-coming/.

Then *New York Times* editor-in-chief Jill Abramson commented, "This is the most secretive White House that, at least as a journalist, I have ever dealt with." "Jill Abramson Talks to John Seigenthaler—Al Jazeera America," Al Jazeera America, Interview Files,

January 21, 2014, http://america.aljazeera.com/watch/shows/talk-to-al-jazeera/interviews-and-more/2014/1/21/jill-abramson-talkstojohnseigenthaler.html.

31. Noah Rothman wrote: "There is one tiny exception to the broadcast networks passing on the opportunity to carry Obama's speech, however. While none of the major broadcast networks will cover Obama's speech live, there is one network that will: Univision. And Obama's address just happens to air right before the Latin Grammy Awards. . . . Surely, this is not about favoritism, though. Univision's lead anchor, Jorge Ramos, does seem like an impartial actor without a political ax to grind." Noah Rothman, "Broadcast Networks Won't Carry Obama's Immigration Address . . . with One Big Exception," Hot Air, November 19, 2014, http://hotair.com/archives/2014/11/19/yawn-broadcast-networks-pass-on-carrying-obamas-prime-time-immigration-address/.

According to Juliet Eilperin, "Paulette Aniskoff, head of the White House Office of Public Engagement . . . had journeyed from Washington to the offices of the entertainment company Live Nation for a strategy session on how YouTube and Vine stars could use their digital celebrity to promote some of the Obama administration's key policies. . . . Barack Obama rose to prominence as a politician who could deliver broad, sweeping speeches with universal themes, and he has leveraged the opportunities of the digital age to maximum political advantage. But often, this now means speaking narrowly to his base voters or to groups disconnected from the mainstream political process." Juliet Eilperin, "Here's How the First President of the Social Media Age Has Chosen to Connect with Americans," Washington Post, May 26, 2015, http://www.washingtonpost.com/news/politics/wp/2015/05/26/heres-how-the-first-president-of-the-social-media-age-has-chosen-to-connect-with-americans/.

32. On May 18, President Obama established a new Twitter account, @POTUS, which should transfer to the next occupant of the White House and will include the benefit of a built-in audience. President Obama, "Hello, Twitter! It's Barack. Really! Six Years In, They're Finally Giving Me My Own Account," Twitter, May 18, 2015, https://twitter.com/POTUS/status/600324682190053376. President Obama set the record for the quickest Twitter user to reach one million followers, achieving that number within less than five hours. Dan Thorne, "President Obama Joins Twitter with @POTUS Account, Breaks Fastest Million Follower Count Record," Guinness World Records, May 19, 2015, http://www.guinnessworldrecords.com/news/2015/5/president-obama-joins-twitter-with-potus-account-breaks-fastest-million-followe-379128. Obama's record was eclipsed by Caitlyn Jenner, who reached a million followers in only four hours and three minutes on June 1, 2015.

33. Traditional media may also enable the power of new media organizations such as BuzzFeed by covering their Obama HealthCare video, for example. Jess Duda, "BuzzFeed's Record-Breaking Obama Video Due To Earned Media Not Social," MediaShift, March 5, 2015, http://mediashift.org/2015/03/buzzfeeds-record-breaking-obama-video-due-to-earned-media-not-social/.

34. Jennifer Mercieca, "The Rhetorical Brilliance of Trump the Demagogue," The Conversation, December 11 2015, https://theconversation.com/the-rhetorical-brilliance-of-trump-the-demagogue-51984; Jennifer Mercieca, "How Donald Trump Gets Away With Saying Things Other Candidates Can't," The Conversation," March 8, 2016, https://theconversation.com/how-donald-trump-gets-away-with-saying-things-other-candidates-cant-55615.

REALITY CHECK

Mr. President,
We Have a Few Questions

STACIA DESHISHKU

All presidential administrations want to manage their message, and the Obama administration was no exception. Whether through legal maneuverings, new media outreach, or limiting the access of reporters covering the White House, the Obama administration often appeared more concerned with providing America a sanitized version of history than with living up to its self-proclaimed motto as the most transparent administration ever. The George W. Bush administration was likewise interested in its public presentation, and so was Bill Clinton's before that. Donald Trump's White House will undoubtedly be the same. And so it goes. Presidents and the press have long found themselves in an adversarial arrangement, as so many of the writers in this book so astutely point out. Even so, the media have a job to do, and that job is to bring what's happening in the people's house to the citizens, who have every right to know what's going on.

To make this happen, and in spite of the fact that administrations sometimes do everything they can to stand in the way (and in spite of the fact that the problem seems to be getting worse), the White House Correspondents' Association has worked doggedly on behalf of the press corps to maintain access to the president and to give the public the chance to see, first-hand, government officials acting in their civic capacity. The association has further insisted that those officials should be willing to answer direct questions, by journalists, about their duties. We do not want to receive photo handouts of important meetings with White House talking points attached. Neither are we interested in perfectly poised pictures and crafted messages better suited to a scripted reality show than news coverage of the American president. But that has been becoming our reality, and more and more it feels as if we are the actors in this show.

The ongoing struggle to cover the White House falls into two categories: restriction and intimidation. Restriction takes form in the ever-dwindling access that the media have to the official activities of the administration, such as meetings with world leaders, the president signing bills into law, and the activities of the Oval Office. Increasingly we are offered photos taken by the president's personal photographer. These beautifully stylized pictures are used to portray an idealized version of events. Indeed, the White House press corps even calls them visual press releases or, more bluntly, propaganda. What they are not is journalism. These are newsworthy events—the kind of occasion that the media have traditionally been given access to cover and that they used to inform Americans about: who the president meets and who is helping inform his decision making, whether on immigration, healthcare, the economy, or the other myriad events that happen on an ongoing basis in a fast-paced world.

The second issue relates to the intimidation of the media. Intimidation cuts two ways: intimidation of the source and intimidation of the journalist. More than ever government officials are hesitant to speak to the media or leave behind any digital trail of contact, as it may open them up to scrutiny. At least seven times during the Obama administration alone, the Justice Department investigated reports of classified leaks to news organizations and secretly subpoenaed the phone records of reporters who they suspected of receiving leaked information. These actions gave reporters and sources pause. Many in government won't even discuss unclassified information with reporters, especially if they haven't cleared those talking points through the White House Communications Office. *New York Times* reporter David Sanger, who has been covering the presidency and foreign policy for thirty years, was quoted as saying the Obama White House "is the most closed, control freak administration I've ever covered." But it's not just federal workers who are intimidated; it's the press corps, too. Presidents do this by restricting access to events unless we agree not to send a reporter to ask questions. Bottom line: play by the administration's rules or get iced out.

As this book is going to print, Donald Trump is entering the Oval Office, and all expectations are that he will take the Obama team's use of social media even further and be even more willing to go around and frustrate the efforts of the traditional press corps. After all, much of his campaign was built on having a hostile relationship with the press. The Obama administration, more than any in the recent past, used the ever-evolving forms of new media to circumvent traditional ones to get their message to Americans. For example, the president sat down with Buzzfeed instead of Bloomberg, with Vox instead of Fox. He talked directly to local TV stations in Dubuque, agreed to be interviewed on *Between Two Ferns*, hosted Google hangouts—you name it, he did it. And that's good. But by creating their own new media avenues to connect with citizens, as so many of the authors in this book have pointed out, the White House walked a dangerously fine line of manufacturing consent through the creation of their own form of journalism. Just look at the 2015 State of the Union interviews with YouTube "stars" that was considered part of the White House's "integrated communication strategy." Yes, GloZell was able to ask the president some questions about the Sony Corporation, which was allegedly being hacked by North Korea, and issues of race and policing, but was the American electorate better informed than if Peter Baker from the *New York Times* had gotten that interview? Better entertained, yes, but better informed, unlikely. The president's desire to talk directly to the people shouldn't be a zero-sum game, because nobody is really informed under the auspices of that kind of either/ or proposition. He could take questions from GloZell and Baker, alike. Talking to the people (or better yet, having a conversation with them) should mean all formats are in play—new *and* old, online *and* off.

AFTERWORD

JON MEACHAM

First, a few facts. George Washington—a president who never faced an opponent for the highest constitutional office in the land—nearly retired after a single term because he was so exhausted by criticism. Thomas Jefferson was forced to read newspaper accounts detailing stories about his sexual relations with a woman he owned. Andrew Jackson grew so irritated by the coverage he received in his party's usual newspaper that he founded his own, often editing pieces before their publication. And these examples don't even get us past the half-century mark of the American experience.

Still, of course, the changes wrought by the rapidly evolving Information Age are important, and those shifts in technology—particularly those that speed up the delivery of news and opinion—are indeed altering the nature of the relationship between a president and the media. Yet the differences in the first decades of the twenty-first century are those of degree, not of kind. Understanding that the story of our time is but a chapter in a long story, not an entirely new saga, should give us some reassurance that the world, while in flux, is not wholly new and thus is not wholly impenetrable.

The presidency, as Franklin Roosevelt once put it, is "preeminently a place of moral leadership," and one cannot exercise moral leadership—or leadership of any kind, really—without mastering the means of communication of one's era. Jefferson and Lincoln, for instance, wrote quickly and well in a culture that was based on the written word. FDR was a powerful presence on the radio. John F. Kennedy and Ronald Reagan were remarkably skilled television performers. And many of us expected, in the now distant days of 2008, that Barack Obama would dominate the digital universe and usher in a progressive era of governance.

The Obama revolution did not happen, and the reason is revealing: the digital world is by its nature unconquerable. There are too many voices, too many platforms, too many tweets. The cacophony of life online has created a cacophonous political life offline. Everyone now has the power to speak, even if few have anything to say. The days of a President Reagan delivering an Oval Office speech to the nation and commanding great attention are gone; our common political culture is fractured.

To be sure, from Jefferson vs. Hamilton forward, American political culture has been forever factionalized. The difference now is that presidential leadership must be exercised in an environment in which the factions never rest. As recently as the administration of George H. W. Bush, from 1989 to 1993, a White House could count on a reliable rhythm to a day. First came the newspapers, then the network morning shows, then the evening news; then the day ended with ABC's *Nightline*. Cable news and talk radio were growing in influence in the Bush 41 years but would not truly explode until the Clinton administration.

It is arguable, in fact, that *the press* as a term is anachronistic. To paraphrase Richard Nixon, we are all reporters and commentators now. As so many of the writers in this volume made clear, open a Twitter or Facebook account, and suddenly you conceivably have the capacity to drive news in the way that was once the exclusive province of formal media organizations.

That is what is new. What is old is the adversarial nature of the relationship between the presidency and those who cover and comment on it. In his book *The Making of the President 1964* (New York: Atheneum, 1965), an account of the Johnson-Goldwater race, Theodore H. White described what he called "the politician's optic." Here is White:

> A politician can read a sentence about himself which begins, say, "Brilliant, effective, statesmanlike John Doe was momentarily confused as he rose the other day . . ." And the adjectives *brilliant*,

effective, and *statesmanlike* shrink to fine print, while the adjective *confused* swells out of the page into poster-size letters. If, on the other hand, a politician reads a dispatch about his enemy which begins, "Richard Roe, dirty, testy, bumbling solon of the old school, was in a civilized mood yesterday as he . . . ," then the adjectives *dirty, testy, bumbling* shrink to pica-size print and the single adjective *civilized* swells to double-sized capitals.

As White concluded, "This is an occupational disease of politicians—just as it is for authors and actors, who similarly live by public approval or distaste." And no matter where critical words appear—in a tweet, in a blog post, from the mouth of a commentator on cable—this "politician's optic" is an enduring reality in our own time.

Another stubborn fact is the press's devotion to division. Many Americans believe those who cover the presidency and politics are driven by ideology, but I have a different view. Reporters, in my experience, are more likely to chase the new or the contentious rather than seeking to adhere to any particular political creed. Hence, journalists who spent, say, the 1992 election cycle portraying George H. W. Bush as an out-of-touch elitist could instantly pivot after Bill Clinton's victory and cover the new White House with ferocity and a weakness for scandal (or even just the suggestion of scandal).

These are universal forces that have found, in the new technology, fresh means of expression. All of which is to say that William Faulkner was right when he wrote that the past is never dead; it isn't even past. There is a natural and inescapable tension between presidents and the press—presidents expect approval, and the press thrives on conflict, novelty, and controversy. So it has been from the beginning, and so, I think, it shall always be.

CONTRIBUTORS

Peter Baker is White House correspondent for the *New York Times* and a contributing writer for the *New York Times Magazine*.

Thomas DeFrank is contributing editor, *National Journal*, and former Washington bureau chief of the *New York Daily News*.

David Demarest is vice president for public affairs, Stanford University, and former White House communications director for President George H. W. Bush.

Stacia Deshishku is deputy Washington bureau chief, ABC News.

George C. Edwards III is University Distinguished Professor of Political Science and Jordan Chair in Presidential Studies at Texas A&M University.

Roderick P. Hart is the former dean of the Moody College of Communication and Shivers Chair in Communication, and professor of government at the University of Texas at Austin.

Rita Kirk is the director of the Cary M. Maguire Center for Ethics & Public Responsibility and a professor of communication in the Division of Corporate Communication and Public Affairs, Southern Methodist University.

Martha Joynt Kumar is a professor in the Department of Political Science at Towson University. Since 1975, Kumar has held a press credential to the White House briefing room, the only academic with such access.

Stephanie A. Martin is an assistant professor of political communication in the Division of Corporate Communication and Public Affairs at Southern Methodist University.

Jon Meacham is executive editor and executive vice president at Random House, a former editor-in-chief of *Newsweek*, and a contributing editor to *Time* magazine.

Jennifer R. Mercieca is an associate professor of communication at Texas A&M University and author or editor of two books, with a book forthcoming on the rhetoric of Donald Trump.

Robert W. Mong is former editor of the *Dallas Morning News*.

Tony Pederson holds the Belo Distinguished Chair in Journalism as professor of journalism at Southern Methodist University.

Stephen A. Smith is professor emeritus of communication at the University of Arkansas and served as a member of the Arkansas House of Representatives and executive assistant to former governor Bill Clinton.

INDEX